Timothy Matlack, Scribe of the Declaration of Independence

Timothy Matlack, Scribe of the Declaration of Independence

CHRIS COELHO

McFarland & Company, Inc., Publishers
Jefferson, North Carolina, and London

LIBRARY OF CONGRESS CATALOGUING-IN-PUBLICATION DATA

Coelho, Chris.
    Timothy Matlack, scribe of the Declaration of Independence / Chris Coelho.
        p.   cm.
    Includes bibliographical references and index.

    ISBN 978-0-7864-7443-1
    softcover : acid free paper ∞

    1. Matlack, Timothy, 1736–1829. 2. United States—History—Revolution, 1775–1783. 3. United States. Declaration of Independence. 4. Statesmen—United States—Biography. I. Title.
    E302.6.M46C64 2013
    973.3092—dc23
    [B]   2013017861

BRITISH LIBRARY CATALOGUING DATA ARE AVAILABLE

© 2013 Chris Coelho. All rights reserved

No part of this book may be reproduced or transmitted in any form or by any means, electronic or mechanical, including photocopying or recording, or by any information storage and retrieval system, without permission in writing from the publisher.

On the cover: Timothy Matlack shown with a printed copy of the 1776 Pennsylvania Constitution; a Council proclamation with his signature and attached state seal; law books; and his old militia rifle and powder horn in the background. Painting. Philadelphia: Charles Willson Peale, 1790. Photograph © 2013 Museum of Fine Arts, Boston; background Declaration of Independence

Manufactured in the United States of America

McFarland & Company, Inc., Publishers
  Box 611, Jefferson, North Carolina 28640
    www.mcfarlandpub.com

For my parents, Mary and Jamie Coelho

Table of Contents

Preface	1
Introduction	5
One. The Failed Crossing	7
Two. Haddonfield and Philadelphia	12
Three. The March of the Paxton Boys	23
Four. Revolution	34
Five. Independence	49
Six. Democracy	57
Seven. The Winter Campaign	69
Eight. The British Occupation	81
Nine. Benedict Arnold Part One (Illicit Affairs)	100
Ten. The Fort Wilson Riot	116
Eleven. Benedict Arnold Part Two (Court-martial)	125
Twelve. A Brief Term in Congress	140
Thirteen. Savannah, Georgia	158
Fourteen. The Revolution of 1800	171
Fifteen. Common Sense Revisited	180
Epilogue	193
Chapter Notes	199
Bibliography	209
Index	215

Preface

In the not too distant future Americans will celebrate a milestone: our two hundred fiftieth Independence Day. The end of America's first quarter millennium will be a time to recover the stories of people who were there at the beginning; individuals who have been left out of our collective memory. Some, who were ordinary citizens, emerged in the Revolution as crucial leaders.

This is the story of the clerk who read Congress's declaration of independence to the crowd gathered at the State House on July 4, 1776. That night he likely helped oversee the printing of the broadside copies distributed the next morning. Later that month, by order of Congress, the clerk engrossed the declaration on vellum. Delegates began signing this finely penned document, *the* Declaration of Independence, in early August.

Timothy Matlack was a Philadelphia beer bottler who inflamed the people in town meetings and taverns. The grandson of an indentured servant, he led a militia battalion at Princeton. He was a disowned Quaker who rose from obscurity to become a delegate to Congress. The son of a farmer, Timothy sent peach trees to Monticello; an amateur scientist, he wrote about a dinosaur bone; a Pennsylvanian, he owned a steel furnace.

The historian A. M. Stackhouse offered this classic description: "Robust in health, brimful of animal spirits and vigor, virile, pugnacious, undauntedly courageous, quick to resent an insult or injury, self-reliant, a good hater, rejoicing as a strong man to run a race."

During the Revolutionary War, Timothy Matlack was a constant force in Pennsylvania. His unflagging dedication to the American cause earned him the admiration and respect of men like Thomas Jefferson and Richard Henry Lee. In this period Matlack was also fundamentally involved in Pennsylvania's upheaval: the fight for control of the province triggered by the battle in Congress over independence.

This is Timothy Matlack's story: from days of youth through apprenticeship, years adrift, ascent, downfall, resurgence, and finally old age. While the years of the Revolution are crucial, this book retraces all the dramatic events of his lifetime.

At the turn of the century Timothy Matlack was involved in a second, peaceful, revolution. After Thomas Jefferson's victory in 1800, Matlack and Pennsylvania's Democratic-Republicans considered their state "the key stone in the democratic arch." Matlack was once again a prominent leader for the victorious side.

Pennsylvania's radicals, and the Democratic-Republicans who followed them, sowed the seeds of an egalitarian American society of the early nineteenth century. The steps they took to rein in the moneyed class were the first in the continuing fight for equality in America. Timothy was the people's tribune.

But Timothy Matlack, as one adversary predicted, has been largely scrubbed from history. For all his contribution to independence and democracy, he has been relegated to very minor status. One reason may be prejudice. The historian Gary Nash writes that in the nineteenth century the radicals were largely ignored by Philadelphia's archivists and librarians. Nash writes:

> The papers of the radicals were lost or never preserved, and most of the officers of collecting institutions were as suspicious of ordinary people elected to high places as were those who, at the time, deplored the 1776 [Pennsylvania] Constitution.[1]

Nash guesses the conservative establishment disapproved of the radicals' desire for a "thorough reformation of American society in the interest of greater equality."

Most prominent among those given the cold shoulder was Thomas Paine. Nash says the nineteenth century was almost over before the Historical Society of Pennsylvania purchased a copy of *Common Sense* "owned by Paine's radical, warm-tempered compatriot, Timothy Matlack." Philadelphia's institutions had long since taken in the papers of such men as "Rush, Pemberton, Dickinson, McKean and Wilson." Nash's observation explains why no Matlack archive has been preserved.

But letters and papers do survive. These are in scattered collections held by the Historical Society of Pennsylvania, the American Philosophical Society, the Library Company of Philadelphia, the Haverford College Library, the University of Pennsylvania's Van Pelt Library, the Free Library of Philadelphia, the Massachusetts Historical Society, the New York Historical Society and the Library of Congress. These institutions made this book possible.

In my research I made extensive use of Peter Force's American Archives. I also relied on diaries and journals, some of which have been transcribed and published, and newspapers, some in their original form, others on microfilm or newsbank. The work of numerous historians was very important in making sense of these accounts. Steven Rosswurm was particularly influential. Matlack studies include A. M. Stackhouse's 1908 essay and Malcolm Bryan's more recent work, deposited at the American Philosophical Society.

I would like to thank Steven Rosswurm, Robert Allison, Pauline Maier, Malcolm Bryan, Bill Robling, Hollister Knowlton, Maureen Gallagher, Sarah Ruiz, James Hiatt, Mary Coelho, Barbara Gardiner, Ken and Marka Conrow, James Piper, Mike Cutchin, Matt Firme, Jonathan Simpson-Bint and Carolyn Davis Mehran. I would also like to thank Valerie-Ann Lutz, Charles Greifenstein (APS), Diana Peterson (Haverford), Daniel Rolf, Sarah Heim, and Ronald Medford (HSP). I especially thank my wife, Gabriela Thomas, for her love, support and patience.

* * *

Timothy Matlack made his share of regrettable choices. On more than one occasion he allowed himself to be used by the opposition for their purposes. And his "manumission" of a woman hurt his legacy as a friend to African slaves and their descendants. But the American people, including those held in slavery, were lucky to have this man on their side. Timothy Matlack lived to see the fiftieth anniversary of the Declaration of Independence. Near the end of his lifetime Americans honored him for his role in helping to win independence and create the United States of America. This is his life.

Introduction

In Congress, a unanimous vote for independence was achieved only over the objections of delegates opposed to separation from the King. In the first week of June those representing Pennsylvania were under specific instructions *not* to go along with secession from the British Empire. In the host province, the ruling class was determined to preserve the status quo. With the authority of Congress, Timothy Matlack and his radical associates deposed the Pennsylvania oligarchy blocking a declaration in contempt of the people's wishes.

With the discredited Pennsylvania Assembly suppressed, Matlack helped write the ultra-democratic constitution, which set the principles for his faction's revolutionary government. Three years later his administration passed the first abolition law in the Western hemisphere.

As Pennsylvania's powerful secretary, Matlack exposed Benedict Arnold's wrongdoing and was a key witness in his court-martial. As a committee man he investigated Robert Morris for predatory trading. Matlack rose to prominence at the expense of an established merchant class. By so doing he made powerful enemies. The opposition harped on the cockfights of his younger days and more recent violence. But the belligerent persona they constructed was not the man he was. Friends and relatives appreciated Timothy's empathy and kindness: this was a man who understood loss and suffering. Matlack's public persona was constructed by those who despised his triumphs, but his private life was marked by tragedy.

* * *

The narrative begins with the Philadelphia militia's attempt to cross the Delaware on December 25, 1776. Then it goes back to his grandfather's arrival in America; his father's tragic story; Timothy's struggles; his love for a young Quaker minister; and his starring role in an intercolonial cockmain. The march of the Paxton Boys is the trigger for Timothy's first association with a militia company. Across the colonies, discontentment with British regulation mounts. After Lexington and Concord, John Dickinson refuses to accede to independence. Matlack's radical wartime government supplants his Assembly.

The government's displeasure with Tories and Quakers escalates during the occupation of Philadelphia. The British Meschianza is a crowning display of excess. Matlack aides the Quakers exiled to western Virginia. His son Mordecai serves on the *Randolph*. Timothy's jailhouse meetings with a British spy expose him to accusations. Benedict Arnold's social contact with Tories leads to Matlack's investigation of his business affairs. Pennsylvania's radically democratic frame of government is the constant target of the elite, and Matlack is its steady defender. The hanging of two merchants is a stark moment in this power struggle. Matlack beats two Quakers with a cane and puts another one in jail. He complains of stress and fatigue.

An economic crisis climaxes in the Fort Wilson riot. Matlack's opposition to price fixing earns him the ire of his fellow Constitutionalists, but following a series of radical victories he is appointed to Congress. Matlack again angers his party by accepting a directorship in the new bank.

The war comes to an end, and so does Timothy Matlack's grip on power. Matlack is forced to resign the office of secretary and defend himself in court against accusations of financial wrongdoing. While cleared of these accusations, he faces more trouble upon returning from a self-imposed exile. During an expedition to explore Pennsylvania's rivers, Matlack meets with the Seneca chief Cornplanter and hears the address of the Seneca women. A yellow fever epidemic strikes Philadelphia. Following the death of his wife, Timothy remarries. Matlack returns to power as clerk of the Pennsylvania Senate. In his second political career Matlack plagues Federalists and Democratic-Republicans by turns, but at the turn of the century he is triumphant as a Jeffersonian democrat.

After receiving a gift, a copy of an old pamphlet, Timothy takes a trip back in time. In 1821, Matlack is honored on the forty-fifth anniversary of independence and reads the Declaration at a celebratory gathering. The Marquis de Lafayette visits him in 1824, and two years later, Charles Willson Peale paints his portrait for a final time.

One

The Failed Crossing

In late June 1776, on a fair afternoon, the five battalions of the Philadelphia militia were called to parade on the grounds at Carpenter's Hall: the "Associators" were preparing to join the war with England. A speaker rose to address the lines. The operations they were to be attached to, he said, were of vast importance: "The present campaign will probably decide the fate of America." At stake was an entire continent; one-quarter of the globe, he told them.

For a moment the men were silent. The magnitude of it was difficult to conceive. But standing there next to each other they understood one thing: they were going out to defend their province, their own country. At home, in Pennsylvania, the speaker offered them something radically new: the rights of men under a democratic government. "You are about to contend for permanent freedom to be supported by a government which will be derived from yourselves."

They all knew this was no ordinary summer, no ordinary year. They were trying to transform the world as they knew it. If they were successful, the speaker concluded, 1776 would be "famed in ... history to the end of time."[1]

A week later Congress declared the United Colonies independent states. The war was now officially a war for independence. But post riders carrying bad news arrived in Philadelphia at the end of August. General George Washington's Continental army had lost a major battle on Long Island. Having liberated Boston in the early spring, his forces conceded New York in the late fall.

Now in December the British army was advancing across New Jersey. The King's forces were marching on Philadelphia. Just four months after Congress signed the Declaration, General Howe's column reached Trenton, thirty miles upriver. Philadelphians who had openly supported independence fled in panic. Congress itself evacuated to Baltimore. A militia captain said of the delegates' flight to safety, "It has struck a damp on ye spirits of many."[2] For Americans with everything staked on liberty, this was a time of crisis.

Retreating ahead of a superior enemy, General Washington transported the remnant of his army over the river to Pennsylvania. Now he prepared his defenses for another assault. From Morrisville Washington ordered General Israel Putnam to take control of Philadelphia. He asked Brigadier General John Cadwalader, commander of the city militia, to defend two important ferry crossings. Washington told Cadwalader to give the enemy "all the opposition in your power," in the event of a landing. But knowing the militia would be overrun by British regulars, Washington warned the officer to "repair to the strong ground near Germaintown" if he found his side "quite unequal to their force."[3]

Cadwalader sent Colonel Timothy Matlack's rifle rangers to guard the Bristol ferry.[4] Those of his men who were fully equipped carried "a good Rifle gun, a powder-horn, a charger, a bullet-screw, twelve flints, a strong pouch, or bag, that will hold four pounds of ball, and such other accoutrements as may be proper for a Rifleman." In 1775 Congress had ordered Timothy's friend, Owen Biddle, to "procure a Rifle that will carry a half-pound ball, with a Telescope sight." But that was a weapon for the future.[5] The five-foot-long Pennsylvania or Kentucky rifles the men did carry could fire a half-ounce ball with accuracy up to two hundred fifty yards or more. Their rifles were effective at twice the range of a musket, but took twice as long to reload.[6]

From the town of Bristol Timothy had a clear view of a large island, once the home of the sachem Chygoes, out in the middle of the Delaware. Timothy knew his grandfather had gone ashore there in 1677, the year English Quakers settled Burlington, New Jersey. But as England and America were now divided, so were the descendants of that immigrant. Timothy was well aware that most of his kinsmen, being pacifist and loyalist Quakers, had great hope the American rebellion would soon be crushed. In the event of a British victory he himself would be hung as a traitor.

* * *

In Trenton, the British commander, General William Howe, considered whether or not to advance on Philadelphia. The fall of the capital city, he knew, would discourage the French from allying with the Americans. An invasion by his army could even end the war. But the traditional season for military campaigning was coming to an end. Howe, who was sympathetic to the American colonies, was ambivalent about proceeding. And so the general decided to forgo an attack and return to New York City for winter quarters.

Howe departed with his main force, but he left a string of garrisons across New Jersey. Crown forces would continue to occupy the conquered state. Three of his outposts, in Bordentown, Burlington and Trenton, were close to Philadelphia. Thanks to the presence of these forces, the numerous

One. The Failed Crossing

loyalists in the region were sanguine. Those of their neighbors who favored independence, on the other hand, feared a long winter of sleepless nights.

But on Saturday, December 21, a "great number of Country Militia" marched through Philadelphia on their way to join the commander in chief. Captain Thomas Rodney was thrilled to see the streets of Philadelphia full of militia and hundreds more pouring in hourly. The enemy was in the Delaware Valley, and patriotic men, Timothy's brothers among them, were ready to fight back.

That same day Thomas Paine published a pamphlet he hoped would excite Americans to fight on through the winter. Paine, an English expatriate, had made a name for himself as a pro-independence writer early that year. The harder the conflict, he now wrote, the more glorious the triumph. The crisis, he said, must be met:

> THESE are the times that try men's souls. The summer soldier and the sunshine patriot will, in this crisis, shrink from the service of their country; but he that stands by it now, deserves the love and thanks of man and woman.

Two days after Paine's work, *The American Crisis*, appeared, General Washington told General Cadwalader he had decided to attack the enemy outpost at Trenton. His battle plan called for three coordinated operations. After dark on Christmas night his own army would cross the Delaware at a point north of the enemy post and march down to attack at daybreak. Pennsylvania militia led by Brigadier General James Ewing, a Scots-Irish frontiersman from Lancaster, would make the second crossing south of Trenton and come up to stop the enemy from escaping in that direction. In the third operation Cadwalader's Philadelphia militia would cross further south, at Neshaminy ferry, and attack Hessian and Scottish units stationed in the vicinity of Bordentown and Burlington. Hessians, as all were bitterly aware, were Germanic soldiers hired by King George III to fight his colonists in America.

Cadwalader's orders were to coordinate points of attack with Colonel Samuel Griffin and General Israel Putnam. Washington told Cadwalader to strike at the same time he would: one hour before daylight on December 26. Washington said he had high hopes the Philadelphia brigade would defeat the enemy forces it encountered and join him in Trenton or Princeton.

On Christmas Day, however, the commander in chief's confidence in the southernmost leg of his operation diminished when he learned Griffin was "very sick abed." To make matters worse, Putnam was still scrambling to muster his force.

Notwithstanding the setback, Washington was determined to proceed with his plan. He wrote, "I am determined, as the Night is favourable, to cross the River and make the Attack upon Trenton in the morning." By favorable he did not mean he expected mild weather. What Washington had in mind was a dark night, which would hide the American movements.

Washington told Cadwalader that if he could not do much on his own, to "at least create as great a diversion as possible." At Neshaminy ferry, at nightfall, Colonel Matlack waited with his advance party. Captain Rodney's small Delaware Company arrived, followed by the rest of the Philadelphia brigade. The militia was finally reinforced by New England Continentals under Colonel Daniel Hitchcock. These soldiers were suffering greatly from "want of shoes, stockings and clothing." The men were supplied with two days' cooked rations.[7] After dark they prepared the transports: eight or nine scows and bateaux (flat-bottom boats).

The night was turning cold and windy. The officers were very concerned about floating ice in the clogged river. They also feared crossing to Burlington, where loyalists might alert the enemy. So the commanders decided to move five miles south to the more remote Dunk's ferry.[8] At about eight o'clock the men formed a column and started their march. Colonel Matlack's riflemen led the right hand file.

At Dunk's ferry the men were confronted with the same conditions. Captain Rodney wrote, "The River was ... very full of floating ice, and the wind was blowing very hard, and the night was very dark and cold, and we had great difficulty in crossing."[9] The men waiting their turn to cross lit fires to fend off the cold despite warnings from officers the flames would be spotted. The Delaware River, a quarter mile wide at this level, churned with tidal flows pushing back against the icy current. Floating ice jammed up along the New Jersey side, and a frozen pack extended out one hundred to three hundred yards from the bank. After three hours, about six hundred troops had made it across, but the transfer of the wagons, horses, and all-important artillery, two six-pound brass fieldpieces, proved impossible.[10] Cadwalader decided the expedition could not proceed without the gunnery and called off the offensive. The men were ordered to return to Bristol. Now officers had to persuade the disappointed and independent-minded men on the New Jersey side of the river that continuing on in defiance of the order was out of the question. Captain Rodney's men, and four Philadelphia companies under Captain George Henry, were the first to cross over and the last to return. A violent storm of windswept rain, sleet, and snow arrived at daybreak to further torment the miserable militia. The men recrossing struggled to navigate through ice which "began to drive with such Force & in such Quantities as threatened many Boats with absolute Destruction."

Washington's former aide, General Joseph Reed, and Major Joseph Cowperthwaite spent the night in a house in Burlington and in the early morning watched through a window as two Hessian dragoons rode down to observe

One. The Failed Crossing

the river.[11] At about 7:00 A.M., Reed heard cannon fire from the direction of Trenton. While neither Cadwalader's nor Ewing's forces were able to transverse the Delaware, General Washington's twenty-four hundred men, horses, wagons and artillery had passed it successfully. Once in New Jersey, Washington split his force into two columns and attacked the Hessian–manned garrison at Trenton from two sides. The American victory was complete. Eight hundred ninety-six enemy soldiers were captured and twenty-two were killed. Washington lost only two officers in the battle itself, but many more of his men died from hypothermia and illness during and after the freezing ordeal of the night crossing, the march to Trenton, and the return trip to Pennsylvania with prisoners.[12]

The good news spread quickly. A demoralized Continental army, badly defeated in New York and forced to retreat through New Jersey, had rebounded to win an unexpected and decisive victory. Whereas the loss of Philadelphia had been feared, crown forces were now evacuating their western-most outposts.

As glorious and thrilling as the news was for the Philadelphia militia, now back in Bristol, the men felt humiliated. Washington's army had won a great victory, whereas they themselves had failed to even cross the river. The men needed rest but they demanded immediate action to recover their spoiled honor.

Two

Haddonfield and Philadelphia

When Timothy Matlack's grandfather landed in West Jersey in 1677 he was put to work building houses in the wooded area along the Delaware River that became Burlington. William Matlack, an indentured carpenter, served the time he owed for his passage, earned a small parcel of land, and married a young woman named Mary Hancock. Now he faced the difficult task of clearing fields for crops. The first English settlers, Timothy said, "cleared little Patches of Land with infinite Labor, cutting up every Tree and Grubb by the Root, until they broke their Hearts with the Labor." The work was "Herculean" and despite the richness of the land "many hardly obtained themselves Bread." The struggle was so difficult "numbers actually returned to England." Those who stayed suffered periods of starvation. Timothy's grandmother Mary said food was sometimes so scarce she was glad to partake of a meal from the hog tub.[1]

The couple's prospects improved when William and two companions acquired a tract of land from the Lenape. The men traded "one match coat, one little Rumlit of Rum, and two bottles of Rum" for "all those plantations at Pimasawquin." Chief Tallaca also pledged "forever to defend" the newcomers from any other Indians laying claim to the land.[2] By this agreement Timothy's grandfather took possession of his share of the fertile bottomland between the north and south branches of the Pennsauken Creek. This land, previously cleared by the Indian women, yielded the crops the Matlacks desperately needed.

William and Mary built a homestead and raised nine children. William taught his six sons farming and carpentry. When the youngest of these boys, Timothy's father, turned nineteen, he set to work clearing his own piece of forested land. Like his father before him he girdled trees to kill them where they stood and hauled away limbs and stones. On the land he freed he planted his wheat and corn. Timothy's father married Mary Haines in 1720, and two girls, Priscilla and Letitia, were born in the years that followed. But the man

Two. Haddonfield and Philadelphia

had a hard time as a farmer. If removing woodland for agriculture could take a decade to complete, he survived the hardest years, but the crops he raised were never more than meager. Timothy's father felt tired and discouraged. And so he decided to take his family and move on.

At Cooper's Creek, Elizabeth Haddon and her husband, the Quaker preacher John Estaugh, had established the town of Haddonfield in the early years of the century.[3] It was here that Timothy's father opened a country store. Matlack Sr. offered dry goods, whiskey and tobacco, but people were accustomed to purchasing their supplies from Sarah Norris, the established shopkeeper in town.[4]

While her husband struggled to support his family, Mary gave birth to her third child, a girl she named Achsah. Another infant arrived two years later, but this time there was trouble: blood was lost and Mary was bled. The little girl, Abi, lived three weeks, and Mary Haines Matlack died the same day her baby did, on a cold day in February 1728.

Timothy's father was left alone with three young daughters to care for. Among the neighbors who came to help was a woman named Martha Burr. Martha was the wife of one of Mary's kinsmen, Josiah Haines. But Josiah soon followed his cousin to the graveyard, and Martha was left alone with *her* children. Timothy's father and mother married in early 1730, and a girl named Sybil was born near the end of year.

Two years later Matlack purchased four acres from a man named John Kay.[5] On one of his town lots he built brew and malt houses. But once again he struggled to find customers. He was forced to take work as a carpenter. The town of Gloucester (now Gloucester City, near South Philadelphia) hired him to build stocks and a whipping post "before the prison windows."[6] But it wasn't enough. The following year he signed a promissory note for the large sum of £100, which he never repaid.

Martha gave birth to a girl named Elizabeth in 1734. Two years later, on May 28, 1736, she gave birth to her husband's first son, Timothy Matlack Jr.

In old age Timothy Matlack said he could not remember when he was born. He lost track of his natal day, but pictures of childhood always stayed in his mind.[7] He saw his grandfather carrying him to school on his back "at a time when there was deep snow."[8] In a different season he saw himself "in a certain Tree standing in John Gill's Orchard, getting Apples, when he could hear John Estaugh preaching in friends meeting house, tho' not so distinctly as to know what he said."

When Timothy was too young to attend Quaker Meeting, his older sisters worshiped with the adults inside. Quakers were taught to avoid such wicked diversions as card playing and dancing. John Estaugh's friend and fellow minister, Thomas Chalkley, warned that cards were "engines of Satan" and "as

many paces as a person takes in the Dance, so many ... steps they take towards Hell."[9] Not relishing a turn with Lucifer, the Matlack girls spent their time copying verse and sewing. Twelve-year-old Letitia made a "distressingly fine" embroidered work, called a sampler, with floral designs, scriptural quotations, and the names of her family members in tiny cross-stitches.

Letitia, it was said, was a great beauty. She was married twice and had children with both of her husbands, but died at twenty-eight. Mysteriously, some thought "poison from her negro" was her doom.[10]

The girls helped their younger brother with his schoolwork, and their father did what he could to help. On a trip to Philadelphia he purchased a dictionary at Benjamin Franklin's print shop. He also bought dozens of copies of Franklin's *Poor Richard's Almanack*: the annual handbook must have sold well in his Haddonfield store.[11]

But Timothy's father continued to struggle. As time went by he was signing more notes for debts he owed, most of them to Minister Estaugh himself.[12] After that good man died on a mission to Tortola, his wife Elizabeth continued to extend credit to Mr. Matlack. She did so despite her awareness she might never be repaid.

* * *

Timothy was eight years old when his family moved to Philadelphia, the largest city in the colonies. His father rented an old house on High Street with a kitchen out back and a shared well in the side alley. Benjamin Franklin and his family lived next door. Out on the street the long Jersey market filled with farmers and wagons on Wednesday and Saturday afternoons. The General Assembly met at the nearby courthouse while carpenters finished a new provincial building on Chestnut Street. Along the riverfront men worked the shipyards and wharves. Laborers, craftsmen and merchants alike filled the city's taverns but the dram shops in Hell Town, the grand jury complained, were attracting too many apprentices, servants and "even negroes."[13]

Timothy's father's servant, an Englishman named Andrew Goodson, escaped soon after the move to Philadelphia. Goodson had always intended to work off his passage, but his health had suffered. The years ahead seemed endless, and others were doing well down south. One night Goodson and three companions—Billy Collemore and the Jones brothers—met at a waterfront tavern. Early in the morning they boarded a seventeen-foot boat fitted

Opposite page: Philadelphia from across the Delaware, with street plan and renderings of the Battery and State House. (1) Christ Church; (2) the State House; (3) the Court House; and (4) the Presbyterian Church. Print. London: Thomas Jeffreys, 1771. Library of Congress, Prints and Photographs Division.

out with an "old Square Spritsail" and a new pine rudder. Posing as castaway sailors, the men sailed down the river and out into the Delaware Bay. In the newspapers Matlack offered a reward for the capture and return of his man. He described Goodson as "Pale, having had the fever and Ague.... Had on when he went away, a blue cloth coat, ozenbrigs Jacket and Trowsers, Thread Stockings, a felt Hat, and no Hair." John Jones, a thick set man, was wearing a red jacket and new shoes. His brother Morgan was short and bowlegged. He and Collemore were last seen wearing beaver hats. A reward of £5 was offered for each runaway. Anyone who returned the boat would receive twenty shillings. But the men and their vessel were long gone down the Atlantic coast.

Timothy went to school. After class he and his friends cut bows and arrows from the hedges surrounding Southeast Square. The boys fished in the creek there and shot at ducks in the pond. When thousands of passenger pigeons flew over the city, Timothy watched people climb up on their roofs to whack at them with sticks. Later he saw wagonloads for sale at the market.

Philadelphia's streets opened up to countryside a few blocks west of the Delaware, and wooded areas were not far away. Timothy's step-brother, Reuben Haines, was with a group of men who chased a bear from Fairmount to Centre Square and shot it down from a cherry tree.[14]

But Philadelphians feared rampant fire much more than rampant bears. Reuben and his stepfather joined the Fellowship Fire Company and hung buckets and bags near their front door. In 1750 their company purchased a "fourth rate" engine from a London merchant for £49.[15] Isaac Williams painted the name "Fellowship Fire Co" on the side of their water pump on wheels, and Matlack Sr. kept a set of keys to its storage shed.

Matlack Sr. opened a new mercantile. In the newspapers he announced his establishment stocked "European and West-India goods, cheap for ready money or short credit." A sign on his house identified it as the location of his shop, the Two Sugar Loaves. Passersby could see that, despite rumors of his struggles, the new man was confident of success: Timothy's father had painted two white peaks of sweetener on his sign and, showily, his initials "T. M." in gold letters. While his career had been anything but brilliant, he was starting his new life with a burst of optimism.

In 1745 Timothy's father purchased a sizable lot on High Street from the overseers of the Quaker School and arranged for the construction of "two good and substantial Brick houses."[16] At the back of the property, which turned out onto the northeast side of Fourth Street, he built new brew and malt houses. Reuben Haines went to work for his stepfather in this new establishment, The Brewer's Horse & Dray.

Matlack Sr.'s prospects seemed to be improving, but he was distracted

Two. Haddonfield and Philadelphia

by unsettled business back in Haddonfield. In the newspapers he announced he would visit that town to collect unpaid debts. On one of these trips he auctioned off cows, sundry household goods, and two copper stills with crain necks and puter worms. The distillery equipment was the costly remnant of a failed rum venture.

While Matlack Sr. spent time in New Jersey, his Philadelphia brewery was losing out to competitors. In his second year in operation the captain of the Tetsworth paid him nine shillings for an order. But George Emlen sold six times more beer to this customer.[17] By now Matlack Sr. was borrowing money from wealthy Philadelphia merchants, family members in the middle ranks of society, and one individual whose status was below all others. In January 1748, Matlack borrowed £20 from Elizabeth Haddon's slave Primus. The borrower wrote out a note in his wild script and the lender signed it with his mark.[18]

Primus, whose owner allowed him to earn money, was better off than other slaves in the area. Ferryman Daniel Cooper's "freedom-minded" Quaco was chained with an iron collar and handcuffs.[19] Quakers were allowed to own slaves if they treated them "with humanity, & in a christian manner." Their 1719 Book of Discipline, however, advised that no member be involved in the trade, "fetching or importing negroe slaves from their own country or elsewhere."[20]

* * *

In 1749, the year he turned thirteen, Timothy Matlack Jr. began a seven-and-a-half-year apprenticeship. He was to learn the art and mystery of the merchant's trade. Timothy's new master was the prosperous Quaker John Reynell. But it was Reynell's business partner, Mary Coates, who signed Timothy's contract along with the new apprentice and his father. The young man's signature, with its looping flourishes, stood in elegant contrast to his parent's effort. His father struggled with quill in hand and nearly misspelled his own last name. The younger Timothy's display of penmanship was a personal statement: the son of a struggling shopkeeper and brewer, he himself was on his way to becoming a *merchant. This* Timothy Matlack would be ordering *his* goods directly from Great Britain and the West Indies. Imagining his bright future, Timothy dreamed of the carriage he would buy and the country estate he would build. With these signs of wealth, Timothy Matlack Jr. would announce his ascension into the ranks of Philadelphia's better sort. But whatever life he imagined for himself, his family's current reality was something quite different. His father's business affairs were as shaky as his pen.

* * *

The following year, 1750, the Matlacks moved into their new brick house on Market (High) Street. Their new home stood cattycorner to the jail and a block up from the popular Indian King tavern. The family's new neighbors included the merchant John Wister and the apothecary Miles Strickland. Now that Timothy had four younger brothers, his mother may have appreciated Strickland's remedies, which included Squire's elixir, Godfrey's cordial and Mary Banister's drops.[21] In July Matlack Sr. announced he had moved to his "brew-house in Market Street ... where he carries on the brewing trade and shopkeeping as usual."[22] Wagons going to the brewery, at the back of the property, used the entrance on Fourth Street.

Having moved in, Timothy's father sublet his family's previous home to Benjamin Franklin. In that house, two days before Christmas, Franklin suffered a severe shock while trying to kill a turkey with "electrical fire."[23] Ben recovered from the scare; the bird was dispatched by conventional means; and both were greeted at the holiday table with laughter. Franklin joked that in trying to kill the turkey he nearly cooked the goose. The Matlacks tried to enjoy their own celebration two blocks away. By this time Sybil, nineteen, had a family of her own. Elizabeth was seventeen, Timothy fifteen, and Titus, thirteen. The younger boys running through the house were Seth, White and Josiah. While this was a happy occasion, the debts remained to be paid.

Eight months later, on August 22, 1751, Sheriff Isaac Griffiths notified the public that a suit by Charles Willing — the merchant, slave trader, and former mayor of Philadelphia — had forced the seizure of Matlack Sr.'s shop and household goods.[24] On the brink of disaster, a last minute agreement with Mr. Willing — and ninety other creditors — won Timothy's father a reprieve. The lenders agreed to execute a bond and warrant of attorney in the amount of six thousand pounds and allow three years continued use of the property "in order and intent to improve the same for the payment of said debts." The lenders also agreed not to "molest, sue, seize, attack or arrest the said Matlack or Reuben Haines" during the three-year respite. As part of the deal Reuben was put in charge of the brewery. The fate of the business, and the Matlack family, was in the hands of the twenty-four-year-old.

An inventory taken at this time listed copper stills, casks, barrels, yeast tubs, coolers, funnels, ladles, pails, a wort pump, liquor back, cart, riding chair, and wheelbarrow. Supplies included eight hundred sixty bushels of malt, nine bushels of barley, thirty gallons of molasses, fourteen barrels of beer and one thousand boards. Three horses, a mare, and two colts were valued at £80, while two cows were worth £5. An upstairs room contained an old desk, arm chair, feather bed, two flock beds, an alarm clock and four common rush chairs.[25] The inspector valued all of it at £678.19.6. Reuben had equipment, raw materials, and, most importantly, a head for business.

Two. Haddonfield and Philadelphia

Matlack Sr. was left a ruined man. The inventory shows he was making rum, and heavy consumption of this liquor may have contributed to his sudden decline. In his final testimony he lamented his many debts. He wished God would prolong his life, to give him time to clear his name, but he hardly expected this blessing. Timothy Matlack Sr. named Reuben Haines executor of his will and his sole heir. Matlack Sr. hoped that if and when his debts were settled a small surplus would remain for his wife and three youngest sons. He hoped these boys would be schooled until reaching a fit age to be put out to apprenticeships. While Reuben undoubtedly hoped to comply with his stepfather's request and help his mother and siblings, lawyers emphasized that this would happen only at Haines's "own indulgence and ability or as he shall think fit." Timothy Sr. failed to mention his other children, Timothy Jr. among them.[26] Timothy Matlack Sr. died in the late summer of 1752 at the age of fifty-seven. His family was left with a sense of sadness and shame.

The young Matlack boys did in fact receive their education, but only as "poor scholars" in Alexander Seaton's charity school. The boys' indigent status took a psychological toll. The hardest hit may have been eight-year-old Seth, who quit school for a time. He later moved to Northumberland County, joined a militia battalion, and was killed in the Revolutionary War.[27]

The current family tragedy was especially painful for the boys' older brother, their father's namesake, Timothy Jr. His father's ignoble end meant he was starting life with a black stain on his name. When he was not feeling sorry for himself he felt resentment and anger.

But Timothy had years left to serve as an apprentice. His master kept him working endlessly at his desk, writing out correspondence and contracts in duplicate. Timothy said he had John Reynell's full confidence and did "*all of his writing.*"[28] Any free time he had was strictly monitored. According to the terms of service he was not allowed to play "Cards, Dice, or any other unlawful Game," nor "absent himself, Day or Night," without his master's leave. He could not "haunt Ale-houses, Taverns, or Play-houses," marry, or "commit Fornication."[29]

Alternatively Timothy was encouraged to attend meetings for worship. Soon he became such a devoted member of the Society of Friends people considered him a candidate for the ministry.

Helping to make his new way of life attractive was Catherine Payton, a twenty-six-year-old traveling minister from England who made Philadelphia her base in the colonies. Catherine's mission was to spread the welcome news of salvation, and Timothy, for one, was ready to listen. Catherine could bring tears to the eyes of hypocrites and inspire fledgling poets to take up their awkward pens. Timothy's ode to Catherine included his admission that her "Youth & Beauty" helped the sacred truths flow with redoubled force. The young man succumbed to the "resistless eloquence" of a voice that brought him "unknown Joy."[30]

Timothy was so enamored he would have been eager to join Catherine's party on a trip to New England. At one stop on this journey, in Nantucket, Catherine wrote that she was accompanied by Mary Paisley and three Philadelphians: Daniel Stanton, Israel Pemberton, and a third, unnamed, man. At Woods Hole, as Stanton and Pemberton made preparations to return home, the third individual expressed his reluctance to part ways with the ministerial ladies. The women were, in turn, hesitant to refuse the company of a young man "remarkably under the baptizing power of Truth." Catherine wrote that this believer had earned her "tender regard." It was agreed the man would continue on the trip, as he might be of assistance. And so the young admirer enjoyed two more weeks in the women's company. Their time together finally came to an end in Boston.

In her memoirs, Catherine Payton offered words of caution for single women who, as ministers, found themselves in the unusual circumstance of traveling alone. When dealing with the opposite sex, she advised, women should avoid sliding into "conversation and behaviour, which tended to engage the affections of young men." If any "forward thought which looks beyond friendship" should surface, she recommended it be checked with some "prudent remarks (yet obliquely)." At the same time, she said, it was best to avoid any austere conduct that might hurt these "tender plants."[31]

It seems unlikely that John Reynell allowed his prized apprentice to travel. Timothy was perhaps not the mystery man Catherine described. But he was clearly one of the green shoots she had in mind. When she left Philadelphia for the last time, on June 5, 1756, Timothy was twenty years old and his feelings ran deep. "My heart is so depressed," he told John Peters. He was suffering from a sense of "unutterable distress." The departure of his idol also triggered a crisis of faith. "In my unguarded hours," he said, "I have been ready to make myself Wings & fly into speculations." But the Lord "humbled me" and "caused me to walk softly." Adding to his turmoil was a state of physical exhaustion which left him vulnerable to illness: "I shall indeavour to rest as quiet as possible" and "cast myself upon his mercyfull Power, for Guidance & Protection." But Timothy was relieved that God "hath not entirely cut off that Hope which supported my Soul under many Afflictions."[32] The heartbroken apprentice would survive.

On May 21, 1757, Timothy Matlack's seven-and-a-half-year apprenticeship came to an end. A week later he celebrated his twenty-first birthday. Finally a free man, Timothy spent as much time as he could in the company of Ellen Yarnall. The daughter of a Quaker minister, Nelly was warmhearted and full of life. Timothy and Ellen married in October of the following year,

Two. Haddonfield and Philadelphia

and their son William, called Billy, was born in the summer of 1759. Timothy and Ellen's second child, Mordecai, arrived two years later.

In naming his sons after his grandfather and his father-in-law, Timothy deliberately shunned his father's name, which was also his own. The shame he felt for his parent was stronger than his own optimism and pride.

* * *

Martha's joy at the arrival of her grandson Billy was lost in the loss of her daughter. When he was born, she was in Haddonfield taking care of grandchildren left motherless.

In May family and friends had gathered in the house where Timothy's sister Sybil lay dying.[33] She had caught an infection, it was thought, while in Philadelphia for Yearly Meeting. About two hours before her death, Sybil asked for a drink of cold water and said: "Lay me down and let me die."

In her final hour of life she recited a prayer heard clearly by the people in the room: "Dearest Father Remember my little ones ... my poor little Babe I commit him unto thee." Then she asked her husband to let her go: "My Dear, give me up. Give me up. This is the end of all Fear."

But then the color returned to Sybil's face. She opened her eyes and asked to be raised up again. Looking around in confusion she asked: "Where have I been, why is it thus, is it possible for men (or me) to die twice?" Her husband said hopefully: "My Dear it may be that the Almighty will please to restore thee to us again." But to this she replied, "I have not desired it." Sybil took a final drink and asked to be turned to one side. Then she "died away like a lamb without sigh or groan."

Sybil's husband, David Cooper, was devastated: "Oh! How is the most delightful flower taken away, in her greatest fragrance, in the morning of her bloom." Sybil left six children, the youngest still a baby. Cooper prepared himself to "take them under his peculiar care, & make them men and women worthy of such a mother."

A few years later his fourteen-year-old daughter took charge of raising her five younger siblings. This Martha, Timothy's niece, served as her father's "housekeeper" until her marriage to Samuel Allinson ten years later.[34]

* * *

Benjamin Franklin and his family had moved across the street from his post office. From where he now lived he had had only to walk next door to pay Matlack Sr. the last £10 due "for rent of the house in the Jersey Market."[35] Now a member of the Pennsylvania Assembly, Franklin hired Timothy Jr. to transcribe onto parchment a massive petition entitled: "To the King's Most Excellent Majesty for Council." The document was a detailed report of the treaties the

Penn family made with various Indian tribes.[36] The work he did for Franklin was a point of honor, but Timothy Matlack hadn't served such a long apprenticeship to become a scrivener.

In 1760 Timothy opened his mercantile. Readers of the *Pennsylvania Gazette* learned that at the sign of the Case Knife, on Market Street near Fourth, TIMOTHY MATLACK was offering goods imported "in the last vessels" from London and Liverpool to be sold "very cheap, for ready money or three months credit."[37] Following his mentor, Mary Coates, Timothy had decided to import cloths and metal wares. The fineries included "taffeties, superfine broadcloth, white linen and black sattin." The other line was anchored by "heart and club German steel, Stidman's ... cross-cut saws, duck, goose and buck shot ... and an assortment of iron mongery." Perhaps Nelly ran the mercery while Timothy stocked the hardware out back.

Matlack's experience with metals led to his purchase of a rudimentary steel mill two years later. Timothy and his friend Owen Biddle paid £155 for the Petty's Run steel furnace in Trenton. Biddle, a watchmaker, was a son of John and Sarah Biddle, the owners of the Indian King tavern. While Timothy and Owen realized steel was the future, the amount they produced at Petty's Run was minimal. The problem, Matlack said, was "few people are aware how much stronger Steel is than iron."[38]

But there was more to the story of Petty's Run. As Timothy later said, "*British* Tyranny restrained us from making *Steel*, to enrich Her Merchants and Manufacturers." In 1750 Parliament set a moratorium on the construction of steel furnaces in America. They did this to protect Britain's steel industry and insure a source of pig iron. In the fall of that year, by order of the governor, Sheriff John Allen of Hunterdon County made a survey in his jurisdiction to enforce compliance. At Petty's Run he reported finding an old iron plating mill and a new steel furnace. The plating mill had been long active, but the furnace was not yet in use. Whether or not it had ever been fired, Benjamin Yard had his kiln in place before the deadline.[39] It was Yard who later sold his business to Matlack and Biddle.

Three
The March of the Paxton Boys

In November 1761, Timothy made a trip to New York City to meet the schooner *Peggy*. He had planned to check on cargo but found the ship late in arriving. Timothy told Thomas Wharton the crossing from "Statton Island to York" had been a "disagreeable, dangerous passage (over the Bay) of three hours and upwards, thro' a hard gale of wind." He said he kept his mare with him to protect her from the British officers at Perth Amboy. The officers, he said, take "any persons horse out of the stable at Taverns and use 'em at their pleasure without asking leave."[1]

The British army had been in North America since the start of the French and Indian War. In 1754 Catherine Payton had seen General Braddock's force arrive in Philadelphia. Most of the fighting between the French and the British had ended by 1760, but Parliament had decided to leave troops stationed in America.

* * *

In late January 1764, Governor John Penn received a report that fifteen hundred Pennsylvanians were collecting arms and powder in preparation for a march on Philadelphia. These angry men said they were coming to kill the "Moravian" Indians being housed in the city for their protection. The western frontiersmen said they had no intention of harming the Quakers who were the Indians' sponsors, but that anyone who interfered would also be killed.[2]

The news was especially troubling in light of the recent massacre of the Conestogas. In December, near Lancaster, six members of this tribe had been killed by armed men. A small number of survivors, those who had been away at the time of the attack, were subsequently locked up in the Lancaster workhouse in an attempt to save their lives. But in another emphatic demonstration of the fury of these Scots-Irish settlers, more than one hundred men rode in and killed these fourteen individuals, the last of their people.

The Conestogas were Susquehannock Indians whose original homelands were on the Susquehanna River. Making their killing especially painful was the fact that this tribe had signed a treaty with William Penn in 1701. This covenant had confirmed Pennsylvania's commitment to peace, and forbade "any Act of Hostility or Violence, Wrong or Injury." Penn, the founder of the province, hoped Europeans and Indians would "forever hereafter be as one head & one heart, & live in true Friendship and Amity as one People."[3] As Penn's heirs and successors, the governor and the Assembly were horrified by the fate of the Conestogas. Governor John Penn offered a reward of £200 for the capture of the ringleaders, but neighbors refused to identify them. Quakers in the Assembly complained that not enough was being done to arrest the perpetrators and demanded western officials be brought to Philadelphia for interrogation.[4]

The western farmers' misdirected action was their furious response to Pontiac's War. Pontiac was the Ottawa leader whose assault on Fort Detroit in the spring of 1763 triggered a string of attacks on garrisons and frontier settlements by Delaware, Shawnee, Huron, Seneca and Mingo warriors. The Indians moved to clear their land by force when the promises made to them by the Kingdom of Great Britain, victorious in the French and Indian War, were not kept: the British failed to demolish forts and evict white settlers in Indian Territory as they had promised to do. As a result of the ensuing bloodshed, "the whole length of the western frontier contracted violently and recoiled upon the eastern settlements."[5] Refugees crowded into towns on the outer edge of white civilization. In their misery, frontiersmen blamed Pennsylvania's Assembly for failing to protect them. Predominantly Scots-Irish Presbyterians, the western farmers even assumed the Quaker-dominated Assembly favored Indians over themselves. The frontiersmen found evidence to support their theories of injustice in the transfer of the Moravian Indians to Philadelphia. These Christianized natives had been put under protection after being threatened by another group of backcountry militants seeking arbitrary revenge. The Moravian Indians were housed in the city's barracks until the "indescribable rage" of some city residents forced the Quakers to move them to the pesthouse on Province Island, at the mouth of the Schuylkill.[6] A second effort to move the Indians to a safe haven in New York failed when the Governor of that colony refused to admit the refugees. The Indians' caretakers were forced to bring them back to Philadelphia.

Now in early February came confirmation the armed vigilantes were in fact on their way. Residents responded to the governor's call to form militia companies to defend the city. One thousand citizens joined foot, horse and artillery companies. Two of Timothy Matlack's friends, Clement Biddle and Joseph Cowperthwaite, organized two hundred Quakers into a militia. Among those who joined this company were John Mears, Benjamin Mifflin, John

Three. The March of the Paxton Boys

Elmslie, Samuel Parker, Henry Shute and William Carter.[7] By taking up arms these men were acting in violation of the Society of Friends' principles of pacifism and non-resistance. War or violence, Friends said, could not be justified under any circumstance.

For twenty-seven-year-old Timothy Matlack, a man devoted to his faith, the current crisis left him with a difficult choice: adhere to Quaker teachings or march out with his peers. On the one hand he risked disownment and on the other unspoken dishonor. The decision he made now would affect the course of his life. While his devotion was real, vigilantes were threatening to kill innocent Indians and menace his neighbors and friends. Timothy felt he had no choice but to answer the governor's call.[8]

In the early morning of March 5, 1764, the city was awakened by a general alarm. Bells rang, drums beat to arms, and residents set out candles to light the way for their defenders.[9] The Paxton Boys had crossed the Schuylkill at Swedes Ford. What followed were scenes of false alarms and panicked confusion. The prominent Quaker Israel Pemberton, founder of the Friendly Association for Regaining and Preserving Peace with the Indians by Pacific Measures, fled town.

But the alarm was called off when it was learned the marchers had stopped at Germantown. Benjamin Franklin led a delegation to meet the hostile visitors, about two hundred fifty in number. Franklin's delegation called their attention to the British troops and militia companies arrayed in defense of Philadelphia. The Paxton Boys agreed to suspend their enterprise and submit their grievances in writing.

The westerners' written address requested, first and foremost, equal representation in the Assembly. To this Pennsylvania's legislators were slow to respond. In 1776 Timothy Matlack would be among the radical leaders who would force their hand.

In the aftermath of the Paxton Boys' march, the Society of Friends came under heavy criticism for the warlike behavior of its members. Whereas Quakers had constantly refused to support the war effort in the west, critics charged, they had sung a different tune when their own members were threatened back east. The Quaker leader James Pemberton responded by calling the men who joined the militia company "unstable youth and lukewarm members."[10] But the episode was remembered during the War of Independence, when Quakers were accused of being hypocritical for claiming conscientious objection despite having armed themselves against the vigilantes. The Philadelphia Yearly Meeting responded eloquently to this charge, saying, "We are led out of all Wars and Fightings by the Principle of Grace and Truth in our own Minds by which we are ... concerned to spread ... the peaceable Doctrines of Christ, to seek the good of all."[11]

For the Quaker named Timothy Matlack, joining a militia company marked the start of a general decline in approved behavior. That summer the Society of Friends said Timothy had become negligent in attending religious meetings while "frequenting company in such a manner as to spend too much of his time from home." The Quakers recorded another serious problem: the failure of his mercantile. Their complaint said: "His business became neglected and having contracted Debts, he became encumbered in his circumstances; that although he surrendered his effects for the use of his creditors there has not been sufficient to satisfy their demands."[12] The punishment was severe. Timothy was disowned. Timothy Matlack had been a devout Quaker and in old age he would return to Friends' Meeting. But at this time in his life he was an outbound prodigal son.

Timothy had been raised to live with Quaker simplicity and to make his living in a lucrative trade. He might have been a successful merchant, thanks to his facility with numbers, but he found himself more interested in the weight of a prize cow, or the distance of a race course, than the price of linen in London. Timothy had once admired Catherine Payton's austere lifestyle. She had been

> Wean'd from the World with all its pleasing Toys.
> Of low Enjoyments & of earthborn Joys[13]

But when he wrote these words Timothy must have been aware that for him, life's pleasures were irresistible. And so, by mutual consent, it was decided Timothy Matlack would no longer wear the Quaker habit or their broad-brimmed hat. He would even have to change his manner of speech.

The news of Timothy's bankruptcy was greeted by some with a sense of tedious familiarity. In little more than a decade's time the son had repeated the father's failure, some thought, in a predictable way. But those close to the family felt only sadness and disappointment. Timothy's failure was a troubling event for his wife Nelly and his mother Martha. Both women were painfully aware of how his father's business collapse had triggered *his* downward spiral.

But Martha had come to the end of her own time. She died a month after Timothy's disownment. In her lifetime Martha Burr Haines Matlack lost two husbands and a daughter. All three had left her with numerous children to care for. Martha bequeathed her property, including a lot on the west side of Fourth Street, to her eldest son Reuben. She made the stipulation that he pay £120 to each of her other children.

* * *

After his father's failure and early death, Timothy found consolation in religion. Now, after his own failure and the loss of his mother, he filled the emptiness in the taverns. In Philadelphia, public houses were ubiquitous. From Front Street to Center Square to Humphrey's Ferry on the Schuylkill, well-known taverns included the White Horse, the Blue Anchor and the Boar's Head. A dram could also be had at the Hen and Chickens, the Death of the Fox, and the Ship-a-Ground. Popular tavern drinks included rum punch, toddy, club, grog and sling. While Timothy tried them all, he did not fall into the abyss. In the alehouses, Matlack found an appealing world. In Philadelphia, the most diverse of the five colonial cities, men of distinct ethnic backgrounds and social classes found themselves sitting together around tavern tables. Public houses were frequented by Germans, Scots-Irish, Swedes, Quakers and the city's other cultures. The men talked trade, politics and sport over rounds of beer, wine and rum punch. This was, after all, a time of "fascination with the public world." And this phenomenon was visible in the "widespread popularity of taverngoing,"[14]

Timothy Matlack joined in with eagerness, and people took notice of the man, whose stature was impressive. His outward personality and friendly manner made him popular. With his acceptance into Philadelphia's tavern world, Timothy found an identity which saved him from this second crisis. He was on his way to becoming a *Public Man*. Matlack's embrace of public life led almost inevitably to his participation in the town meetings and committees of the climactic years of the American Revolution. The first Continental Congress was only ten years away.

* * *

In the aftermath of the French and Indian War, British-Americans living in the thirteen colonies became increasingly disgruntled with British colonial rule. Especially despised were searches for smuggled goods legalized by the Navigation Acts and taxes imposed by the Stamp Act. The Stamp Act required that newspapers, pamphlets and many documents be printed on stamped paper made in England. The duty stamps raised revenue to pay for the thousands of troops left stationed in North America after the war.

As the first tax on commercial activity within the colonies, not trade, the stamp levy triggered a violent response in New England and demonstrations throughout the colonies.[15] Resistance, however ununified, led to an intercolonial meeting the year following Timothy's disownment and public emergence. On October 19, 1765, leaders from nine colonies met in New York and issued a Declaration of Rights. The Stamp Act Congress said no taxes could be imposed on the colonists as Englishmen without "their own consent, given personally, or by their Representatives." The congress also stated that "the People of these Colonies are not, and from their local Circumstances cannot be, Represented in the House of Commons in Great-Britain."[16]

Merchants on both sides of the Atlantic actively protested the new tax. In early November Philadelphia's traders, including eighty Quakers, signed a nonimportation agreement (as a failed merchant Timothy could not participate).[17] The economic resistance was effective. On a rainy night in April 1766, Matlack rode out to tell his friend Jacob Hiltzheimer the Stamp Act had been repealed for certain.[18]

Good will for the British monarch now returned to Philadelphia. In June the Matlacks and Hiltzheimers joined a banquet on the banks of the Schuylkill for King George III's birthday. A toast to the King's health, first offered by Dr. Franklin in London, "gave great satisfaction to the Company."[19]

With the stamp crisis over, Timothy and his friend Jacob got back to doing the things they enjoyed most. They took rides along the rivers, shot pigeons, traded horses and fished. The two joined clubs and societies, including the patriotic Liberty Fishing Company.[20] They also went to the theater. In February 1767, the American Company was at Southwark Theater. On a clear and cold Monday night Matlack and Hiltzheimer rode Jacob's sleigh down to see *Cato*.[21] Two weeks later Timothy and Jacob went back to the theater with their wives for a production of *Romeo & Juliet*.[22] Nelly was pregnant on this occasion, and the Matlacks welcomed their daughter Catherine in April. Catherine was the couple's fourth child (a girl named Sybil had arrived two years earlier).

* * *

Two years after taking charge of the Matlack brewery, Reuben Haines had signed a new agreement with his remaining creditors. In August 1754, these thirty-five lenders had confirmed their acceptance of a one-quarter payment upfront, a second quarter payment within two years, and their share of £500 at closure.[23] All were repaid and the brewery was saved. All were reimbursed, that is, except for the man left out of the deal: the slave Primus. Over the years Matlack Sr. paid his lender 7.5 percent interest, and Haines continued making payments, which Primus signed for with his mark. But his £20 were never returned, and after a few years he simply stopped coming around. Perhaps he was too old to travel. Or he had come to the end of his own time.

By now Reuben had transformed the failed Matlack operation into Haines & Twells, the largest brewery and malt house in Philadelphia.[24] Reuben's customers included Governor John Penn and, years later, President George Washington.[25] Reuben was now a wealthy man with land holdings. When Haines organized the speculative purchase of two thousand acres in Cumberland County, at the head of Penn Creek, he brought his step-brother Timothy in on one hundred fifty.

In May 1766, Reuben set Timothy up in a bottled beer business. Haines supplied the beer, which Timothy described as "remarkably pale, and very good." As far as the bottles, Caspar Wistar's New Jersey glassworks could have been the source. Wistar, who died in 1752, was Reuben's father-in-law. Another possible supplier was the Manheim Pennsylvania Glasshouse operated by Henry William Stiegel. Stiegel, who first advertised in Philadelphia in February 1765, made bottles as large as eight quarts.[26] A third possibility is that Matlack's bottles were stoneware.

> The best *BOTTLED BEER*, is fold by
>
> # Timothy Matlack,
>
> At the old BREW-HOUSE in 8 xth-street, near the State-House, at Nine Shillings and Six pence per dozen.
> If the bottles are immediately exchanged the usual allowance will be made.
> For exportation, it is wired and packed free of any expence, except the cask.

Timothy Matlack's bottled beer advertisement as it appeared in the *Pennsylvania Gazette* in the spring of 1768. Newspaper advertisement. Philadelphia: *Pennsylvania Gazette*, May 19, 1768, Issue #2056. Free Library of Philadelphia, infoweb.newsbank.com.

Timothy's store, opposite the Indian Queen tavern, was most likely located on the property Reuben inherited from their mother. Timothy's price was six shillings per dozen, not including the returnable bottles.[27] The bottles could be packed for export, and the corks were stamped TIM MATLACK PHILAD.

Philadelphians were accustomed to think of beer as a temperate alternative to rum and whiskey:

> What means this fury in my veins?
> This fire that hisses thro my brains?
> The bottle I resign.
> Firm to pursue this better plan.
> To drink small beer and make the man.
> Fair Temperance!
> Ever thine.[28]

While Quakers condoned the moderate consumption of beer, which was made from their barley, they were very unhappy about the social ills linked to alcohol. The Society of Friends complained about "the increase in vice occasioned by the enormous increase of taverns and tippling houses."[29] The immoral behavior they had in mind included "excess of drinking, swearing, cursing, lying, unlawfull or unseemly keeping company with women." Coupled with taverns and drinking, in the Quaker view, were gambling and sport. The Book of Discipline ordered members not to "run races either on horseback or on foot, lay wagers, or use any gambling or needless & vain sports or pastime, for our time swiftly passes away, and our pleasure & delight ought to be in the Law of the Lord."[30]

For Timothy Matlack, horseracing was a passion. In the taverns, beer lathered horse talk, which reached a fever pitch ahead of Philadelphia's spring and fall races. In early September 1767, Matlack and Hiltzheimer "measured the new race ground again & very exact, & find it wants 144 yards of 2 mile."[31] After the men plowed the corrected course they went down to the lower ferry to pick up Selim, a thoroughbred owned by the wealthy New Yorker James Delancey. In October, with race day approaching, Delancey himself arrived with more horses. On the day of the big event, Selim won the one hundred-guinea purse.

Captain James Delancey, a war hero who inherited his father's lucrative dry goods business and vast estates, could easily afford the leisurely lifestyle of a gentleman. Timothy Matlack, on the other hand, could not afford to mimic the way the better sort lived. In March 1768, Matlack appeared before Judge Waln in the Court of Common Pleas. He was being sued by the London merchant William Neate for unsettled debts.[32] The insolvent defendant was unable to make restitution and was confined to debtor's prison. Jacob Hiltzheimer paid his friend a visit in jail.[33] At this moment in time, few could have imagined that in just eight years Timothy Matlack would be one of the most powerful men in Pennsylvania.

Timothy's confinement was short. He must have received help from Reuben Haines because he was out by April enjoying a ride down to Marion Meadow. In May he and Jacob rode to Hiltzheimer's Schuylkill pasture to retrieve a mare named Spark and her new colt. Later Hiltzheimer sent two men down to Virginia to pick up the Delancey thoroughbred Juniper. Upon the stallion's arrival, Jacob wasted no time introducing him to his mare, Molly B.

After a second stay in debtor's prison, in the spring of 1769, Matlack's situation seemed to improve. That summer he opened his own brewery. Matlack announced he had relocated to "the old BREW-HOUSE in Sixth-street, near the State-House." At his brewery Matlack offered employment for a cooper: an artisan who would make his barrels. He offered a shop, with accommodations for a small family, in exchange for work.[34]

Timothy was already a master of the brewer's trade. He later wrote that a "wort of malt and hops, fermented at 65° and separated from its yeast in due time, becomes spontaneously fine, and even perfectly bright ... soft and free from bitterness."[35] Brightness, he explained, was a term used to express the difference in clarity between fine and that "perfect transparency in which liquors are, alone, tasted in their purity."

Timothy also sold Madeira. Wine, like beer, was a favorite drink in Philadelphia from the earliest days. William Penn had himself made a fruitless effort to plant vineyards. Matlack found an excellent customer in a man who

Three. The March of the Paxton Boys

once observed there could be no "good living where there is not good drinking." Perhaps in preparation for a trip to Europe, in March and April 1763, Benjamin Franklin purchased forty-seven quarts of Madeira from Matlack. Benjamin paid his bill, eight pounds, four shillings and six pence, in May 1764. He sent half of his supply to his son William, the Royal Governor of New Jersey.[36]

Following Pennsylvania's apple harvest that fall, Matlack offered to buy "a quantity of the best CYDER from any person who can deliver it in Philadelphia, before it begins to ferment." The last qualification did not mean he planned to sell apple juice: fermentation was a process he wanted to control himself. Matlack later published a guide to making hard cider, that "excellent liquor capable of perfection." Demand for cider spiked during the fall races. Jacob Hiltzheimer recorded the results of the Jockey Club race held on Thursday, September 28, 1769:

> At noon started for the £100 purse the following horses: James DeLancey's bay horse, Lath; Mr. McGill's bay horse, Nonpareil; Governor Sharp's gray mare, Britannia; Richard Tidmarsh's gray mare, Northumberland. Lath won.

After more races on Friday and Saturday, Hiltzheimer, Matlack and their friend Dan Wister were burning with horse fever. On Sunday the threesome purchased Maryland Governor Sharpe's three-year-old gray mare Britannia. Hiltzheimer noted his share cost him a hefty £18.2.8.[37] Horseracing was surging in popularity across the middle and southern colonies. Aristocrats were running their thoroughbreds at Leeds Town, Annapolis, New Jersey, New York and Philadelphia. In Pennsylvania, however, some observers were about as pleased with the rise of the equestrian sport as they were with the return of "strolling stage players." Quakers complained that "scenes of reveling and debauchery continue(d) ... for several days ... after the last Races in the Centre of the Seat of Government." They demanded that such offenses against God as "drunkenness, whoredom, and other uncleanness" be stopped. It was their strong wish, they said, that "cards, dice ... masks, bull (and bear) baitings, and cockfightings be discouraged and severely punished."[38]

But Timothy and his companions were as passionate about cockfighting as they were about horseracing. In the middle and southern colonies, as in England, the sport was very popular among rich and poor alike. One authority later wrote:

> In England cock-fighting is confined to no particular class. High and low alike engage in it. Amongst the noblemen, the most noted cock-fighters were Lord Derby and Lord Shefton, and their fowls go by their names ... some of the fowls raised by the common and poorer class of citizens, are in some respects superior, as more care is generally taken in their raising.[39]

The Bostonian Josiah Quincy complained that in the South "young men of fortune" were obsessed with cockfighting and horseracing:

> To hear them converse you would think that the grand point of all science was properly to fix a gaff and touch with dexterity the tales of a cock while in combat. He who was at the last match, the last main, or last horse race assumed the airs of a hero or German potentate. The ingenuity of a Locke or the discoveries of a Newton were considered as infinitely inferior to the accomplishments of him who knew when to shoulder a blind cock or start a fleet horse.[40]

In Pennsylvania, in response to the "huge popularity of [cockfighting] with people of all ranks of society," the Assembly repeatedly legislated against the sport.[41] In 1774 the first Continental Congress would also insist Americans abandon such unpatriotic diversions as cockfights and theater. But aficionados persisted. J.W. Cooper later said of the game fowl, "Amongst poultry he is what the Arabian is amongst horses, the high-bred short horn amongst cattle, and fleet grey-hound amongst the canine race."

In 1770 Philadelphia hosted a big intercolonial cockmain, a well-attended event likely organized by Dan Wister and a tavern owner named Joseph Richeson. The two men had had prior business dealings, including the sale of a black horse. Wister was a member of a hard-drinking group of privileged young College of Philadelphia graduates. A classmate told a correspondent the Society of Friends had disowned those who were Quakers for "sottishness and immorality." The Meeting had also "condemned 'D.W.' for keeping game cocks to the value of £25." The informant added the eye-opening rumor that Wister had paid "a Girl £50 to strip Stark naked before him."[42] Wister's lavish lifestyle ended in bankruptcy.

Tavern owner Richeson was later involved in a counterfeiting plot. Sheriff's men were unable to arrest him "on account of his telling them to keep their proper distance." After this standoff he skipped town.

A gamecock with gaffes. Book Illustration, Media, Delaware Co., PA: Cooper and Vernon, 1859, The Historical Society of Pennsylvania (HSP).

Three. The March of the Paxton Boys

The big cockmain pitted James Delancey against a local man of more humble origins. On Tuesday, March 6, a clear sunshine day, "James Delancey Esq from New York, and Timothy Matlack, had a great cockfight at (Captain) Joseph Richeson's [tavern] on Germantown road."[43] Timothy Matlack was probably the best known heeler in Philadelphia. In this blood sport he made a big name for himself: for some a hero, for others a villain. Delancey came equipped with "twenty fighting Cocks ... all arm'd with steel & ready for war."[44] Perhaps Delancey pitted English birds, such as Derbys or Sheftons, while Timothy Matlack handled roosters bred in Maryland and Virginia. Cooper described "a large grey cock of Virginia, as pretty and fine a fowl as we ever saw. His weight was six and a half pounds, had black eyes, and turkey colored legs, stands up on his pins like a prize fighter, he had a fine large tail, long hackle feathers, in a word he was as beautiful feathered fowl as I ever saw."[45]

At the big event spectators drank, gambled, and got out of hand. The day's entertainment ended in a mass brawl.[46] Word got around about the spectacle, and the future Declaration signer Francis Hopkinson wrote an elegy to Delancey called *The Cockfighter*. Hopkinson lamented the New Yorker wasted his talents on that "barbarous" and "cruel" sport just to come away with the title of "first Cock-Fighter in the land." "Unborn Chickens," he said, "would curse Delancey's name."[47]

Win or lose, Timothy Matlack was now a man known to everyone. In his newspaper ad he replaced a description of his beer with his own name in large type. Matlack's cockfighting fame, or infamy, would follow him throughout his political life. His enemies took every opportunity to link him to the discredited sport as well as those participants who came from society's lowest ranks. The Tory poet Jonathan Odell ridiculed that "game-cocks and negroes were his whole delight."[48]

Four

Revolution

Pennsylvania's merchants and lawyers loved sporting and drinking as much as the province's journeyman tailors, cordwainers, sailors and laborers. But as the century advanced the better class was distancing itself from the poor and middle population. As their share of the wealth increased dramatically, elites built large houses and purchased expensive carriages. In Philadelphia they secluded themselves in new establishments like the London Coffee House and City Tavern.

In the economic downturns of the period the wealthy did not suffer. But at the other end of the spectrum, growing poverty was the cause of widespread misery. Growing resentment of the better sort was exacerbated by the fact that the ruling class controlled government at the expense of the city of Philadelphia and the western counties. The wealthy had constructed an oligarchy by denying equal representation in the Assembly to a majority of the population.[1]

A disagreement over how to fight a new wave of taxes opened a critical phase in this class conflict. Following the rejection of the Stamp Act and its internal tax on colonial business, Parliament's Townshend Acts set duties on paper, paint, lead, glass and tea. Colonists were allowed to import these goods from Great Britain only. The point of the new law was not to raise revenue so much as to confirm Britain's dominance over its North American colonies: other control measures in the new acts made this clear.

John Dickinson, the former Pennsylvania Assemblyman and Stamp-Act-Congress delegate, called the Acts unconstitutional in his popular *Letters from a Farmer in Pennsylvania*. Timothy Matlack's former master, John Reynell, told a correspondent in England that Americans would never agree to being taxed by a Parliament in which they were not, and never could be, represented. Representation being the point of English liberty, he asked, how could the colonists surrender?[2] Reynell wrote that if England retained the right to tax, he and his fellow colonists would no longer be "free Englishmen but vassals and slaves to Great Britain." Reynell said he would give up his beloved tea and put on a leather jacket until Parliament reversed itself.[3] His wife bought a spinning wheel and began to make her own homespun cloth.

In February 1769, Reynell and a merchant group agreed to suspend imports from Britain until the Townshend Acts were repealed. Under pressure, more Philadelphia's merchants joined the new boycott in March. Reynell was chosen chairman of the merchant's committee that would carry out the protest. Reynell was proud of his committee's effort to protect the rights of colonists as subjects of the King.

In July 1769, a shipment of Irish malt arriving on the *Charming Polly* spurred Philadelphia's brewers to action. At a town meeting chaired by Reynell the brewers presented their signed agreement not to purchase the grain. The ship was forced to recross the Atlantic with its cargo intact.[4] While Reynell and his fellow resistance leaders were determined to protect American interests, Quaker elders were shocked by this episode. From their point of view, Reynell and his group had gone too far. Israel Pemberton wrote his brother:

> If thou seeth the papers thou wilt find they have been so wild as to collect ye inhabitants, and by their resolve oblige an honest man from Yarmouth with a cargo of malt ... to take back his cargo.[5]

The Quaker rulers now threatened to disown members who continued to resist taxation by methods "contrary to the peaceful spirit and temper of the Gospel." Under pressure from the Society of Friends, the Quakers on the merchants committee, including John Reynell, resigned.

In April 1770, Parliament repealed most of the Townshend duties but retained the law's broader control policies, including the customs service. In July, at a town meeting, Charles Thomson castigated New York merchants for lifting their boycott on untaxed English goods. But the issue was complicated: Pennsylvania was paying duties on large imports of sugar and molasses from the British West Indies, while New York was not allowing in any taxed goods, including tea, wine, rum, sugar and molasses. In New York, Timothy's brother White Matlack signed a petition to continue nonimportation.

While the partial repeal of the Townshend duties did not meet colonial demands, Philadelphia merchants voted to end nonimportation in September. This decision angered artisans and craftsmen. Mechanics of all trades were called to action by new resistance leaders:

> Let us step forth like Men sensible of our true Interest, and while we glory in the despicable Name of Mechanic, let us, by our Prudence, Moderation and Unanimity, command Respect, and convince the great Ones that truly wise and honest Men, worthy to represent a free People, can be found amongst us.[6]

Whereas in the past the middle sort would have deferred to their betters, mechanics now acted on their own by holding a town meeting and forming a committee. The future secretary of Congress, Charles Thomson, said the object of forming these patriotic committees was to organize the middle and lower sort and stop merchants from dropping resistance measures whenever they pleased.

Those in opposition to the merchants and lawyers who traditionally held power included artisans and tradesmen of every variety. These included cordwainers, wheelwrights, tallow chandlers, printers, coopers, blacksmiths, whitesmiths, stone cutters, brick layers, skinners, cabinet makers, gilders, distillers, hatters, barbers, ship chandlers, carpenters, butchers, bakers, potters, bricklayers, nail smiths and brewers. In Assembly elections in November the tradesmen expressed their discontent, and rising independence, by electing a tailor.[7]

Laborers reacted to the end of nonimportation with violence. That same month sailors brutally attacked a customs collector who had seized smuggled goods. This man was tarred and feathered and "duck'd" in the Delaware.[8] Philadelphia merchants, many of whom were Quakers, began to worry that control of the province slipping from their hands.

* * *

In 1773, Timothy and his fellow brewers led a public action against Philadelphia's elite, who controlled the city's Crown-chartered municipal corporation. The corporation had come up with a plan to extend the farmer's market shed which stood in the middle of Market Street between Front and Third Streets. The Matlacks' first house in Philadelphia faced this structure. The protest arose when the corporation said it would extend the shed up to Fourth Street. Matlack's particular interest was, of course, in the brewery on the affected block. His father had opened the Brewer's Horse & Dray in 1745, and Reuben Haines had turned it into Haines & Twells. Timothy wrote, "The great Western trade of this city was at that time carried on by merchants residing in market Street, between Third & Fourth Streets, almost exclusively, and the largest brewery & malthouses of the city were on the same street, and their supply of barley, at that time, was by waggons from the westward." The brewers said the planned extension would block the giant horse-drawn Conestoga wagons that delivered western goods to their block. The elite members of the municipal corporation responded, saying their charter gave them the right to build in the street and divide the rents paid by vendors among themselves.

Building materials were removed quietly at night. When workers for the corporation completed vertical piers for the shed, protestors threatened to overturn them. The corporation responded by indicting protest leaders for riot. Matlack said that "a man of distinguished talents & generally much esteemed, called on the Citizens indicted and as a friend, advised submission as the only means of escaping severe punishment." The protest leaders, however, insisted they would not only appeal any conviction all the way to the Crown, but would ask that the corporation's charter be revoked. With the threat of violence, the market addition was never built, and "the revolution soon after commencing, the indictment was never tried — and the charter died of itself."[9]

The threat of violence loomed large in the late fall of 1773 when merchants acting as agents for the British East India Tea Company were pressured to resign. The Townshend duty that had been retained was the one on tea. In early December 1773, a town meeting told the Quaker merchants James and Drinker they would not be allowed to import a shipment of English tea leaf. Then on Christmas Eve, a special edition of the *Pennsylvania Gazette* carried the news of the Boston Tea Party (as the harbor incident later became known). Men protesting the tea tax had boarded three British ships and thrown three hundred forty-two chests of East India Company tea into the bay. Two days after this news arrived in Philadelphia, at another town meeting in the State House yard, the people determined that the tea ship *Polly* would not be allowed to unload its cargo.[10]

Timothy Matlack officiated at a patriotic social gathering held one month later. On this February afternoon, thirty men turned out at the slaughterhouse to weigh a prize steer owned by Jacob Hiltzheimer. Timothy recorded the exact weight of every part of the animal, named Roger, in his friend's diary. The men were pleased to find that its four quarters, for example, weighed an impressive thirteen hundred pounds. Timothy authenticated the figures with the notation that the cow had been "weighed and measured in the presence of T Matlack."

Two days later Hiltzheimer and his wife took a ride in their sleigh down to Mullins to meet Timothy and Nelly for dinner. Jacob wrote that he "had a beefsteak off my big steer Roger." Timothy's toast was, "May the Friends of America be fed with such beef and may her enemies long for it and be disappointed." Timothy meant that the colonies should deny the British Empire unlimited access to America's vast resources.

In early May 1774, Philadelphians learned that in retaliation for the Tea Party, Parliament had ordered the closure of Boston's port to trade shipping by force of a naval blockade. On May 16 Paul Revere arrived in their city with an urgent appeal for solidarity. Resistance leaders Charles Thomson, Joseph Reed and Thomas Mifflin scheduled a meeting for May 20 to determine Pennsylvania's answer. Crucial to their plans was the attendance of the influential John Dickinson. But Dickinson, increasingly nervous about the course of events, wanted out. Thomson and Reed later claimed his sudden conservatism could be traced to his wife, the daughter of a wealthy Quaker merchant, and his mother. Dickinson's mother, they said, was worried about her son's fate as a traitor to the crown. She reportedly warned, "Johnny you will be hanged, your Estate will be forfeited ... you will leave your excellent wife a widow and your charming children orphans."[11] Prior to the Boston meeting Reed and Thompson determined not to leave Dickinson alone "least his wife or mother would speak with (him) and overthrow ... all that had been done. [The women] were in an adjoining room, appeared very uneasy and only waited for such an opportunity."[12]

Their manly anecdote made the rounds in the years that followed. John Adams joked, "If I had such a mother and such a wife, I believe I should have shot myself." Men like Adams enjoyed a laugh at Dickinson's expense, but the leaders of the rebellion knew they would be severely punished if their movement failed. According to another popular story, John Hancock warned his fellow congressmen, "We must be unanimous, there must be no pulling different ways; we must all hang together." To this John Penn, the delegate from North Carolina, or Benjamin Franklin, replied: "Yes, we must, indeed, all hang together, or most assuredly we shall all hang separately."[13]

The meeting on Boston's request for solidarity, with Dickinson in attendance, approved the very moderate plan of action the four leaders had conceived in advance. Pennsylvania's response was met with disappointment by New Englanders and local mechanics alike. The latter felt a growing sense of frustration with their resistance leadership.

It was Virginia that issued a call for a Continental Congress, to be held in Philadelphia, to determine a united course of action. In Pennsylvania, preparation for the Congress set up a summer-long battle between those who wanted an aggressive delegation, to commit their province to the strong protest measures favored by Massachusetts and Virginia, and those who did not. The measures were likely to include another boycott, which was, in general, a threat for merchants and an opportunity for mechanics.

On June 18 Matlack and Hiltzheimer attended a massive town meeting at the State House. Eight thousand people packed the yard. Resistance leaders called for a convention to choose and instruct Pennsylvania's delegation. But mechanics considered their overall strategy too slow and cautious. The artisans felt the leaders ultimately answered to conservative merchants and lawyers. The results of the town meeting were not at all to the liking of the craftsmen, who wanted more spirited resolves.

The convention was held and its delegates came up with a very specific structure for an agreement between Great Britain and the colonies that could end the conflict.[14] But Pennsylvania's conservative Assembly ignored these recommendations: it wrote very general instructions for Pennsylvania's delegates, which it selected from among its own members. The Assembly announced the delegation would be headed by its own leader, Joseph Galloway. Galloway was later one of Philadelphia's most notorious loyalists.

On Monday, September 5, 1774, Jacob Hiltzheimer marveled, "In the forenoon the General Congress met at Carpenter's Hall, in this city, forty odd in number they have chosen Peyton Randolph, one of the Virginia gentlemen to be Chairman, and Charles Thomson (who is not one of the delegates) to be their Secretary."

In October, Congress resolved to send a formal address to the King asking him to restore harmony to the Empire by giving his royal attention to "the grievances that alarm and distress his Majesty's faithful subjects in North America." John Dickinson, who won a seat in the Pennsylvania Assembly in October and immediately joined the delegation in Congress, wrote the conciliatory version of the King's Address preferred by the majority of the members; men who did not believe their Congress represented a rebellion. Congress approved Dickinson's respectful document on October 25 and ordered an engrossed (formally transcribed) copy be prepared with urgency. The appearance of this important state paper had to be elegant and refined, as would properly reflect the gravitas of the Congress. Secretary Thomson assigned this urgent task to Timothy Matlack. Matlack was known to Thomson as the talented scribe who had done work for Benjamin Franklin. Now Timothy labored through the night preparing *two* copies of the address, both of which were signed the next day, the last day of Congress. One copy was supposed to go out on the *Britannia,* on October 27, but the ship's departure was delayed. The second was carried on the *Mary and Elizabeth,* which cleared port on November 14.[15] In London, Benjamin Franklin received the identical documents. He presented one to Lord Dartmouth. Dartmouth said the King was "pleased to receive it very graciously and to promise to lay it, as soon as they met, before his two Houses of Parliament."[16] The Address was laid before the House of Commons on January 19, 1775, and the House of Lords the next day. But, Franklin told Thomson, "It came down among a great heap of letters of Intelligence from Governors and officers in America, Newspapers, Pamphlets, Handbills, etc., the last in the last, and was laid upon the table with them, undistinguished by any particular recommendation of it." Congress never received an answer.

Anticipating their address might be ignored, Congress had made a plan to be heard economically. This was a boycott to seek redress for numerous grievances suffered under Great Britain's "ruinous system of colonial administration." Congress had agreed that after December 1, 1774, the North American colonies would no longer import, directly or indirectly, any goods, wares or merchandise from Great Britain or Ireland. Also banned were East India Company tea from any part of the world; molasses and coffee from the British West Indies; and wine from Madeira. Congress also agreed to halt exportations to ports in the empire starting in September of the following year.

The delegates' agreement spelled out how colonists were to manage their economic activity and personal conduct during the boycott. Congress said the people were to "encourage frugality, economy, and industry, and promote agriculture, arts and the manufactures of this country, especially that of wool." They were also to discountenance "all horse-racing, and all kinds of games, cock fighting, exhibitions of shews, plays and other expensive diversions and entertainments."

But with the first Congress ending in October, there would be no intercolonial authority to oversee the boycott. Compliance would have to be enforced locally. Congress assigned this work to existing committees of correspondence, set up by the Stamp Act Congress. These committees were to inspect the custom houses in their respective colonies and report any "material circumstance." Oversight of the agreement on an individual level was to be placed in the hands of new committees which Congress said would now be chosen in every city, town and county. These "committees of inspection" were given the power to observe the conduct of all persons in position to violate the boycott and to make publicly known those that did so that they might be universally condemned as the enemies of "*American* Liberty."

The election for Philadelphia's committee of inspection was held on November 12. The competing tickets included a moderate and conservative list of men and a radical one. The radical ticket won by an overwhelming majority. Men in the middle ranks, those who made their living by their handiwork, had taken control of a important committee network. Left out were the traditionally dominant ruling-class merchants and lawyers. Timothy Matlack was elected to join the Committee of Inspection when its membership expanded the following summer.[17]

Quaker elders were disturbed and distressed by what was happening. On January 5, 1775, the Society of Friends reminded its people to withdraw from any activity that violated Quaker principles. Some of its members were supporting the boycott from their seats in the Pennsylvania Assembly while others sat on the various committees. Two weeks later a second statement from the society condemned all persons involved in the "usurpation of power and authority" through "combinations, insurrections, conspiracies and illegal assemblies." While some in the Quaker community disagreed with these edicts, conservative elders held firm control of the Society's proclamations. Observers who distrusted this powerful group felt that wealth and politics were the driving motives behind their statements, not religious belief.[18]

Four. Revolution

* * *

Riders carrying jolting news from Boston arrived in Philadelphia late in the afternoon of April 24, 1775. A company of seven hundred British soldiers under Lieutenant Colonel Francis Smith had marched out from Boston to capture weapons and ammunition stored north of the city. After an engagement enroute, at Lexington, the British regulars were stopped at Concord by militia minutemen. As the British withdrew south they took heavy fire. Back at Lexington, Smith was reinforced by Lieutenant Colonel Hugh Percy. Percy was forced to use artillery to disperse large numbers of militia at Cambridge before escaping to Charlestown.

Philadelphians reacted en masse. On April 25 eight thousand people assembled in the State House yard and resolved to "associate together, to defend with arms their property, liberty, and lives against all attempts to deprive them of it."[19] This was no statement of intent but a call to arms answered immediately by all sectors of society. In the city's open spaces the Associators organized companies, elected officers and drilled. Two weeks later thousands of Associators paraded for the delegates arriving for the second Congress. The colonial leaders were impressed by Pennsylvania's show of force. One told a friend in London, "The very Quakers in this and other provinces are in arms, and appear in the field every day in their regimentals, and make as good a figure as the best; you may be sure we are in earnest when they handle a musket."[20]

Captain Joseph Cowperthwaite was in command of a light infantry company of Quakers called the *Blues*, for the color of the cockades on their hats. Charles Biddle said, "We went out every day to exercise, and took great pains to make ourselves qualified to act our parts as soldiers when called into the field."[21] The Society of Friends was not amused by this second martial rebellion from within. This time it did not hesitate to discipline those who had strayed from its pacifist teachings. The Society began disowning hundreds of members in July.[22]

The Second Continental Congress opened on May 10 with delegates from New Hampshire, Massachusetts Bay, Rhode Island, Connecticut, New York, New Jersey, Pennsylvania, Maryland, Virginia, North Carolina, South Carolina, and New Castle, Kent and Sussex on Delaware in attendance. Lyman Hall had been admitted as the representative of the Parish of St. John's in Georgia, but did not yet represent that colony as a whole. Timothy Matlack, now clerk to Congress, took an oath to keep his knowledge of the proceedings secret.

On June 15 Congress appointed George Washington general and commander-in-chief of the army of the United Colonies. Two days later Matlack completed his commission, which said:

> We, reposing special trust and confidence in your patriotism, valor, conduct, and fidelity, do, by these presents, constitute and appoint you to be General and Commander in chief, of the army of the United Colonies, and of all the forces now raised, or to be raised, by them, and of all others who shall voluntarily offer their service, and join the said Army for the Defence of American liberty, and for repelling every hostile invasion thereof: And you are hereby vested with full power and authority to act as you shall think for the good and welfare of the service.

The document was signed by a man who had thought of *himself* as a leading candidate for the army command: the president of Congress, John Hancock. General Washington departed immediately for Hancock's hometown. In Boston, two days earlier, the British had won a pyrrhic victory in a battle on Breed's Hill for control of Bunker Hill. In this engagement one hundred British officers were killed along with one hundred twenty-six regulars. Over eight hundred British soldiers were wounded. On the American side one hundred forty men were killed and another two hundred wounded.

In early October 1775, Congress made Timothy Matlack Storekeeper of Military Supplies.[23] Tents, linens and other supplies were put under his care. In September Philadelphia's Committee of Inspection announced the names of eleven men charged with cracking down on vendue masters (auctioneers) who were selling imported goods in violation of the boycott. Matlack was one of the eleven. The Committee was becoming a powerful force. Charles Thomson complained that the men who sat on this board "were suddenly raised to power, and who exercised an uncontrolled authority over their fellow-citizens, were impatient of any kind of opposition."[24] The Committee's power rested in the militia, and Timothy Matlack had also been named secretary of the Committee of Officers of Philadelphia's three militia battalions.

* * *

In Pennsylvania the patriotic rush to join the militia after Lexington and Concord tapered off that autumn like warm weather. Mechanics said that while they themselves continued to turn out, the better sort had stopped drilling. The committees now pressured the Assembly to make militia service compulsory for all, with fines for exemptions "adequate too the Dangers, Loss of Time and Expence" faced by those who served.[25] The Quaker hierarchy responded to this with a petition which said any such obligation threatened freedom of conscience and the right to nonparticipation in war guaranteed by the laws and charter of the province. With this charter William Penn and the Quaker community had sought to create a society free of the wars of the old world. The Society of Friends reminded the public:

Four. Revolution

> It is well known that for above one hundred years past, we, as a religious society, have declared to the world that we could not, for conscience sake, bear arms, nor be concerned in warlike preparations, either by personal service or by paying any fines, penalties, or assessments imposed in consideration for our exemption from such services.[26]

Quakers were not the only pacifists in Pennsylvania, but they were the most powerful and vocal group. They stated their concern that a militia bill would "widen or perpetuate the Breach with our Parent State" and invite the persecution of the Society of Friends.[27] This address triggered an emergency meeting of the Committee of Inspection, and Timothy Matlack was named to a subcommittee charged with writing a response. On the last day of October 1775, the committeemen marched to the State House to present their response, and the Assembly ordered their statement be read immediately.[28] The committeemen charged that Quakers wanted the "friends of liberty to fail in the present, glorious struggle." They said Quakers, "many of the wealthiest among us," should not be exempt from paying fines while others carried the burden of war and risked death in the process.[29] The Society of Friends and pro-independence Americans were destined to live in a state of conflict for the duration of the war.

In November, under intense pressure, the Assembly issued militia articles which made fines for nonparticipation applicable to all Pennsylvania residents, except ministers and servants. While the new law did not scale these payments to taxable wealth, as the committees had requested, leaders urged militiamen to sign the articles. The reason was they feared a British assault on Philadelphia more than inequity.[30] News had arrived of King George III's Proclamation for Suppressing Rebellion and Sedition. The King had ordered all British officials to suppress an "open and avowed" American insurrection.[31] The King also said he intended to respond with an armed force, which could include "foreign participants."

While His Majesty assumed rebellion leaders were seeking to establish an independent empire, the American population was only starting to imagine that their colonies might fight to become autonomous. The people, whether Whigs or Tories, were just beginning to see what Thomas Jefferson, for one, considered inevitable. The next step for Congress, he thought, was an assertion of separation from Britain. Now John Dickinson took immediate action to prevent anything of the kind. The Assembly leader wrote instructions to Pennsylvania's delegation (of which he himself was a member), which said:

> Though the oppressive measures of the British Parliament and administration have compelled us to resist their violence by force of arms, yet we strictly enjoin you, that you, in behalf of this colony, dissent from, and utterly reject, any

propositions, should such be made, that may cause, or lead to, a separation from our mother country, or a change of the form of this government.[32]

While delegates in Congress prepared for a protracted internal fight over independence they took steps to build a naval fleet for "the Defence of America." In December Congress ordered the construction of thirteen frigates, including the thirty-two-gun *Randolph*. In seeking specifications for a second fleet the Marine Committee's secretary, the ubiquitous Timothy Matlack, asked the builder of the privateer *Hero* for the vessel's exact dimensions. Matlack submitted these to Chairman John Hancock, and the committee agreed to build one hundred twenty-four-foot gunships.[33] While awaiting delivery of the fleets, Congress acquired what vessels it could and had a rudimentary navy operating by the end of the year. On January 4, 1776, Matlack issued the Marine Committee's order to "every Officer in the Sea and Marine Service and all the common Men belonging to each ... that they immediately repair on board their respective Ships." The order said those who did not appear would be deemed deserters.[34] The navy was ordered to "surprise and take Lord Dunmore with his Associates" at Norfolk. Lord Dunmore, the Royal Governor of Virginia, had assembled a regiment of hundreds of runaway slaves by offering freedom to those who joined the British. By the time the American force was ready to sail for Virginia, the appearance of the British ships *Liverpool* and *Roebuck* in the Chesapeake Bay convinced Congress to cancel the operation.[35]

Congress now made Timothy Matlack commissary and clerk-in-chief of the Committee of Claims. It was his responsibility to respond to requests for military supplies. The delegate Richard Smith made note of a typical order submitted to Commissary Matlack: a request for balls and flints for Maxwell's companies, then preparing to march to Canada. Smith noted that Matlack was "this person who it is said was once a Quaker Preacher [and] is now Col. of the Battalion of Rifle Rangers at Philadelphia."[36]

Early in January 1776, the city had added two more battalions to its militia brigade. Timothy Matlack had been elected colonel of the Fifth Battalion of Riflemen. The Fifth Battalion was called the "shirt" battalion for the simple hunting tunic its men adopted as their affordable uniform. In a year's time Matlack's rifle rangers would find themselves fighting British regulars on a frozen battlefield.

On January 10, 1776, Philadelphia was abuzz over a pamphlet titled *Common Sense*. In this booklet an anonymous author argued Americans should put an end to British rule of their continent. The author was soon identified as an English immigrant named Thomas Paine. Quaker leaders, for one, were shocked by Paine's message and responded emphatically. On January 15 the Society of Friends published a four-page newspaper insert which expressed their "abhorrence of all such Writings ... designed to break off the happy connection we have heretofore enjoy'd, with the Kingdom of Great Britain, and our just and necessary subordination to the King."[37] This address triggered retaliation. The Quaker merchants John Drinker and the Fisher brothers were called before the Committee for refusing to accept continental money. Back in December 1774, Drinker's goods, which the Committee said he imported in defiance of the boycott, had been seized and stored in its warehouses. Now the merchants were condemned as "enemies of their country" and forbidden from doing business with city inhabitants.[38]

On February 14, 1776, Paine published an expanded edition of *Common Sense*, which included his response to the Quaker address. Paine, the son of a Quaker, started his rebuttal by agreeing, "Our plan is peace for ever." He observed that "if the setting up and putting down of kings and governments is God's peculiar prerogative, he most certainly will not be robbed thereof by us." But, he said, the Quaker statement was a "slap in the face." The King had attacked Americans "beneath the shade of our own vines ... in our own homes, and on our own lands," and therefore "we can see no end to it but in a final separation."[39] The Society of Friends, he said, was dabbling in political matters best left unmeddled.

Quaker elites were accustomed to wealthy lifestyles protected by their political power in Pennsylvania and their trade networks in the Empire. In their home province they were wary of rivals. A newspaper essayist explained that the diversity of people in Pennsylvania, and "all the effects which the passions and prejudices of religion and country inspire," was an underlying cause of the province's internal conflict:

> The people of Pennsylvania are diversified more than the people of any other state in the union. The inhabitants are composed chiefly of Quakers, Episcopalians, Presbyterians and Lutherans. There are a few of Society of Roman Catholics, Mennonists and Moravians; but they are too inconsiderable to give the least complexion to the politics of the State. The majority of the inhabitants are Germans, Irish, English and their descendants.

Welsh, French Huguenots, Swedes, and Dutchmen had also formed communities in Pennsylvania, and a few hundred Jews lived in Philadelphia. But the people Quakers feared most were the Scots-Irish Presbyterians, who now dominated Pennsylvania's revolutionary committees. These two groups had battled for control of the province in the 1760s, and Quakers saw the American cause as a path to dominance for these rivals.

Moderates and conservatives took note that Paine's new edition of *Common Sense* had appeared two days prior to Committee elections. The vote on February 16 gave radicals greater control of the committee network. Timothy

Matlack was made a committee officer and added to a policy-making subcommittee. His promotion came at a crucial moment. A unanimous declaration of independence in Congress would require striking John Dickinson's instructions to the Pennsylvania delegation to "utterly reject" any such proposition. But Dickinson had no intention of removing his wedge. So John Adams and other radical leaders in Congress asked Philadelphia's committeemen to take action. The Committee now told the Dickinson-controlled Pennsylvania Assembly it had no right to bind the delegates against the people's wishes. The committeemen also said the Assembly seats long withheld from the city of Philadelphia and the eight western counties must finally be added. But members of the Assembly were well aware that if they agreed to these new seats, new men might take control of their body, rewrite the instructions blocking a vote for independence, and replace their delegates in Congress. Control of the legislature was crucial to avoiding this sequence. They failed to respond.

The Committee of Inspection now took more aggressive action. On February 26 Matlack and three other committeemen handed John Hancock a paper for the approval of Congress.[40] The Committee said it planned to call a provincial convention which would act where the Assembly had failed to do so. This convention would take it upon itself to authorize the new Assembly seats and write new instructions for Pennsylvania's delegates in Congress. Philadelphia's elite, who viewed themselves as society's better sort and natural rulers, were shocked by the volley. Joseph Reed, the former aide-de-camp to General Washington and future leader of Pennsylvania, said the committeemen were "violent spirits" who acted rashly by sidestepping his own, deliberate, resistance strategy. Joseph Shippen, whose wife was a member of the loyalist Galloway family, singled out Timothy Matlack as a leader:

> Tim Matlack and a number of other violent wrongheaded people of the inferior class have been the Chief Promoters of this wild Scheme; and it was opposed by the few Gentlemen belonging to the Committee—but they were outvoted by a great majority.[41]

The Committee's convention call provoked fear that Pennsylvania was about to face "the greatest Confusion, Anarchy and Disunion." In early March the moderate resistance leaders Reed, Mifflin and Thomson convinced the Committee to rescind its plan by promising the Assembly would take action. The Committee agreed but continued to press its agenda. On March 14 the Assembly acknowledged the Committee's power by agreeing to add seventeen new Assembly seats. While these places were a fraction of the number needed for equal representation, they were potentially enough to shift power. In the campaign battle that followed Matlack met on a daily basis with James Cannon,

Thomas McKean, Dr. Thomas Young and other rising radical leaders. James Cannon, a schoolteacher, was Secretary of the Committee of Privates. Dr. Thomas Young was a New Englander who had worked with Samuel Adams in the Boston resistance. Thomas McKean was a Pennsylvanian serving as a delegate to Congress from Delaware and Chairman of the Committee of Inspection.

But the men were not successful. In a close race, three of the four radical candidates for Philadelphia, including Owen Biddle, lost. The disappointed leaders said the outcome was the result of the sheriff's early closure of the polls, the blockage of German votes, and the absence of soldiers. Radicals won the vast majority of new seats for the western counties, but failed to gain control of the Assembly. While John Adams had hoped this election would "give a finishing Blow to the Quaker interest," there was more work to be done.[42] In the critical months of May, June and July 1776, John Adams and Samuel Adams collaborated with McKean, Cannon, Matlack and others on a decisive plan. Christopher Marshall, Thomas Paine, Dr. Benjamin Rush and David Rittenhouse were also among the men leading the next phase of the struggle. Now their objective was to shut down the Assembly.

* * *

By the spring of 1776, Washington's Continental army had forced the British to evacuate Boston. While this was thrilling news for Philadelphians, confirmation that the King was sending thousands of Hessian soldiers to fight in America provoked fear and outrage. The Hessians were subjects of the Landgrave of Hesse-Cassel. The Landgrave was a prince said to maintain a French theater, as well as opera and ballet companies, at his court. To help pay expenses he rented out his army.[43]

On May 6 alarm guns announced approaching British warships, and Philadelphia's militia companies formed ranks at the State House. John Adams saw an opportunity. In Congress he introduced a resolution asking the colonies opposing independence to temporarily repeal or suspend their delegates' instructions. His measure was defeated.[44] On May 8 a British man-of-war, *Roebuck,* and a frigate, *Liverpool,* appeared downriver and exchanged fire with Pennsylvania's gunboats. The next day a second skirmish, now closer to town, drew thousands of spectators to the Delaware.[45] War had arrived.

On May 10 Adams introduced a resolution which would give the Philadelphia Committee the authority to repudiate Pennsylvania's Assembly. Adams proposed that each of the United Colonies "adopt such Government as shall ... best conduce to the happiness and safety [of the people] ... where no Government sufficient to the exigencies of their affairs has been hitherto established."[46] But the language he used was weak, and John Dickinson responded simply that he would concur with the resolution since Pennsylvania already enjoyed such a government. On May 15 Adams introduced a crucial preamble to his resolution, which was, effectively, a call for independence:

> Whereas ... the whole force of (Great Britain), aided by foreign mercenaries, is to be exerted for the destruction of the good people of these Colonies ... it is necessary that the exercise of every kind of authority under the said Crown of Great Britain should be totally suppressed, and all the powers of government exerted under the authority of the people of the Colonies ... for the defence of their lives, liberties and properties.[47]

All understood that if Adams' resolution, with its blunt preamble, passed a vote in Congress Pennsylvania's Assembly might be quashed. Standing in for John Dickinson, who was away, James Wilson responded, "Before we are prepared to build a new house, why should we pull down the old one?"[48] To this Samuel Adams answered, "Our petitions have not been heard, yet answered with fleets and armies." Maryland's delegates staged a walkout but the Adams resolution passed. Adams had done his part. That same evening Philadelphia's pro-independence leaders gathered in the Committee Room at Philosophical Hall. They had in their hands the authorization of Congress to suppress the Assembly and create a new government authorized by the people. Now they made preparations to hand the ruling elite their final defeat.

Five

Independence

In what must have seemed like another lifetime, Timothy Matlack aspired to join the ranks of Philadelphia's aristocracy. As a young man he dined at the estate of the wealthy Galloways. On one occasion Matlack and Hiltzheimer went there to see Dan Wister's barn raised. After dinner the men enjoyed a bull bait.

But now Timothy denied any ambition to count himself among the better sort. "Riches were never a main object with me," he claimed, "and I believe never will be." Perhaps he understood that as a brewer his place was among the mechanics and artisans in the middle ranks of society. Below his class the lower sort considered Matlack their hero. Now he was leading them all in a revolution.

Matlack and his fellow radicals had been given the authority to shut down the Assembly. Once in control of the province they would send new delegates and instructions to Congress. While their first objective was to commit Pennsylvania to independence, Matlack, Cannon and Rittenhouse saw the possibility existed to give the people the power to govern themselves. William Penn had granted this right, but the oligarchs had taken it away. Independence and self-governance, Thomas Paine said, were the people's natural rights.

While democratic government was the last thing John Adams wanted to see in the colonies, his priority was independence. Dickinson and his Assembly were blocking a unanimous vote in Congress and had to be displaced. What government the new men set up in Pennsylvania, after a declaration, was a secondary concern for the Massachusetts leader.

Across the colonies Friday, May 17, 1776, was "Congress Sunday," a day reserved for fasting and prayer. In Philadelphia, committee leaders took the opportunity to distribute a petition calling for a town meeting on Monday morning. A broadside entitled *The Alarm* spelled out their agenda. Pennsylvania, they said, must have a government resting on the authority of the people and a convention of their representatives was the proper forum for its creation.

On Monday morning a massive crowd gathered in a downpour for the town meeting. The people agreed the Assembly derived its charter from "our mortal enemy the King of Great Britain." The Adams resolution, which said that power was void, received three cheers. Next the instructions to Pennsylvania's delegates in Congress—to oppose separation from the mother country—were read to the disapproval of all. The crowd agreed these directions represented "a dangerous tendency to withdraw this province from that happy union with the other colonies, which we consider both as our glory and protection." Finally the mass meeting authorized a conference of committees to organize the election of delegates to a convention. The convention would in turn set up the new government.

Congress watched the day's proceedings from their chamber in the State House. John Adams reported, "We have had an Entertaining Maneuvre, this Morning in the State House Yard.... The Weather was very rainy, and the meeting was held in the Open Air, like the Comitia of the Romans.... Coll. McKean, Coll. Cadwalader and Coll. Matlack the principal orators."[1]

In the face of this popular action Pennsylvania's old guard, content with its power and wealth, clung to the status quo. The elite feared a world in which "rank amateurs of dubious backgrounds, suspect intentions and irresponsible programs would suddenly become the leaders of their community."[2] In response to the town meeting the merchants and lawyers circulated a petition supporting the Assembly. The appeal was "much promoted by Quakers." But their efforts to raise signatures met with active resistance.[3] Dr. Benjamin Rush reported that "two emissaries ... were detected at Lancaster and York carrying the Remonstrance. One of them fled; the other ... (was) obliged to go off without gaining a single convert to Toryism."[4] In other places the petition was torn to pieces or burned. Hundreds of people in Philadelphia who had initially signed crossed out their names.

Radicals, meanwhile, carried out an effective campaign across the eastern counties and into the backcountry. Timothy Matlack and James Cannon rode to Norrington to meet county committee members. In western Pennsylvania the radicals conjured violent scenes from Pontiac's War: "Fire, sword, desolation.... Parents and children weltering in their blood—Infants torn with savage brutality from their mothers wombs, and made the food of dogs!!!"[5] The Assembly, they reminded frontiersmen, had failed to react to this bloodshed. The fury of the drive stunned the eastern elites, but the worst was yet to come. The final push for independence and new government was about to carry away their comfortable world.

Radicals realized the seats they had won in the by-election made it possible to temporarily shut down the Assembly. By absenting themselves they denied a quorum. On May 24 an impotent clerk wrote to "absent members, requesting their attendance in Assembly as soon as possible."[6]

Now the Virginia Convention passed a resolution requesting Congress to declare the colonies free and independent states. On June 7 Richard Henry Lee read a resolution Samuel Adams called "the most important that was ever agitated in America."[7] Lee proposed:

> That these United Colonies are, and of right ought to be, Free and independent States, that they are absolved from all allegiance to the British Crown, and that all political connection between them and the State of Great Britain is, and ought to be, totally dissolved.

But Pennsylvania's delegates requested a delay in voting on the Lee resolution. James Wilson explained that although the "majority of the People of Pennsylvania were in Favour of Independence ... the Assembly ... was against the Proposition."[8]

The following day, under heavy pressure, the Pennsylvania Assembly sent new instructions. These allowed the delegates to agree to "further compacts" and "Treaties with foreign Kingdoms and States." The new directives, which did not include the word "independence," permitted a vote for separation by not prohibiting one.[9] The new instructions signaled that John Dickinson was attempting to save his Assembly from extinction. But Philadelphia's committee leaders took immediate action to ensure his legislature did not recoup its authority.

On June 10 the five Philadelphia battalions staged meetings to demonstrate their support for new government. A published account of this peaceful action focused on Matlack's Fifth Battalion. Colonel Timothy Matlack, it said, asked his men to vote on a series of questions. The first was: "Is it the determined resolution of this corps to support the said Resolve of Congress with their lives and fortunes?" The men said yes. The second question was: "Is it the determined resolution of this corps to support the proceedings of the [May 20 town] meeting aforesaid, at all hazards?" Again there was no dissent. Now a third question, said to be unplanned, was posed by the Colonel. He asked "whether they wished the province of Pennsylvania to be a free and independent State, and united with the other twelve colonies represented in Congress?" The vote was unanimous, and "all present shewed their hearty approbation of the whole transaction by three huzzas."[10] And so, as all read in the newspapers, Colonel Timothy Matlack's battalion voted for independence on June 10, 1776.

Fourteen months after Lexington and Concord, Timothy Matlack was one of the most recognizable men in Philadelphia. He was a leader of a movement seeking separation from Great Britain and self-rule for the people of Pennsylvania. From the obscurity of his past he was on a path to prominence no one could have foreseen. Now people watched him perfect the art of revolutionary political mobilization. He was a commissary for Congress, a committee leader, and a militia Colonel. The end of the fight for a declaration of independence was at hand, but the War of Independence was just beginning, as was the battle for control of Pennsylvania.

In June a "numerous body of Tories" cut off communication to Dover, Delaware, by blocking the road through Sussex County. In Philadelphia Whigs thought these loyalists were trying to "give disturbance and break our measures." Christopher Marshall hoped "the pit they dug, they themselves will fall into." On June 13 Colonel Matlack ordered fifty haversacks and canteens from the Committee of Safety. The next day "powder and ball were sent ... under escort of a company of Colonel Matlack's Battalion." By the time the artillery arrived the loyalists had dispersed. The hole was filled in and the road reopened.

The War of Independence was a civil war fought without geographic boundaries. British-Americans who actively opposed independence lived in each of the five cities, the small towns, and across the countryside. Colonists loyal to the Crown formed their own militia companies to oppose the rebellion by force. Other Tories acted as conspirators and spies. Americans who supported independence were boxed in by enemy combatants: they faced militant loyalists dispersed from north to south, British and Hessian soldiers crossing the eastern ocean, and Crown-allied Indians on the western frontier.

On June 14 the Assembly adjourned, stating it would reconvene in August.[11] But in truth, the radicals had finally quashed Pennsylvania's proprietary government. The Philadelphia committee met that same day to choose delegates to the Conference of Committees. The Conference opened four days later with Franklin, McKean, Matlack and Dr. Rush heading the city's deputation. More than one hundred committeemen from across Pennsylvania packed Carpenter's Hall. The Conference immediately addressed the crucial vote looming in Congress. The Assembly was gone, but its appointees were still seated in Congress, free to vote against independence. The Conference announced: "We, the deputies of the people of Pennsylvania ... unanimously declare our willingness to concur in a vote of the Congress, declaring the united colonies free and independent states."

Next the delegates reiterated that Pennsylvania's government had not been "competent to the exigencies of our affairs." The Conference was calling a convention to form a "new government in this province on the authority of the people only."[12] The election for convention delegates, it said, would be limited to Associators who had been assessed for taxes. Voters would also be required to foreswear allegiance to King George III. These rules eliminated Tories and Quakers but increased the suffrage by lifting the property requirement that made it difficult to qualify as a voter. A large number of white males were about to become voters for the first time.[13]

In closing the week-long Conference the representatives informed the people of Pennsylvania that the "sudden and unexpected separation of the Assembly" had forced it to act as the temporary government. Its major act of governance, it said, had been to respond to the request of Congress for forty-five hundred more militia.

Now the Philadelphia militia, the Associators, gathered on the grounds of Carpenter's Hall for the speech that would send them off to the war. The speaker asked them, with their zeal for liberty, to concur with the Conference's convention plans:

> You are about to contend for permanent freedom to be supported by a government which will be derived from yourselves, and which will have for its object not the enrollment of one man, or class of men only, but the safety, liberty, and happiness of every individual in the community.[14]

The democratic values of the Conference attendees were real. The author of the speech, most likely Thomas Paine, offered an inspiring vision of a new and just world. Paine added the clairvoyant prediction that

> the present campaign will probably decide the fate of America. It is now in your power to immortalize your names by mingling your achievements with the events of the year 1776 — a year which we hope will be famed in the annals of history to the end of time, for establishing upon a lasting foundation the liberties of one quarter of the globe.[15]

With the Conference at an end, the men walked up to the Indian Queen for a triumphal banquet. Later that day Thomas McKean read the meeting's statement on independence to Congress.

On July 2 Timothy Matlack, Christopher Marshall and four others were named to a new board called the Committee of Secrecy. This committee would act as a rival to one that had survived the Assembly's demise: the Committee of Safety.[16] Matlack's new committee said it would examine "all inimical and suspected persons that come to their knowledge."

That same day Congress voted in favor of the Lee resolution and declared the united colonies independent states. The vote took place without the delegation from New York, whose revised instructions had been delayed by the approach of British forces. John Dickinson, once inspirational as the Pennsylvania Farmer, was reduced to absenting himself. His abstention, along with Robert Morris and Charles Humphreys, cleared the way for Pennsylvania's 3–2 vote.

Dickinson was completely aware of how his action would be received. He wrote, "My Conduct, this Day I expect will give the Finishing Blow to my once too great, and now too diminished Popularity." John Adams once described Dickinson as "a shadow—tall, but slender as a Reed—pale as ashes. One would think at first sight that he would not live a month."[17] But while Dickinson was discredited, he was no dead man. And his return to power would be bad news for Timothy Matlack.

On July 3 Congress edited Thomas Jefferson's draft of a declaration of independence. Three weeks earlier, in anticipation of an affirmative vote, Congress had ordered a committee of five to prepare a pronouncement. Jefferson had written a proclamation and his fellow committee members, especially Benjamin Franklin and John Adams, had worked on his text. Now, sitting as a committee of the whole, the rest of Congress honed his document. On July 4, satisfied with the changes they had made, the delegates adopted "A Declaration of the Representatives of the United Colonies of America in General Congress Assembled." Congress asserted:

> That these United Colonies are, and of right ought to be, FREE AND INDEPENDENT STATES; that they are absolved from all allegiance to the British crown and that all political connection between them and the state of Great Britain is, and ought to be, totally dissolved.

In a long indictment Congress listed atrocities suffered by the American people. The King had "plundered our seas, ravaged our coasts, burned our towns, and destroyed the lives of our people." Congress complained the he had fomented domestic insurgents—slaves—against the colonists. His Majesty had also stirred up "merciless Indian Savages" who fought under "indiscriminate Rules of Warfare." And now King George III was "transporting large armies of foreign mercenaries to complete the works of death, desolation and tyranny." These egregious acts, and many other complaints, had forced Congress to "dissolve the political bands" connecting the two people.

Congress ordered the Declaration printed and copies sent to "the several Assemblies, Conventions, and Councils of Safety, and to the several Commanding Officers of the Continental Troops, that it be proclaimed in each of the United States, and at the head of the Army." This process started immediately. Anthony Morris said Timothy Matlack "read the Declaration of Independence... from the State House steps."[18] Morris was standing in the crowd, as was Charles Biddle: "On a memorable Fourth of July 1776, I was in the Old State-House yard when the Declaration of Independence was read."[19]

After Matlack's impromptu reading, while people milled about excitedly, he may have accompanied Thomas Jefferson to John Dunlap's print shop on Market Street. Congress had asked Jefferson's committee to "superintend and correct the press," and it was perhaps the author himself who carried the official text to the printer. Matlack would have gone as a surrogate for Secretary Thomson, who was busy in Congress. Jefferson, who was interested in typography, would have enjoyed overseeing the press. But Dunlap and his staff worked late into the night. It was probably the secretary's assistant who stayed into the wee hours. Perhaps Matlack conveyed proofs to Jefferson and Thomson for their inspection. Crucial errors were caught and corrected, and the printer's broadside was ready by morning.[20]

* * *

Also on July 4, in Lancaster, representatives from the state's fifty-three militia battalions met to elect two brigadier generals. Militiamen in the rank and file voted alongside officers for their choices. In Philadelphia a group of committee men, militia officers, and congressional delegates from the middle colonies met to plan a militia call out. The men agreed to send the entire militia to New Jersey.

The campaign for Convention delegates was also under way. In a surprise maneuver the Committee of Safety, that remnant of the Assembly, ordered the Declaration be read and proclaimed on July 8, the day of the election. The Committee of Safety sent letters to Bucks, Chester, Northumberland, Lancaster and Berks counties requesting Congress's proclamation "be published on Monday next at the places where the election of Delegates are to be held."[21] By sidling up to the popular cause, moderates and conservatives hoped to gain support for their ticket and control of the Convention. Matlack's Committee of Inspection responded by organizing patriotic entertainments in support of its own list. These were also scheduled for Monday, July 8.

On Monday morning the rival committeemen met at Philosophical Hall and walked over to the State House in procession. In the State House yard Colonel John Nixon, of the Committee of Safety, proclaimed the Declaration of Independence in front of a large crowd. The people responded with loud huzzas. John Adams told a friend the Declaration had been read "from that awfull Stage, in the State House Yard, by whom do you think? By the Committee of Safety! the Committee of Inspection, and a great Crowd of People."[22]

That afternoon the reading was repeated for the five Philadelphia battalions, assembled on the common. Adams said the men "gave us the Feu de Joy, notwithstanding the Scarcity of Powder. The Bells rung all Day, and almost all night."[23] The patriotic crowd pleasers organized by Matlack's committee were capped by the burning of the King's Arms on a bonfire of casks. Christopher Marshall enjoyed the "Fine star-light, pleasant evening. There were bonfires, ringing bells, with other great demonstrations of joy."[24] All who participated enjoyed the day. Adams noticed that "even the Chimers Chimed Away."[25]

Adams also reported the results of the day's vote for Convention delegates. "The Election for the City was carried on amidst all this Lurry, with utmost Decency, and order. Who was elected I can't say; but the List was Franklin, Writtenhouse, Owen Biddle, Cannon, Schlosser, Mattlack, and Khull (all of these were elected)." Of this triumph, John Adams said, "Thus you see the effect of Men of Fortune acting against the Sense of the People." Looking forward with optimism he wrote, "Next year we shall do better. New Governments will bring new Men into the Play, I perceived: Men of more Mettle."[26]

Six

Democracy

In most of the colonies the original resistance leaders controlled the revolutionary governments. In Pennsylvania the situation was different. A second tier of democratic-minded leaders was organized and powerful enough to take over.[1] The moderate Whig Charles Thomson, unhappy with this turn of events, blamed John Dickinson for what had happened. Thomson scolded, "I cannot help regretting ... that you have thrown the affairs of this state into the hands of men totally unequal to them." Thomson said of the people:

> They did not desert you. You left them. Possibly they were wrong, in quickening their march and advancing to the goal with such rapid speed. They thought they were right, and only "fury" they show'd against you was to chuse other leaders to conduct them.[2]

The new Pennsylvania leaders faced a difficult situation. Their new state was joined with twelve others in war, and the enemy's strength was overwhelming. A report said five hundred British vessels, carrying thirty to fifty thousand soldiers, were, at that moment, crossing the Atlantic.[3] These troops would be joining the many already in New York.

On July 14, 1776, Washington ordered the Pennsylvania militia to report to camp at Perth Amboy, New Jersey. Here they would guard the coast against excursions by General Howe's forces, stationed just across a narrow waterway on Staten Island.

Colonel Matlack had been purchasing arms for his battalion. He received forty rifles made by Thomas Palmer on July 6 and five more made by John Pollard a few days later. Matlack led his battalion to their post before hurrying back to Philadelphia for the start of the Convention.[4]

On July 15 the elected representatives of Pennsylvania's eleven counties and the city of Philadelphia gathered for the start of the Convention. The men named Benjamin Franklin President. Franklin lent the meeting a measure of the gravitas and authority it desperately needed. But the opening of the

Convention signaled the end of the old political order. The delegates made this clear with an immediate housecleaning in Congress. Dismissed were the two men who voted against independence: Andrew Allen and Thomas Willing. The Convention also removed two of the three men who absented themselves from the vote: John Dickinson and Charles Humphreys. Retained were the three men who voted for independence: Benjamin Franklin, John Morton and James Wilson. Robert Morris also kept his seat. The Convention named Dr. Benjamin Rush, George Clymer, George Ross, Col. James Smith, and George Taylor as new delegates.

The Convention's instructions to its delegation expressed a new fear. The representatives were afraid a standing army would become the source of lasting power for its officers. The Convention's preference was for a navy:

> We recommend to you to use your utmost power and influence in Congress, to have a due attention paid to the establishing and maintaining a respectable naval force; as such a force is absolutely necessary to every trading nation, and is the least expensive or dangerous to the liberties of mankind.[5]

The Convention's purge continued. The Committee of Safety was next to go. To replace this body twenty-five men were named to a new Council of Safety, which would take responsibility for managing the war. Of the men named only Matlack, Rittenhouse, Cannon and a handful of others sat on the committee over the next few weeks. Timothy Matlack kept up a frantic search for rifles, inspected the old jail, investigated the facts in the case of Colonel James Easton, and wrote an ordinance for his release.[6]

The men of mettle now faced the task of replacing a seventy-five-year-old constitution, Pennsylvania's Charter of Privileges, with one of their own invention. In the Convention the business of writing a constitution got under way. But James Cannon, Timothy Matlack and David Rittenhouse and their democratic plans met immediate resistance from a group led by George Ross and George Clymer. Also prominent in this faction were Col. James Smith and John Bayard. In the opening week the opposition group seemed to gain the upper hand: Cannon, Matlack and Rittenhouse were all left off a key drafting subcommittee. But power shifted with the late arrival of western delegates. The three democratic leaders were added to the subcommittee, which would draft the frame of government.

At this moment in time there was, of course, no *national* constitution. Ratification of the first one, the Articles of Confederation, was four and a half years away. The writing of state charters was therefore "a matter of utmost gravity."[7] In Pennsylvania, radical leaders supported by the Scots-Irish had taken control of this critical task. This situation was a nightmare for the moderate and conservative elite that had long controlled local politics. Quakers had feared the American cause would create a path to dominance for the Scots-Irish Presbyterians, one hundred thousand or more, who had settled in the state. The Scots-Irish were in fact a driving force behind independence in all of the colonies and the "main pillar supporting the Revolution in Pennsylvania." A visitor from New England called them "the most God-provoking Democrats on this side of Hell." Scots-Irish support gave the Convention leaders the strength to move ahead with their democratic experiment.

Cannon, Matlack and their fellow radicals wanted a single Assembly of the people to serve as the legislative branch of government. They wanted no upper house, which they feared would become the realm of aristocrats. Those opposed to this idea argued that the checks and balances of a bicameral system were needed.

With their early advantage slipping away, moderates and conservatives were quick to dismiss the preparedness of the Convention's delegates. One member said the body was full of "numsculs, not a sixth part of us ever read a word on the subject of government."[8] The Rev. Francis Alison said the delegates were "honest, well-meaning Country men" not equal to the task before them.[9] One visitor complained that his lodgings were full of "Convention men, most of them profoundly ignorant," who were making "a new code of Laws for the Province." He sneered, "O, Happy people ... that has such wise guides."[10]

Before the Convention James Cannon *did* say men of "unsophisticated understanding" were the best choice for delegates.[11] Men of great fortune, he said, were improper persons to frame a new government. Cannon's plan was to fill the Convention with the artisans, mechanics and frontiersman who would support his radical ideas for democratic government. But to *lead* these delegates, Cannon, Matlack and their associates wanted a highly educated core. On July 3, in Philadelphia, both had lectured a meeting of militia rank-and-file on the subject of Convention delegates. Christopher Marshall reported: "James Cannon, Timothy Matlack (and) Dr. Young flourished away ... upon the qualifications they should be possessed of, viz; ... Great learning, knowledge in our history, law, mathematics, &c., and a perfect acquaintance with the laws, manners, trade, constitution and polity of all nations, men of independent fortunes, steady in their integrity, zeal and uprightness."[12] Radical leaders in the Convention did include scientists and scholars such as David Rittenhouse, James Cannon, Owen Biddle, William Henry, Robert Loller and Robert Whitehall.[13] Others were prominent men such as John Hubley, William Van Horn, John Jacobs, Col. John Bull, Frederick Kuhl, George Schlosser, Jonathan Hoge, Jacob Stroud and Thomas Porter. Judge George Bryan pushed for a unicameral legislature from outside the meeting.

Timothy Matlack, beyond his school years and apprenticeship, was a self-educated man. He owned a Book of Hours (a fifteenth-century Roman Breviary) and a copy of *The Seasons* by James Thomson.[14] On the subject of government he had undoubtedly read his Locke. Adam Smith's *Wealth of Nations* had been published in Europe four months earlier. On a later date Matlack described the effect of supply and demand on the price of steel. Timothy enjoyed scientific experimentation, math problems, and the tinkering habits of an inventor.[15] He was his party's sharpest penman and would in later years be hired for legal and architectural work.

The debate over unicameralism was representative of other conflicts in the Convention. A dispute over qualifications for public office led the delegate Thomas Smith to complain

> Our principle seems to be this: That any man, even the most illiterate is as capable of any office as a person who has had the benefit of education; that education perverts the understanding, eradicates common honesty, and has been productive of all the evils that have happened in the world."[16]

Where education was used as code for wealth, Matlack, Rittenhouse and Cannon did not want it as a requirement for office. The men agreed with a little-known New England pamphleteer who considered property qualifications for officeholders a source of corruption. He wrote, "Let it not be said in future generations that money was made, by the founders of the American states, an essential qualification in the rulers of a free people."[17]

* * *

On July 19 affirmation by the New York delegation made the Declaration unanimous. Now the delegates agreed to sign a fair copy. Secretary Charles Thomson assigned Timothy Matlack the task of preparing a finely engrossed Declaration.[18] Although completely occupied by the Convention, the Council of Safety, and his rifle battalion, Matlack made time for this important work. Perhaps in the evening hours, on his desk at home, he arranged a large sheet of parchment in front of him, along with his quill and ink stand, a copy of the printed Declaration, and perhaps his own handwritten copy of the text (if he had one).

At the top of the printed sheet a date was fixed in history. And so Matlack copied: "In Congress, July 4, 1776." The printer, John Dunlap, had typeset the Declaration's original title, "A Declaration by the Representatives of the United States of America in General Congress Assembled," on five lines. Matlack inscribed the revised title, "The Unanimous Declaration of the thirteen united States of America," on one. The decorative lettering of his title was formal and elegant. The single line looked aesthetically balanced and saved space at the bottom for the all-important signatures. In his title Matlack

Six. Democracy

emphasized that which was new. Long since united as thirteen colonies, the new *States* of *America* were now making a *Unanimous Declaration*: a proclamation of independence.

Penned on animal skin with a feather quill, physically of that moment in time, the Declaration of Independence announced that the American States were preparing for the future. The document said that the United States, standing along the eastern waters, would fight for the right to move across the mountains, into the far territory. In the west the new country would secure life, liberty and happiness for the people. In 1804 Thomas Jefferson would transact the Louisiana Purchase and send explorers to trace the course of rivers he hoped would carry the American people as far as the Pacific Ocean.

Matlack worked quickly through the body of the document because he was needed back at the American camp at Perth Amboy. He made two errors, a misspelling and a missing word, which were corrected in the margin. The finished document was presented in Congress on August 2, compared at the table, and signed by the members present. Others signed in the months ahead. Five of the nine delegates who signed for Pennsylvania were the men appointed by the Convention.

* * *

Pennsylvania's temporary government, the Convention, was operating in a state of confusion, trying to cope with innumerable demands. On July 30 Matlack and Biddle were assigned to find out if Congress's Board of War or Pennsylvania's Council of Safety was responsible for building fortifications at Billingsport. On August 1 Colonel Matlack was ordered to find out whether the Council of Safety had authority over the State Prison. The Council of Safety was forced to deal with the lack of a judiciary system, since the courts had been effectively shut down by supporters of the ousted Assembly. In response Council named all twenty-five of its members, plus thirty-seven others, Justices of the Peace.

On August 2, the day of the signing of the Declaration, Matlack was in New Jersey assessing the Amboy and Elizabethtown camps. The officer in charge, General Hugh Mercer, informed Colonel Matlack that only two hundred seventy-four men had signed up for Washington's new mobile "Flying Camp" militia reserve. Pennsylvania's Associators, he said, were not only shunning the Flying Camp, they were leaving their own battalions in large numbers. General Mercer said those who remained were also "clamorous to return home." Mercer asked the New Jersey Convention to send guards to the Delaware ferries to stop the militia from crossing.[19] On August 5 Mercer told Washington, "Colonel Matlack is gone to Philadelphia, to represent the temper of the Associators to the Convention, that some speedy method ...

may be adopted, to facilitate the recruiting business."[20] Back in Philadelphia on August 7, Matlack recommended that "sufficient bounty" be employed in the raising of Pennsylvania's quota of the militia reserve (six thousand men). At the same time the Council of Safety was forced to deny a rumor, planted by Tories, that the "number of [American] troops now in New-Jersey is too great, and that many are in consequence discharged by the Generals."

The shorthanded Convention struggled to balance constitution writing and war management. Even as it grappled with the militia problem it asked officers who were also delegates to return. Matlack had no choice but to shuttle back and forth across New Jersey.

The militia continued to leave camp. General Washington sent an address thanking those who stayed for their spirit and perseverance in the glorious cause. General Roberdeau followed up with a vivid appeal to honor:

> Here is the spot to make your defense. If you have a mind to keep the enemy from ravaging your country, fight them on the seashore.... There is no difference in effect between retreating and being defeated. Consider it well, gentlemen. Think for your country's good; look but across the water; and for your honor's sake never let it be said that an army of sixpenny soldiers, picked up from prisons and dungeons, freed from transportation, the whipping-post, and the gallows, fighting in the worst of causes and for the worst of kings, bore the fatigues of war with stouter hearts than you.[21]

Near the end of August Congress agreed to lend Pennsylvania one hundred thousand Continental dollars. The Council of Safety immediately forwarded $30,000 to Colonel Matlack and Colonel Slagle for bounty pay. The Convention had named these two officers Commissioners to the Flying Camp. The recruiting effort, however, was failing fast: most of the currency went unused.

Two weeks earlier the Convention had approved the first section of the Pennsylvania Constitution: the Declaration of Rights. In drafting their statement, Cannon, Rittenhouse, Matlack, and associates kept Virginia's example close at hand. Virginia's Declaration of Rights said

> That all men are by nature equally free and independent, and have certain inherent rights ... namely, the enjoyment of life and liberty, with the means of acquiring and possessing property, and pursuing and obtaining happiness and safety.

The Convention's drafting committee had a second authoritative document for reference. Thomas Jefferson had also taken inspiration from George Mason's work in Virginia. His Declaration of Independence stated:

> We hold these truths to be self-evident, that all men are created equal, that they are endowed by their Creator with certain unalienable Rights, that among these are Life, Liberty and the pursuit of Happiness.

The drafting committee made Virginia's "inherent rights," and Jefferson's "unalienable Rights," Pennsylvania's "natural, inherent and inalienable rights." The committee said

> That all men are born equally free and independent, and have certain natural, inherent and inalienable rights, amongst which are, the enjoying and defending life and liberty, acquiring, possessing and protecting property, and pursuing and obtaining happiness and safety.

The Convention committee, again echoing Virginia, said these rights also included unimpeded religious worship, trial by an impartial jury, and freedom of speech. The Convention agreed with Virginia's preference for militia "composed of the body of people, trained to arms." But it stated more specifically that "the People have a right to bear Arms for the defence of themselves, and the State." The Convention also said those who were "conscientiously scrupulous" could not be compelled to bear arms.

A clause which claimed the state's right to discourage the possession of enormous property — or redistribute wealth — was voted down by the Convention.[22] Timothy Matlack likely joined those opposed. He later told James Pemberton, "I have ever considered personal liberty and safety as the first object of civil government, and the possession and security of property the next."[23] Timothy Matlack was in fact a moderate voice within the radical camp.

But the Convention also issued an ordinance which said those convicted of aiding the King, or coming out publicly against the measures of the United States, would forfeit their "lands, tenements, goods and chattels, and be imprisoned for a term not exceeding the duration of the war."[24] The rights of treasonous individuals would not be protected by jury trial or habeas corpus, and the only avenue for appeal was to the Council of Safety.[25] And so, due to the demands of war, the Convention contradicted its Declaration of Rights before its Constitution was finished.

The British had amassed thirty-two thousand well-trained soldiers on Staten Island and a massive armada in the New York harbor. To oppose this force General Washington had fewer than twenty thousand men. On August 27 Washington's troops were badly defeated in the Battle of Long Island. The Americans' losses were massive: three hundred men killed and over one thousand captured. The rest of the army escaped to Manhattan under the cover of rain and fog. Long Island was the first in a string of defeats—followed by Kip's Bay, White Plains and Fort Washington — which forced the American army to retreat across New Jersey.

On September 10 Timothy Matlack was back in Philadelphia. That day the members heard a report of the Battle of Long Island. This came with a request for blankets, the men having "thrown them away in the engagement." The Convention assigned Matlack to review the military affairs of the state, update regulations for the militia, and increase penalties for non-Associators.

After two months in session, radicals in the Convention faced further opposition to their constitutional plans. Matlack, Cannon, Rittenhouse and their faction believed strongly in political equality and majority rule. To protect the welfare and safety of Pennsylvania's inhabitants, they said, a "just, permanent and proper" government must be "derived from, and founded on the authority of, the people only."[26] The men wanted a Paineite framework which would, with minimal structure, translate the will of the majority into legislation. This could only be guaranteed, they said, with a broadly elected single-house assembly. As a safeguard, and to ensure unity across the United States, Pennsylvania's new Assembly would be subject only to the *American Congress*.[27]

The leadership triumvirate's democratic theory of government took inspiration from Thomas Paine's famous pamphlet. *Common Sense* contained his plan for a large national Congress, of at least three hundred ninety delegates. Paine made no mention of an upper house.

In the early part of the year Paine's ideas had triggered attacks from the moderate and conservative elite. The author of a pamphlet titled *Plain Truth* predicted independence would trigger a nightmare situation in Pennsylvania since "our constitution would immediately degenerate into democracy."[28] John Adams also lashed out at Paine, whom he called "a keen Writer but very ignorant of the Science of Government."[29] Adams was not shy about expressing his strong dislike for Paine's "absurd democratical notions" and his "crude, ignorant Notion of a Government by one Assembly."

Pennsylvania's radical democrats now ignored Mr. Adams. On September 11 a twelve-page frame of government for the Commonwealth of Pennsylvania was published for the consideration of the people. Of the forty-nine sections printed that day, forty-seven were included in the final charter. Not forgetting his own experience, Timothy Matlack must have fought for Section 28, which said, "The person of a debtor, where there is not a strong presumption of fraud, shall not be continued in prison after delivering up, *bona fide*, all his estate, real and personal, for the use of his creditors." The Convention did keep this rule as part of the final Constitution.

On Saturday, September 28, the Convention closed with the signing of the Pennsylvania Constitution, by far the most democratic in the new nation. Canon, Rittenhouse and Matlack closed out business by settling incidental expenses, revising and printing the minutes, and writing a public address "setting for the reasons which induced this Convention to make the several Ordinances and Resolves which they have passed." In this address the trio explained that the people had granted the Convention the right to act as the government of the state.[30] Finally the Convention ordered the Council of Safety, headed by the same three men, to prepare materials for the printing of paper currency for the state, to be ready for the first meeting of the new Assembly. The frame was transferred to the Council, which would serve as the state's next acting government, until elections were held.

The Pennsylvania Constitution of 1776 expanded the suffrage to all twenty-one-year-old freemen who had been assessed for taxes. Virginia and Massachusetts were among the states that continued to limit the vote to property owners. The frame's controversial Section 15 said that all proposed bills must be preprinted for the consideration of the people, with reasons and motives for them clearly explained. Elites frightened themselves with visions of taverngoers passing judgment on every proposed law. In response to earlier opposition to this clause the Convention had assigned Matlack and two others to "revise and bring in a substitute," but any changes failed to quiet opponents. This "taproom veto" and similar rules were immediately attacked by conservatives and moderates. And while Pennsylvania had always had a single legislative body, the conservative elite treated the frame's unicameralism as a shocking innovation.[31] To protect their interests the wealthy wanted an upper house to check the lower one. But Matlack and his radical group had purposely combined republicanism and democracy to break ruling-class control of Pennsylvania.

Radicals had won the fight and pushed through their ultra-democratic frame of law. John Adams later conceded, "Matlack, Young, Canon and Paine had influence enough to get their democratical plans" adopted in Pennsylvania. Their Constitution, he said, was copied by Georgia and Vermont.[32] For Adams, democracy was synonymous with popular rule, which he thought threatened civil disorder and bred tyranny.[33] When his state wrote its Constitution four years later, it installed a Senate, to represent property owners, as a second legislative body. In the face of heavy criticism Pennsylvania's Convention leaders appealed for unity, but the controversy over their Constitution was just beginning.

On October 3 the new Constitution was printed on blue paper and inserted in the newspapers. But support for the frame in the radical camp was slipping away. Many of those formerly allied with Matlack's side, including Rush and McKean, were now in opposition. Their group became known as Anticonstitutionalists.

As the two sides prepared for a political fight, Matlack, Cannon, Rittenhouse, Thomas Wharton Jr., and ten other men were managing the state's war effort from their seats on the Council of Safety. Matlack was out in the counties during the first two weeks of October enlisting the recruiting sergeants who would fill the state's quotas for Continental troops. He also visited Pennsylvania troops stationed in New York. During his absence rumors that General Howe would invade Pennsylvania tormented the Council and Congress alike. On the day of Matlack's return, the Council of Safety received a letter from General Lee warning that Hessians were headed for their state. The Council asked General Adam Stephens of Virginia, and a group of Philadelphia officers, to help pick sites for defense works. But the alarm and ensuing panic were short-lived; a small number of Hessian and English prisoners arriving under escort were the apparent cause of the rumor.[34]

Council was also dealing with numerous cases of individuals identified as loyal to the King or otherwise offensive to the cause. Matlack reported he was at the Coffee House when a Captain Hare made a show of purchasing three silver dollars with a large number of Continental bills. Hare was publicly chastised for his performance, which had a detrimental effect on the value of paper money.

Anticonstitutionalists said they wanted immediate changes to the new frame. Another defector, Christopher Marshall, attended a meeting in mid–October with a "large number of respectable citizens" to plan for "setting aside sundry improper and unconstitutional rules laid down by the late Convention."[35] The new party's plan for introducing constitutional changes was paradoxically democratic. Its members said they would publish their proposals "for the perusal and approbation of the whole State at large" ahead of a town meeting.

The opposition town meeting attracted fifteen hundred men to the State House yard on October 21, 1776. The main speakers against the charter were John Dickinson and Thomas McKean. James Cannon, Timothy Matlack, Dr. Thomas Young and Colonel James Smith of York County spoke in its favor. The frame's defenders were not successful. By a "large majority" the town meeting agreed to specific changes it wanted made to the new laws. This work, it said, would be done by the new Assembly.

On November 5 Philadelphians rejected Matlack, Rittenhouse and their fellow Constitutionalist candidates for the Assembly. While their party won a large number of seats across the state, Anticonstitutionalists gained enough to block quorum. The opposition used this leverage to extract an agreement for a new Convention.[36] For their part Constitutionalists were able to appoint John Jacobs as speaker and Timothy Matlack as clerk.

Radical democrats, now known as Constitutionalists, lost the Assembly vote because angry Associators stayed away from the polls. Militiamen were furious that the burden of the summer campaign had fallen entirely on their shoulders. Their families had suffered severe hardships, they said, while non-Associators were not penalized for avoiding service.[37] To cap the injustice, the Convention had fined those who left camp before the end of their six-week term. This penalty was imposed at the request of Washington's commanders, who detested the militia's pattern of desertion. But for the men themselves, the ordinance was a betrayal. The Convention had said every member of society, including conscientious objectors, was bound to contribute to the war by serving or paying an equivalent. But militia veterans now considered these empty words: they blamed the injury they had suffered on their own leaders.

* * *

The disaffection of the militia became a critical concern when General Howe began crossing New Jersey. The new Assembly and the Council of Safety had no choice but to work together to prepare Philadelphia's defenses. One man able to bridge the two sides was the Council member and Assembly Clerk Timothy Matlack.

With the British coming, Pennsylvania's rudimentary government prepared for war. The Council purchased weapons, ammunition, food, clothes and blankets; hired wagon teams for the supply line and express riders for communications; constructed defense works and batteries; and called out the Associators. In late November the Assembly said it would collect fines from men who failed to muster. It also said it would try to relieve pressure on the active militia by rotating battalion ranks in four-week shifts. The Council of Safety, which had been buying and storing salt, resolved to sell this important commodity at a loss to the militia that turned out for duty. Matlack's Council of Safety requested bounty payments for signees, and the Assembly agreed two weeks later. It said men who turned out before December 20 would receive twenty dollars, those who were out before December 25, seven, and those were ready to march by December 30, five.[38]

On November 27, riders brought news that the British navy had sailed out of New York to either join the attack on Philadelphia or "amuse the southern States and prevent them sending any assistance."[39] On December 2 Philadelphians learned the British army had reached Brunswick, New Jersey, and the Council of Safety closed the city's shops. People loaded their wagons in preparation for departure. Drums beat and all were in "hurry and confusion." In the midst of the frantic activity one observer said Quakers "moved little of their goods as they seem to be satisfied that if Gen. Howe should take this City, as many here imagined that he would, their goods and property would be safe."[40] Sarah Logan Fisher, a Quaker, confirmed, "Many people moving out of town, but we are as yet preserved in stillness."[41] Thomas Rodney, the militia captain and future Congressman, called the Fishers, his in-laws, "very great tories."[42]

Congress struggled with the lack of American naval vessels available to fight the British ships that had appeared in the Delaware Bay. The frigate *Randolph*, for one, had launched in July 1776, days after independence was proclaimed. But Captain Nicholas Biddle, a brother of Charles Biddle, refused to take her into action without a full complement of sailors. Robert Morris said he "scolded the [naval] Officers like a bitter Whore for their dilatoriness; they say they wish to Fight & not run, I tell them they must run until they can fight."[43] Captain Biddle was, however, no slouch. His brig *Andrea Doria* was part of a squadron that captured the island of New Providence [Nassau]. In the same command he also captured two ships from Scotland transporting four hundred Highland troops to Boston.[44] The *Randolph* and her men would see action soon enough.

General Washington and his demoralized army were now in Pennsylvania. General Putnam took command of the city on December 8 and the Council of Safety placed Brigadier General John Cadwalader at the head of the five battalions of Philadelphia Associators.

The wealthy Cadwalader had commanded an aristocratic militia company known as the *Greens*. One member of his "silk stocking" company recalled afternoon exercises at the Cadwalader mansion, "where capacious demijohns of Madeira, were constantly set out in the yard where we formed, for our refreshment before marching out on exercise."[45] Some may have observed that by providing fine wines at his home, Cadwalader was circumventing militia rules and regulations, which said, "No Company or Battalion shall meet at a Tavern on any days of exercise; nor shall march to any Tavern before they are discharged."[46] But Cadwalader was a true Whig who led with bravery at Princeton. In 1778 he fought a duel against Thomas Conway, a leading participant in the so-called Conway Cabal, a series of communications among men who favored replacing General Washington with General Gates. Cadwalader wounded Conway in the mouth.

Preparations for war had one unexpected benefit for the authors and supporters of the Pennsylvania Constitution: it put a stop to talk of a new convention.

Seven

The Winter Campaign

On the day of Washington's victory at Trenton, Cadwalader sent word to the commander in chief his men were pushing for a second, face-saving, expedition. Now his men got their wish. At about 10:00 A.M. on December 27, 1776, a mile or two above Bristol, the Philadelphia militia began crossing the river for a second time. But while Cadwalader's force was crossing to New Jersey, word arrived that Washington's army was back in Pennsylvania. In a letter he wrote that night, Cadwalader told Washington that upon receiving this news he had thought it prudent to turn back. Colonel Joseph Reed, however, had insisted it was best to continue and "recommended it warmly, lest it should have a bad effect on the militia, who were twice disappointed." After a heated argument among the officers—in which Matlack undoubtedly sided with Reed—the operation went forward.

Once in New Jersey the decision was made to move the militia south to Burlington. On this march Colonel Matlack's riflemen scouted about two hundred yards ahead of the lead infantry, moving through the woods on either side of the road in single file.[1] The light infantry followed in four columns of double file, then the artillery, then the main column in platoons. The brigade arrived in Burlington at about nine o'clock. The enemy had evacuated the town and surrounding area.

From the landing point in New Jersey General Reed and a small reconnaissance party, including Joseph Cowperthwaite, rode in the opposite direction, up the river road by way of the Crooked Billet and White Hill to Bordentown. On this ride he observed "almost every House on the Road had a red Rag nailed up on the Door which the Inhabitants upon this Reverse of Affairs were now busily pulling down."[2]

The main force left Burlington the next morning and arrived in Bordentown in the afternoon. That night part of the brigade camped at nearby Crosswicks. Sargent Young said the woods there were "quite alive with men, all are illuminated with large fires."[3]

After four or five days in the field the men were motivated but sleeping poorly during the long, cold nights. In vivid contrast to the ragged militia was Philadelphia's First Troop of Light Horse, now arriving on the scene. This troop was composed of twenty-one wealthy young men riding matched chestnut horses and wearing fancy brown uniforms with "snow-white facings, high-topped riding boots, and small round black hats with silver cords and a jaunty buck's tail."[4]

From Bordentown Colonel Matlack went out at the head of a detachment of one hundred riflemen, one hundred light infantry, and one hundred "active young men." His mission was to pursue and harass the rear of the enemy column, said to be moving slowly up the Old York road under the heavy burden of plunder. Cadwalader told him, "If you should meet with any of General Washington's army, the field word is Victory, the sign, a white piece of paper in the officers hats— put the same in your hat."[5] Colonel Matlack led his men forward aggressively. Reed reported that despite the "Severity of the Weather, Badness of the Roads, being also unprovided with Tents they push'd on that Night to Allentown." There Colonel Matlack learned the enemy had moved north to Brunswick and decided to continue the pursuit. In Cranbury Matlack's party captured a group of loyalists following the King's troops. Reed reported:

> Col. Matlack pressed so close that next Morning early he surprised a Party of [Tories] who by this Time supposing themselves out of Danger had stayed a few Moments behind the Troops.[6]

The loyalists taken prisoner included a merchant from Trenton and two Philadelphians: Campbell, possibly a tea merchant, and Pearson, probably a mad hatter. The prisoners were being held in a house when Issac Pearson was spotted trying to escape through a window: "They shot two balls over his head to stop him, but as he persisted in making off, the next two were ordered fired at him and one of the balls passed thro' his breast and he fell dead on the spot." Matlack's men brought his body in the next afternoon. It was generally agreed the man had been very actively in favor of the enemy. The circumstances of his death, Reed said, "struck the Tories with more Dismay than 20 Executioners by Law would have done."[7]

Among Matlack's prisoners was Edward Shippen Jr. The eighteen-year-old son of Pennsylvania's chief justice, Shippen had been in New Jersey when the fighting started. He said two friends, John and William Allen, had convinced him to cross enemy lines to avoid being impressed into the American militia. The Allen boys had continued on to British-occupied New York prior to his capture. Washington later ordered his release.[8]

On December 30 General Reed led seven members of the aristocratic

Seven. The Winter Campaign

Light Horse on a reconnaissance of the back roads to Princeton. Reed's small force surprised and captured twelve British dragoons—light cavalrymen—lunching in a farmhouse. Under questioning these soldiers revealed that Lieutenant General Charles Cornwallis was amassing eight thousand men at Princeton in preparation for an attack on Washington's army, which had returned to Trenton. A young man who came into camp gave a detailed overview of the British defenses at Princeton. Cadwalader made a map based on this intelligence and forwarded it to Washington.

On December 31, the commander in chief sent a large force up the Post Road to delay the British column. On the first day of 1777 these American units engaged the enemy at Eight Mile Run, six miles south of Princeton. The two sides fought all morning, and companies of British light infantry and Hessian jaegers suffered significant casualties before retreating. The Americans pulled back when threatened by a large force of grenadiers, and fighting ceased for the night. Washington and his officers debated sending Cadwalader's brigade up the old York Road to attack the British garrison guarding a large war chest at Brunswick. The officers also considered whether to fight Cornwallis at Trenton or retreat south to Bordentown. But knowing how a withdrawal would be viewed, and the damage it would do to paper money, Washington decided to make a stand at Trenton. And so he summoned Cadwalader's brigade to Trenton. Washington ordered the Philadelphia militia to march the eight-mile distance overnight and arrive by 5:00 A.M. on the morning of January 2."At any rate do not exceed six."[9] But the brigade set out after midnight and muddy roads made for very slow progress. In the darkness the column extended for miles. Exhausted marchers following the shadows in front of them had plenty of time to worry about the danger ahead. They knew that when the sun rose they could find themselves squinting at bright red uniforms and long steel bayonets. The peril was actually greater than they understood: Crown forces were under strict orders to take no prisoners.

* * *

Seven thousand Americans amassed on Mill Hill and extended their lines along Assunpink Creek. The focal point was a stone bridge linking Trenton's Queen Street and the road south. Cadwalader's brigade arrived with its artillery: two brass six-pounders and two iron three-pounders. Washington had thirty to forty artillery pieces.

On January 2, at about 10:00 A.M., drums announced the enemy was approaching. North of Trenton, Colonel Edward Hand's Pennsylvania Rifle Regiment ambushed the British column in a wooded area south of Shabbacunk Creek. At three in the afternoon the King's forces were still a few miles from Trenton. In the late afternoon, a half mile outside of town, a small American detachment of infantry, rifle and artillery met their foes at Stockton Hollow.

The main body of American forces, arrayed from the Delaware River on their left to Phillip's Mill on their far right, made final preparations to defend their position. The Assunpink, which carried as much water as a small river, was crossable at the bridge and three fording points. Cadwalader's Philadelphia Associators guarded the ford at Henry's Mill, one mile up from the bridge.

As darkness approached, the defenders at the bridge spotted American troops running chaotically in their direction. At about five o'clock British and Hessian infantry trying to cross the ford on the American left were repelled back. In a second assault, targeting the bridge, British artillery attempted to clear the way for Hessian grenadiers. Behind them British infantrymen advanced and retreated in waves.

Seeing that the British were moving up more troops for a third attack, Washington summoned Cadwalader's brigade to the bridge. Washington ordered the militia commander to "fly to the support of that important post." Here Colonel Matlack's riflemen, with their long range, may have taken a position near the front line. When the British came down "in a very heavy column to force the bridge," his men found themselves fighting in their first engagement. It was American artillery, however, which delivered the destructive force that stopped the British assault.

As the day's fighting ended the two sides prepared their camps and took care of their casualties. The American side, it was reported, suffered fifty casualties, while three hundred sixty-five British and Hessian soldiers were killed, wounded or captured.[10]

General Cornwallis felt certain an all-out assault the next day would be a triumph. Washington and his officers saw that he would reinforce his army by ordering more troops and artillery from Princeton. Knowing this, they assumed a second day of fighting at Assunpink would end in defeat. Washington's only option seemed to be that dreaded retreat to the south. But then he and his officers devised a plan to circumvent Cornwallis's position in the night and attack the British forces at Princeton in the morning. The enemy strength there would be reduced by the battalions being summoned to Trenton. If successful at Princeton, the American army would continue on to Brunswick to make an attempt on the war chest. From there they would move to the safety of the American camp at Morristown.

Cadwalader's map marked a path through the woods which led to a lightly travelled back road to Princeton. Washington and his officers decided the army would take this route to pass quietly around the British. To speed the night march, officers sent the army's heavy wagons south to Burlington. To decoy the enemy, five hundred men were left behind to light campfires and make noise with picks and shovels, as if digging works for the next day's engagement. But the ruse was not entirely successful: rolling wagons alerted the British something was up. Cornwallis received reports of mass movement in the American rear but decided a night attack was coming. He sent troops into defensive positions for an onslaught that never came.[11]

In the darkness, American officers assembled their troops in whispered confusion. The column got under way, moving south and away from the enemy, but sometime in the night a large number of Pennsylvania militia, members of a brigade organized by Thomas Mifflin, panicked and fled. These young men were spotted the next day all the way down in Burlington.

The rest of the army turned east and followed the rough path through the isolated woods. Horses struggled to pull the artillery over the track and men pushed and pulled and begged them along. The Americans skirted a settlement called Sandtown and continued north along the edge of Great Bear Swamp. The night was dark and cold and the men were exhausted. Cadwalader's men were making their second night march in a row.

Close to daybreak Washington's force arrived at a "small wood, south of a Quaker meeting," near Stony Brook. Here Washington organized his men into three divisions for the assault on Princeton. General John Sullivan's division was ordered to "wheel to the right" at Saw Mill Road, follow this back road to Princeton, and attack from the east. Colonel Thomas Mifflin's and Colonel Nicholas Hausegger's brigades were ordered to "wheel to the left" and follow Stony Brook up to the Post Road. Their first mission was to disperse the small force defending the bridge at this intersection. Leaving men to break down the span, they were to make a circuit around the countryside and flank the enemy batteries from the west. The third division, the brigades led by General Mercer and General Cadwalader, was to follow behind Sullivan's division and hit Princeton "straight on" from the south.[12]

A half hour after sunrise, Sullivan's division had marched past a farmhouse owned by Thomas Clark. At this point officers in the rear of the column spotted two or three British light-horsemen on a hill to their left about a mile distant. The riders, facing east, were shading their eyes, trying to make out who they were. Washington ordered Mercer to attack what he apparently thought was a "detachment sent out from Princeton to reconnoiter."

But Cornwallis had ordered *two regiments* to reinforce him in Trenton. Lieutenant Colonel Charles Mawhood had started out from Princeton before sunrise at the head of a column of foot soldiers, cavalry, artillery, and supply wagons. The horsemen were part of this large force.

Advancing down the Post Road, Mawhood had crossed the bridge over

Stony Brook. On a hill to the southwest, his scouts brought him their report. Captain William Hale wrote, "We discovered the Rebel Army in two columns, entering a wood on the other side of a Rivulet we had just passed."[13] Mawhood now turned his wagons around and sent them back to Princeton. He himself doubled back with his regiments to gain the high ground south of the town, between the Post Road and the back road.

Mercer's brigade had been the last to move out "owing to some delay in arranging Cadwaladers men."[14] Having received his new orders, Mercer rushed forward with one hundred twenty men to intercept what he thought was a scouting party. On a hill beyond Thomas Clark's farm, his men "observed a light-horseman looking towards us, as we view an object when the sun shines directly in our faces."[15] The General ordered his riflemen to pick the rider off but before they could get a shot off the dragoon wheeled and galloped away. The scout reported Mercer's approach to Mawhood, who immediately redirected the bulk of his force, about four hundred men, off the road to their right. He placed these men in a line "behind a long string of buildings and an orchard" on William Clark's farm. Spotting the American detachment crossing in front of them, dismounted dragoons rose from behind a bank of earth and fired. Taken by surprise, General Mercer "immediately formed his men with great courage and poured a heavy fire in upon the enemy." The dragoons retreated, and the Americans advanced to a fence and fired again. Captain Hale reported the loss of seven men, perhaps in this volley.[16] The engagement turned on a British bayonet charge and a bloody mess of close fighting. Among the casualties was General Mercer, who took multiple bayonet wounds. Outnumbered, the Americans fled in confusion. Retreating chaotically, Mercer's men ran head on into General Cadwalader's brigade, which was coming through the "skirts of a wood."[17] Seeing Cadwalader's force, about fifty British foot soldiers took position "behind a fence and a ditch in front of the buildings before mentioned." Attempting to set his battle line, Cadwalader sent Jacob Morgan's battalion to the left flank and Matlack's riflemen to the right. When their first volley had no effect he ordered his divisions to "double up" and reload as they advanced. But the militia was out in the open, "in the face of the enemy and under a shower of grape shot." Captain Rodney said the British had "extended themselves that every man could load and fire incessantly."[18] Under this pressure Cadwalader's line broke and "fell back upon the column" throwing "the whole into confusion." It was Captain Joseph Moulder's artillery that temporarily stopped the enemy. Cadwalader tried to reform his line, joining "one man after the other to it," but "the fire was so hot they again broke."

Now Washington ordered Hitchcock's New England Continentals and Hand's Pennsylvania riflemen to detach from Sullivan's division and attack

Mawhood's left flank. The commander in chief himself rode down to rally the militia. Far back in the woods Cadwalader managed to reform part of his brigade. He led these men "obliquely to the right, passed a fence, and marched up to the left of the enemy." Other officers formed "two small parties" of militia that "bravely pushed up in the face of enemy fire." Cadwalader's force was hit with multiple volleys, and two men were killed and several wounded.

Colonel Hitchcock now attacked the enemy straight on while Colonel Hand approached from the northeast. At the same time part of Colonel Mifflin's brigade arrived from the southeast. Under heavy platoon fire the British finally "threw down their weapons and ran." Hale said, "A resolution was taken to retreat, i.e. run away as fast as we could."[19] The Americans "pushed forward towards the town spreading over the fields and through the woods to enclose the enemy and take prisoners."[20] Washington himself rode forward for a time, on the trail of running red coats, enjoying a certain sense of euphoria.

The rest of Sullivan's division took Princeton. British infantry abandoned their position at a ravine called Frog Hollow and surrendered at a breastwork near the College. The troops inside Nassau Hall also surrendered after a brief engagement.

The Battle of Princeton was over, but the American army was in a vulnerable position. Cornwallis was coming up from Trenton. Only two hours after the engagement at Nassau Hall, the British column reached the bridge on the Post Road at Stony Brook. Here Cornwallis was delayed by a detachment from Mifflin's brigade, which had cut down the bridge, and Captain Thomas Forrest's battery.[21] This unit stopped the British long enough for Washington's exhausted army to move out from Princeton.

General Washington still hoped for an immediate attack on the British post at Brunswick, but his men were in no condition to fight again that day. That night, January 3, an exhausted Philadelphia militia camped out in the cold—without tents or blankets—at Somerset Court House on the Millstone River. At Pluckemin, the following night, they were again left exposed to the elements. Officers slept in houses, but the men were left out in the open. From the Pluckemin camp Washington wrote:

> I fear those [militia troops] from Philadelphia will scarcely submit to the hardships of a winter campaign much longer, especially as they very unluckily sent their blankets with their baggage to Burlington. I must do them the justice, however, to add, that they have undergone more fatigue and hardship than I expected militia, especially citizens, would have done, and at this inclement season.[22]

Philadelphia's Associators had good reason to leave and many started to do just that. For those who stayed the situation did not improve. It was not until January 8 that Sergeant Young and the waggoners in Burlington received orders to transport the militia's blankets and supplies to the American camp in Morristown. With the wagons expected in a few days, Colonel Matlack submitted his roll and requisition. This was a tragic report. The Fifth Battalion was down to less than half its original size. Matlack had only one senior officer on duty: a major, perhaps Lawrence Herbert or George Miller. Of his three captains only Andrew Geyer was accounted for. Under Geyer were three lieutenants and nineteen "rank and phile." The same number of lieutenants and fourteen men were the remnant of Captain Townsend's company. And just two lieutenants and fifteen men were all that were left of Captain Woolery (Ullrich) Meng's unit. And so, three weeks into the campaign, Colonel Timothy Matlack's Fifth Battalion had been reduced to fifty-nine men. Seventy or more were dead, injured, sick, or otherwise absent.

Five of those remaining, including the colonel himself, needed shirts. Eight men requested shoes; two, blankets; and one, a pair of stockings. But none of these necessities arrived on the wagons from Burlington.[23]

With the Philadelphia militia's four-week tour nearing its end, the men were ready to go home. Officers told them they could not leave because they were needed in the field. Cadwalader gave a speech which Charles Willson Peale said had little effect. Sergeant Young wrote: "Our men are uneasy on the account of their staying. A great deal of Swearing and taking the Holy Name of God in vain."[24] On January 15, Young said he "slept but poorly on account of the ungodly behaviour of our Men. All uproar on account of [not] going home. Colonel Nixon has passified them by giving them his Honor that they shall be Discharged in ten Days. Some are pleased and some are angry."

The militia could not be discharged because replacement troops had not arrived. Officers squeezed between General Washington's constant demands and their men's endless complaints were as angry as anyone. Cadwalader asked Matlack to draft a letter to Philadelphia's Council of Safety. Matlack demanded strong measures be taken to recruit new men and get them out quickly. The militia, he said, was outraged and humiliated that others had been allowed to stay home while they risked their lives in a brutal winter campaign. In one especially harsh passage he warned that a failure to take strong action could lead to a military takeover of the state. This coup threat was not necessary idle. The final letter made it clear state authorities were in danger of inviting this drastic measure:

> We wish to see the Civil Authority regulate and direct all our public measures, and should greatly lament the necessity which may compel the Military Power to take the direction into their hands in order to save this Country from absolute ruin — but you may depend that the Military will exert its authority whenever

Etches print. Germany: Daniel Berger, Daniel Chodowiecki, 1784. Library of Congress, Prints and Photographs Division.

the weakness, languor or timidity of your councils shall render it their duty so to do, and all the world will justify them in it.

This passage was actually Cadwalader's stiffened version of Matlack's draft. Matlack had written, less forcefully, "You may depend that they will exert their authority whenever they find it absolutely necessary from the weakness, languor, or timidity of your councils."

Timothy must have felt intense discomfort attacking the Council of Safety. He was of course a member of that civil authority as well as clerk of the Assembly. But he had to consider the political situation. Anticonstitutionalists had crippled the Assembly and convinced voters not to name an Executive Council. If the government was nonfunctional, he was not to blame. After weeks in the field, Colonel Matlack was in full military mode. To restore government authority, he wrote, the Council of Safety and the Assembly must oblige men from the city and three eastern counties to enter the service immediately or forfeit their estates and be banished forever. On January 15 Matlack submitted the edited letter to Cadwalader's adjunct with the instructions: "Gen. Cadwalader desires Lt Sam C Morris will copy this tomorrow morning early as it is to be sent off for Philadelphia at 8 o'clock." The letter was signed by Brigadier General John Cadwalader, Colonels John Bayard, Jacob Morgan and Timothy Matlack, Lt. Colonel John Nixon, and Majors Meredith, Knox, Bradford, and Cowperthwaite.[25]

General Washington followed up with his own missive. Militiamen, he said, were risking their lives to defend those who failed to "even make a pecuniary satisfaction for the exemption of their persons."[26] The Council of Safety forwarded both letters to the Assembly. The Assembly requested Timothy Matlack's "immediate return from the army, to attend his office here."

Still in the field on January 21, 1777, Matlack and his diminished battalion had moved south. From Raritan he reported to Cadwalader, "Agreeable to your orders I pushed forward on Friday as far as to McGattrees." There he had learned American scouting parties were watching the British lines at Brunswick. The next day, at Bound Brook, his battalion camped at Millstone River to await intelligence that might aid an attack at Brunswick. On Monday morning an alarm rang: a British foraging party was in the area. Five or six hundred Crown troops had moved three guns onto a hill fifty yards above a bridge over Millstone River. Matlack's battalion was on the scene but it was General Philemon Dickinson who was credited with leading a small company of New Jersey militia and Pennsylvania Riflemen against the enemy. Dickinson reported, "When our men found it impossible to cross [at the bridge], they went down the river, broke through the ice, waded across ... flanked the enemy" and "routed them."[27] This engagement was another in a string of

Seven. The Winter Campaign

American victories that winter, and this time a Dickinson was the hero. The general's troops recovered forty-three wagons, one hundred horses, one hundred fifteen head of cattle and sixty or seventy sheep.[28] General Washington reported to Congress:

> General Dickinson's behaviour reflects the highest honour upon him, for tho' his troops were all raw, he led them thro' the River, middle deep, and gave the enemy so severe a charge, that although supported by three field pieces, they gave way and left their convoy.

Matlack told Cadwalader, "Brigadier Gen Dickinson has gained universal applause by his spirited and at the same time prudent conduct; to which is justly attributed yesterday's great success." Matlack's comments implied that his men played a role in the operation. But one fact made it impossible to claim any credit: his battalion had subsequently disintegrated. Matlack's men, he said, had been complaining that their shirts were worn out and "their backs ... were galled very sorely." Worse, to their mortification, they were "getting lousy." Another problem was a shortage of food and drink. The riflemen had scuffled with "Independent Companies" over a "prize of Cyder which they had seized." Tired, cold and hungry, the last of his men had gone home. Just five men had agreed to stay and Matlack had discharged these few. He had had no choice but to disband his battalion. Now he pleaded with his superior: "I beg you will (do) me the justice to believe I have (done) all that has been in my power for the public service & lament that I could not do more."[29]

Back in Philadelphia, Matlack had time to recover and reflect. He realized the winter campaign had been a great success. He was proud of Washington's Christmas counterattack on the western edge of New Jersey and the American offensive that drove the British back to the other end of the state. Philadelphia's militia had participated in the standoff at Assunpink Creek and the victory at Princeton. The citizen-soldiers of the old Quaker province, Matlack said, had earned special credit: "The Militia of the City of Philadelphia and of the State of Pennsylvania has enabled General Washington to strike a Blow which has greatly changed the Face of our affairs."[30] Washington himself gave credit where credit was due:

> The readiness with which the militia of Pennsylvania have shown in engaging in the service of their country, at an inclement season of the year, when my army was reduced to a handfull of men, and our affairs were in the most critical situation, does great honor to them.[31]

Another officer, writing in the *Pennsylvania Evening Post*, was more specific about what the Philadelphia militia accomplished:

Great credit is due to the Philadelphia Militia; their behaviour at Trenton in the cannonade, and at Princeton was brave, firm, and manly: they were broken at first in the action at Princeton, but soon formed in the face of grape-shot, and pushed on with a spirit that would do honor to veterans.

The Associators had performed especially well at Princeton. In that battle, Sergeant Young wrote, "the Militia behaved to [a] Miricle." In the Revolutionary War the militia almost never regrouped after a panicked flight. In this battle, however, Philadelphia and Pennsylvania Associators came back after leaving the field. Inspirational officers, effective fighters, and fear of failure all played a role.[32] But what finally pushed the men forward was pure rage. The men were infuriated by the abhorrent behavior of the enemy, conduct which had carried over from New York. Young was shocked by one incident: "One officer who was wounded in one of his Legs a (British) soldier came and Knocked his Brains out with the Butt End of his gun." In another: "A young lad that was wounded they stabbed 3 times in his side with his Bayonet." These brutalities so exasperated the militia that "seeing two Hessians behind a tree ran at them, shot one and Run the other through..."[33] Sergeant Joseph White, a member of an artillery company from New England, wrote of the American troops at Princeton, "I never saw men looked so furious as they did running by us with their bayonets charged."[34] At Princeton, extreme anger overcame utter fear and the enemy was overrun.

Eight
The British Occupation

For loyalists, the favorable turn of events for the American army was not good news. The Quaker Sarah Logan Fisher said the victory at Trenton "greatly elated our Whigs, & as much depressed the Tories." On January 23 the Council of Safety announced returning soldiers would be quartered in the homes of non-Associators. Fisher feared that Quakers in particular would be forced to receive these uninvited guests: "If they carry it into execution, it will be almost too great to bear, as they are ... so intolerably dirty that even ... the stench of their dirt is great enough to cause an infectious sickness."[1]

For their part, militiamen coming back from the field were angry to discover others had prospered by avoiding military service. All in authority knew the military burden had not been equally shared. Washington made it clear that strict participation rules and resolute oversight were needed. With a spring campaign looming and Philadelphia a likely target, he warned that "weakness, languor, or timidity" on the part of the Pennsylvania Assembly was unacceptable. Washington said a new militia law was needed urgently. The Assembly, he said, could no longer remain silent.

Timothy Matlack was home in time to join his wife Nelly for their son's send off. Mordecai was leaving on his first cruise as a midshipman in the Continental Navy. The fifteen-year-old would be serving on Captain Nicholas Biddle's *Randolph*. However well respected the captain, the Matlacks had special cause for concern: the *Randolph*'s crew had been filled out with imprisoned British seamen. The ship set sail on February 3, 1777.

Timothy tried to keep his mind on the political fight at hand. Anticonstitutionalists in the Assembly had crippled his new government by denying quorum.[2] Now his side found an opportunity to break the deadlock. Washington's victories, the threat of a British invasion, and the discovery of a treasonous letter convinced the public to support the government. The letter in question was written by John Dickinson, who had been elected to Assembly by Philadelphia County. Prior to the Battle of Trenton, Dickinson had unpatriotically advised his brother: "Receive no more Continental Money on your Bonds and Mortgages. The British Troops having conquered the Jerseys.... Be sure to remember this. It will be better for you." With Dickinson embarrassed, Matlack's party ordered new elections to fill the Assembly seats left vacant by non-attendees. Constitutionalists also convinced voters to elect a Supreme Executive Council. This Council was the executive branch of government created by the Convention. Radicals in the Convention, distrustful of a powerful governor, had devised this board as a democratic alternative to a one-man executive.

Radicals won a victory in the February by-election. On March 5, 1777, in a joint session of the Assembly and the new Council, Thomas Wharton Jr. was elected President of the Supreme Executive Council, Captain General and Commander-in-Chief of the Commonwealth of Pennsylvania. One Quaker said sarcastically, "some call him Governour."[3] Sarah Logan Fisher described the celebration with bitterness: "The cannon fired & bells rang, & an elegant entertainment was prepared for him & his Council at the City Tavern where they dined, & in order to heighten the farce, in the evening [were] fired rockets and bonfires."[4] In her private diary Fisher continued to make her loyalties clear: "I sincerely hope & believe that before long General Howe will subdue their rebellious spirit & give them but little reason to rejoice."[5]

The next day the new president and his Supreme Executive Council heard the petition of Timothy Matlack, "praying to be appointed Secretary to this Council." Timothy's application was accepted and he "took the Affirmation required by the Constitution to Qualify him for his Office of Secretary of this Commonwealth." His first task was to "procure drafts of Licences for Public House Keepers, and Commissions for the several Officers of Government."[6]

But Matlack's government had little time to organize. The opposition regrouped in a matter of weeks and launched another push for a constitutional convention. Ignoring their own efforts to obstruct administration, especially in the judicial system, Anticonstitutionalists said the 1776 Constitution was destroying an orderly society.

The two sides organized their political forces. Constitutionalists formed the Whig Society in response to the opposition's Republican Society. Matlack's group called the Republicans "wealthy-militia-avoiding-supporters-of-the-Crown."[7]

But in June, under the threat of a British attack, the opponents reached a deal to suspend debate on the Constitution and put the question to a referendum in October.[8] And so, as in November, enemy movement thwarted the aspirations of Anticonstitutionalists. Was the threat real? General Howe *had* moved inland from the Raritan River, and Washington *had* shifted his army south from Morristown to Middlebrook to flank what looked like the

Eight. The British Occupation

start of a second march across New Jersey. But on July 3, 1777, Philadelphians learned Howe had pulled his army back to Staten Island; now it appeared he would advance north up the Hudson.[9] James Wilson, for one, felt his side had been either very unlucky or very well manipulated:

> If a regular system was formed between General Howe and the friends of our Constitution, his motions could not have been better timed for them than they have in two different instances. When an opposition has been twice set on foot, and has twice proceeded so far as to become formidable, he has twice, by his marches toward [the] Delaware, procured a cessation.[10]

Radicals, however, could soon deny having wagged the dog. The British did not move north. By the end of July their ships had rounded Sandy Hook and entered the mouth of the Delaware: Philadelphia was in fact their next target.

* * *

On July 4, 1777, Philadelphia celebrated the first anniversary of independence.[11] At noontime the American ships and galleys in the Delaware assembled near the city. The colors of the United States and streamers flew in the wind. Thirteen cannon from each of the ships were fired along with one from each of thirteen galleys. A Hessian regimental band captured at Trenton, featuring six prized hautboists, made some "fine performances suited to the joyous occasion." Following an elegant dinner for Congress in the afternoon, "the troops were paraded thro' the streets with great pomp." If all this was a recruiting event, as Tories believed, its effectiveness was hurt by the fact that "many of [the troops] were barefoot & looked very unhealthy."[12]

In the evening, bells were rung and thirteen rockets fired on the commons. The city was illuminated late into the night. Quakers who refused to light up their homes were punished. Sarah Fisher said her family suffered fifteen broken windows, "[Nicholas] Waln 14 [panes destroyed], T Wharton a good many more, & Uncle Logan had 50 cracked & broken, & all for the joy of having gained our liberty."

While disapproving of Quaker loyalism and pacifism, Timothy Matlack did not condone the vandalism. Although estranged from the members of his faith, Timothy never rejected his heritage. As if to prove this point, in mid–August, Timothy published an invitation to his kinsmen to celebrate an anniversary:

> Such of the numerous descendants of William Matlack, who choose to celebrate the anniversary of his arrival on this continent, will please to recollect that on Monday the 25th instant, one hundred years shall be completed since that time.[13]

Timothy Matlack was proud of his grandfather and the large Quaker family that carried his name. Quakers, Matlack reminded the patriots who despised them, were among the first Europeans to arrive in the Delaware Valley. All who came later owed them a debt of gratitude.

But any festivities Timothy organized for the Matlack centennial were disrupted by the arrival of two armies. On August 24, 1777, after a Sunday shower, General Washington and his Continental army marched through Philadelphia. On August 25, General Howe landed eighteen thousand British troops at the head of the Chesapeake Bay, fifty miles south.

That same day Congress received certain papers which, it said, proved Quakers were supporting the enemy. Having discovered this act of treason, Congress ordered Pennsylvania and Delaware to "apprehend, disarm & secure ... the notoriously disaffected," and seize the "fire-arms, swords, and bayonets" in the possession of loyalists.[14] The Congressional committee that wrote this order—John Adams, Richard Henry Lee and William Duer—did not stop there. Adams was particularly irritated by wealthy Philadelphia Quakers, who he said "love money and land better than Liberty or Religion." Adams' committee now handed Pennsylvania authorities a list of Quakers it wanted arrested. The Supreme Executive Council collaborated on the list, which passed through the hands of its secretary. But Timothy Matlack did not equate Quakerism and Toryism: he knew a growing faction supported independence. These Friends did not agree with the royalist statements issued by their Society's elite rulers. Matlack also understood that if Congress wanted to target militant loyalists it made no sense to go after pacifists. When the list arrived on his desk, Secretary Matlack took action in at least one instance to protect a friend. By adding "Jr." to the name Owen Jones he substituted the healthy son for the infirm father.

The Supreme Executive Council arrested the Quakers named and detained them at Carpenter's Hall. As the site of the 1774 Congress to resist British tyranny, this location was a poor symbolic choice. The Society of Friends immediately protested an "arbitrary, unjust and illegal seizure." Congress responded by publishing the eleven treasonous documents that supposedly made the case against the detainees. But only one of these papers was previously unknown. Said to have been found on Staten Island, Congress claimed it proved the Spanktown Yearly Meeting had provided the enemy with intelligence. But Congress was embarrassed to learn it was a fake: no such meeting existed. Looking for a way out, Congress requested that the Supreme Executive Council give the prisoners a hearing. This the Council declined, citing a lack of time. On September 9 the councilmen condemned the Quakers as "enemies of the American cause" and exiled them to western Virginia. In this period the isolated wilderness of western Virginia was a long

Eight. The British Occupation

journey from Philadelphia. Sarah Fisher claimed "a voyage to England would appear a trifle to it."

Council was not eager to carry out its exile order. It said the prisoners would be released if they signed an oath of allegiance which read: "I _____ do swear (or affirm) that I will be faithful and bear true allegiance to the Commonwealth of Pennsylvania as a free and independent state." The Quakers refused, however, saying they could neither swear nor affirm any oath. Quakers said the arrests were arbitrary since "no other crime [was] alleged against them than that they looked upon themselves to be subjects of Britain."[15]

Philadelphia merchant Owen Jones, 1711-1793, was saved from exile by Timothy Matlack, who replaced him with his son. This shows the Quaker broad-brimmed hat. Historical Society of Pennsylvania (HSP).

Offended that their offer of clemency had been spurned, Council ordered the prisoners be transported to Winchester, Virginia, "in a manner ... consistent with their respective characters." But the removal of the Quakers turned into an ugly scene. The men "were dragged into wagons by force by soldiers ... & drove off surrounded by guards and a mob." Sarah Fisher, whose husband was among the prisoners, was left in a state of turmoil: "Oh, can any pen paint my feelings at this time. But sometimes a gleam of hope darts in my mind."

Degrading handbills were handed out along the road to Virginia.[16] In Reading the detainees with greeted with "rocks and jeers." In Carlisle mounted militiamen hurled insults. Finally on September 28 the Quakers received an unfriendly reception at their destination. Over-burdened local authorities turned to Governor Patrick Henry and Congressman Richard Henry Lee for advice on handling the prisoners. In Philadelphia Sarah Fisher woke up feeling "very low indeed this morning & sunk almost below hope."

* * *

On September 11 General Howe defeated General Washington at Brandywine Creek, twenty-five miles southwest of Philadelphia. The British commander surprised Washington by sending part of his army on a long flanking march around the American right. As many as thirteen hundred American soldiers were killed, wounded or lost to sickness or desertion.

Now city residents feared the British would cross the Schuylkill at Swede's Ford, which was near the home of Christopher Marshall Jr. and his family. In a letter to his father, Christopher Jr. said he and his wife did not know what to do. Their district, he said, was overrun with Continental army wagons and sick men. He expected "the dismal sound of canon" at any moment.

Early in the morning of September 19 an alarm spread through Philadelphia: the British had crossed the river and were advancing on the city. People panicked. Sarah Fisher watched "wagons rattling, horses galloping, women running, children crying, delegates flying."[17] The last mentioned escapees "moved off before 5 o'clock in the morning." Jacob Hiltzheimer agreed: "Congress and all other public bodies of men, was gone by daylight." But the alarm was false: the British had appeared at the ford but had not crossed the river. Congress arrived in Lancaster where they rested before continuing on to Yorktown.

On September 20 British battalions followed Tory guides to an American encampment in the woods near Paoli. Four hundred fifty American soldiers were killed or wounded in a devastating, late-night, bayonet attack illuminated by burning tents and wagons. Following this massacre Howe outmaneuvered Washington again and marched his army to Germantown, north of Philadelphia. In scenes of chaos and anarchy Tories began seizing Whigs by "loyalist citizen's arrest."[18] Sarah Fisher hoped for the end to the rebellion: "I was much favored not to be at all fluttered, tho' it was an event I had so long wished to take place."

On September 26 General Howe sent part of his army down to occupy Philadelphia. Hiltzheimer wrote, "This day the English got into Philad." British Light Horse led the procession followed by Lieutenant General Lord Charles Cornwallis, infantry, and a marching band. Next came artillery, Hessian grenadiers, and another "large band of music but not equal in fineness or solemnity to the other." Following the second band came "baggage wagons, Hessian women, & horses, cows, goats, & asses brought up the rear." The regiments encamped on the commons and "three hours afterwards you would not have thought so great a change had taken place. Everything appeared still & quiet."[19]

After another British victory, in the Battle of Germantown, Howe set up a line of defense north of Philadelphia from the Schuylkill to the Delaware. Now the commander faced the task of feeding his army and the city's remaining population. His force was hemmed in by Continental troops while American forts were blocking British supply ships. Food and fuel were hard to find and harder to pay for. By the end of October British soldiers had gone eight

Eight. The British Occupation

Timothy Matlack's residence on East Orange Street, Lancaster, Pennsylvania, circa 1777. Courtesy LancasterHistory.org, Lancaster, Pennsylvania.

weeks without their clothes, blankets and tents. The wealthy Sarah Fisher managed to buy "two live hogs, a quarter of beef, & a bushel of turnips." She worried Philadelphia would soon run out of bread, "not a barrel of good flour to be bought at any price." Shortages of meat, butter, eggs and wood were severe. The poor, as always, were worse off than anyone. Fisher wrote:

> Such is the lamentable prospect of distress that the rich have not for themselves, nor have they in their power to relieve the cries of the poor, for money will not procure the necessities of life, for as the English have neither the command of the river nor the country, provisions cannot be brought in.

Matlack was in Lancaster with the government. On October 20 Christopher Marshall Sr. was "alarmed by Timothy Matlack" with the news Howe had evacuated Philadelphia. General Washington was in full pursuit. Marshall went happily back to bed but had "not lain long when Major Wertz came with boy, candle and lantern, on the same errand. I then arose and conversed until he went away then to bed. Not long there before Robert Taggert came with his lantern." Finally Marshall and his house guest got dressed and went out to join the "many heartily rejoicing." While the news of the British evacuation was false, there was real cause to celebrate in the days ahead. General John Burgoyne had surrendered to General Horatio Gates following the Battle of Saratoga.

In July, Burgoyne's British forces had advanced south from Quebec to take control of the Hudson Valley and divide New England from the rest of the colonies. On October 7, at Bemis Heights, twenty-five miles north of Albany on the Hudson River, Burgoyne's troops were defeated by a large American force under Gates. Ten days later Burgoyne surrendered his entire army near Saratoga.

In Philadelphia some loyalists were having second thoughts about their devotion to the empire. The British occupation had been a nightmare. Sarah Fisher, who had "so long wished" for the British to occupy her city, complained the troops were "plundering & ruining many people." In seeking supplies British soldiers were making no effort to distinguish between Whigs and Tories, and some who supported the King were left devastated. "[Joseph] Morris lost everything almost he had, nothing left but the shirt on his back."[20] Three thousand soldiers went out under Cornwallis on one foraging expedition which lasted a full week. Christopher Marshall said the British took "droves of cattle, sheep ... poultry, butter, meal, meat, cider, furniture, and clothing of all kinds, loaded upon our own horses."[21] There were also reports of sexual misconduct. Sarah Fisher heard "very bad accounts of the licentiousness of the English officers in deluding young girls."[22] Marshall said British and Hessian soldiers had been "stealing boys above ten years old [and] deflowering virgins." Before the end of the occupation, the harshness of the British occupation converted many a loyalist into a patriot.[23]

By January 1778, the American forts had fallen and supplies were flowing into the city. Loyalist merchants opened stores in the shops deserted by patriots and were soon profiting from a surge in trade. Local delicacies and exquisite imports were in great demand as a busy season of plays, concerts and dances got underway. Festivities included a parade staged by Irish soldiers on St. Patrick's Day. James Allen's wife said everyone was "gay & happy." Local socialites such as Peggy Shippen thrived at parties hosted by the likes of Major John Andre and "attended with every degree of luxury and excess."[24] While many thought the festive atmosphere in Philadelphia entirely inappropriate, state authorities in Lancaster were enjoying some fun of their own. *Their* social gatherings were likewise frowned upon by the likes of Christopher Marshall:

> Last Sixth Day another Ball or Assembly in Lancaster, where, it's said, cards were played at a hundred dollars a game. President [Thomas Wharton] there. O poor Pennsylvania! [25]

Eight. The British Occupation

However much Timothy Matlack may have enjoyed card games, he was in no condition for much diversion. The exertion of the last four years had taken its toll. Timothy fantasized about getting away from the war and Pennsylvania politics. In a letter to a cousin in New Jersey he complained of mental fatigue and physical exhaustion:

> The human mind, if it is right to judge from my own weakness, was not intended to be very strenuously exerted for any great length of time without some rest ... it is, I believe, natural to all men to seek for a retreat from hurry and over much employment in the decline of life: This I can't consider at a great distance from me.

But in March 1778, the end of the war was five years away. Matlack's ultimate retirement from public office would not come until 1822, forty-four years later. Now, as the last of the 1776 radicals still in office, Timothy Matlack was the symbol of Pennsylvania's revolutionary government. Benjamin Rush told John Dickinson, "Matlack alone remains in power and influence, of all the authors and pillars of the Constitution."[26]

* * *

Mordecai Matlack's first cruise on the *Randolph* had ended a year earlier in Charleston, South Carolina. Fourteen or fifteen men had died of sickness during the five-week voyage. Captain Nicholas Biddle called the trip "one of the most disagreeable Passages that ever I experienced." In a bad storm the frigate sprung its foremast, he said, before the mainmast gave way with the deck. "As it blew a fret of wind and a very high Sea ... to see [the mainmast] stagger from side to side with the rowl of the Vessel was as unpleasant a sight as ever I wish to behold." The crew rigged jury masts just before a "Gale of Wind would have undoubtedly put us ashore." Despite this frightening episode Biddle called the *Randolph* "the very Best Vessel for Sailing that ever I knew. I hope soon to be out in Her again."[27]

In Charleston, Captain Biddle struggled to repair the *Randolph*. As soon as the broken mainmast was replaced, lightning split the new one, and it too had to be exchanged. Recruiting for new men progressed slowly until the bounty was increased to fifty dollars. Biddle signed two hundred ten men, including officers and boys, but other ships were "detected in carrying off my People." The captain was forced to fire on the privateer brig *Fair American* to retrieve two of his sailors.

The *Randolph* and her new crew finally crossed the Charleston Bar and cleared the harbor for a second cruise on September 1, 1777. On the third day out, thirty leagues southeast of the city, the *Randolph* came upon a small fleet which "fired on us for about an Hour as we ran down before the wind upon them." The Randolph fired a few broadsides, and the flotilla struck their flags and surrendered. Taken captive were the twenty-gun *True Briton*, the eight-gun *Severn*, and the brigs *Charming Peggy* and *L'Assomption*. The Frenchman was released, and the *Randolph* returned to Charleston with her prize. The captured ships were carrying rich cargoes of rum, sugar, ginger and logwood. Agents sold the ships and their cargoes for about sixty thousand pounds sterling. Their commissions and expenses amounted to twelve or fifteen thousand. Each of the *Randolph*'s crew members, including Mordecai Matlack, received a share of half the remaining balance. In his report to Robert Morris, Captain Biddle made special mention of his first and second lieutenants, William Barnes and John McDougall.[28] The Captain was pleased enough with his sixteen-year-old midshipman to award him a fine sword.[29]

While back in port, Captain Biddle had a "very narrow escape from Fever that laid Violent hands on me." During his illness "to Comfort Me in my distress the *Randolph* was sunk in Careening and lay under water two Weeks before they could get Her up." In a New York newspaper a Briton reported the frigate had sunk on September 8, while turned on her side for cleaning, and "lay full of mud the fifth of October, and there was little hopes of her floating again."[30] But by mid–November both Biddle and the *Randolph* recovered from their ordeals. Biddle asked his brother James to get "What Prize Money May be due to Me from the Northward ... and Make use of it for the Family."

On the night of January 15, 1778, Charleston was engulfed in a fire that destroyed two hundred fifty houses amid heavy looting. The advance of the blaze was finally halted by blowing up several houses. The Gazette thanked Captain Biddle, who, along with a party of his crew, "assisted, as did most of the masters and sailors belonging to the other vessels in the harbor."[31]

In January 1778, the British ships *Craysford*, *Perseus* and *Hinchenbrook* were holding Charleston harbor in a blockade. In early February 1778, Biddle agreed to lead a fleet — the *Randolph, General Moultrie, Notre Dame, Fair American* and *Polly*— to liberate the town. But once again there were delays. Crewmen were slow to sign on despite the offer of bounty money and £21 monthly pay. By the time the crews were filled and the American squadron got over the bar the blockaders were gone. So Captain Biddle took his fleet south to the West Indies in search of the enemy. His armada cruised for a time in the latitude of Barbados and stopped several French and Dutch vessels. One afternoon in early March, Captain Charles Morgan of the *Fair American* and other officers dined aboard the *Randolph*. The men "spent the day Merrily." Biddle told his companions he feared no single-deck gunship. A few days later, sometime between one and three o'clock in the afternoon, the *Randolph* spotted a sail to windward and ordered his squadron to haul on the

Eight. The British Occupation

wind and stand for her. Captain Blake, officer of the marines aboard the *General Moultrie*, reported: "About 7 o'clock the Randolph, being to windward, hove to; the Moultrie being then about 150 yards astern and rather to leeward also hove to, the *Notre Dame* rather to astern and to leeward of us."[32]

At about eight o'clock the approaching British ship fired a shot just ahead of the *Moultrie* and hailed, asking her name. Captain Sullivan replied deceptively she was the *Polly* from New York (and therefore a friend). It was at this point, Captain Blake said, the Americans could see they were facing a ship with two decks of guns: their opponent was a massive British ship-of-the-line. The giant enemy vessel ranged up alongside the smaller *Randolph* and got on her weather quarter. Asked what ship she was Lieutenant Barnes called out "This is the *Randolph*." An officer on the British ship replied that she was the *Yarmouth*. Now a battle erupted with an exchange of broadsides.

The sixty-four-gun HMS *Yarmouth* had seen action in the battles of Cuddalore, Negapatam and Pondicherry in 1758 and 1759. She carried twenty-six thirty-two-pound cannons on her main gun deck and another twenty-six eighteen-pounders on her upper deck. The Americans were facing an extremely dangerous opponent.

The *Randolph* was almost immediately caught in crossfire. This happened when Captain Sullivan of the *General Moultrie* ordered his crew to fire at the *Yarmouth*'s stern. The *Moultrie* fired three broadsides but the enemy moved forward and the last shot, Captain Blake reported, hit the *Randolph*. Blake reported he "mentioned with some warmth to our Capt that instead of assisting we were firing into the *Randolph*." The *Moultrie* "immediately made sail to get ahead and engage [the *Yarmouth*] on her bow, but before this could be effected the *Randolph* blew up." Now it was the *General Moultrie* that was in danger: "The enemy was then yawning to get her broadside to bear which would rake us fore and aft." The *Moultrie* made sail and escaped. The *Randolph* was destroyed and sank.

Onboard the *Randolph*, about twenty minutes into the battle, Captain Biddle was wounded in the thigh. He was seated in a chair on the quarterdeck, being dressed by the surgeon's mate, when his ship exploded in a shower of burning debris over the ocean. An enemy ball from the *Yarmouth*, or friendly fire from the *Moultrie*, must have ignited her powder magazine, which detonated. More than three hundred seamen, marines and infantrymen were killed.[33] Four survivors were apparently picked up by the *Yarmouth*.

Among the dead was twenty-eight-year-old Captain Nicholas Biddle. Charles Biddle went to Charlestown to settle his brother's affairs. Charles wrote that he had wanted to join the crew of the *Randolph* but had been refused by his brother. Nicholas had thought it "too Much for his Mother to risque two sons in the ship." Captain Morgan had "from his first Arrival been lavish in praise of N. and Never Mentioned him without tears."³⁴ The *Pennsylvania Packet* wrote: "Never was a man here more sincerely esteemed or lamented than Captain Biddle ... an officer and a gentleman. He died in the midst of glory, fighting for his country against a very superior force, with all the gallantry of the bravest."

Also among the dead was seventeen-year-old midshipman Mordecai Matlack. Timothy Matlack was devastated by the loss of his son. In the aftermath of the accident Timothy tortured himself thinking about the explosion and the damage it had done to Mordecai's lifeless body. Two years later he tried to give a tribute to his son in a speech but broke down in tears:

> I mourn a darling Son, once the fond Hope and Comfort of my Heart—That dreadful fatal Blast which sent the *Randolph* to splinters, scattered his mangled Limbs in the Air and they fell, blacked and disfigured, a prey to the Fishes of the Sea.—I mourn his Loss but would preserve his Name.—Beloved by all that knew him, esteemed and highly honored by his brave Captain, he fell in the most glorious cause—

* * *

After Mordecai's death Nelly took comfort in a visit from her son Billy. She and Timothy had a third daughter by now, named Martha. Martha's older sisters were Sybil and Catherine. The girls were called Libby, Kitty and Patty.

Nelly was busy with the comings and goings of family, friends, boarders and numerous visitors calling on the secretary. Thanks to her husband's income, she had the means to pay for domestic help. One Lancaster neighbor, on the other hand, seemed to be doing all of her household work herself. Christopher Marshall said his wife started her day in the kitchen baking bread, pies and meat. Then she cleaned the house and attended to the orchard,

> cutting and drying apples, of which several bushels have been procured, add to which her making of cider without tools, for the constant drink of the family, her seeing all our washing done, and her fine clothes and my shirts ... all smoothed by her, add to this her making of twenty large cheeses ... and daily using milk and cream, besides her sewing, knitting, &c.

Christopher Marshall admitted his list failed to do his wife justice. He had stopped short, he said, because "entering [her services] minutely would take too much of my time."³⁵ Timothy later commented: "Female Industry deserves the Highest Reward." He thought women should be honored and loved and that their hands will make us truly rich.

In April 1778, Nelly welcomed four visitors from Philadelphia: Susanna Jones, Phebe Pemberton, Polly Pleasants, and Elizabeth Drinker. The group had come to Lancaster to petition for the release of their husbands, who were among the exiled Quakers.

Eight. The British Occupation

Following the death of his son, Timothy seemed anxious to help the men. He told Owen Jones Jr., "There are very many motives which conspire to induce me to render you every service in my power with cheerfulness and pleasure."[36] Jones Jr. had asked him for assistance after being accused of passing a gold coin. The authorities considered this an effort to undermine the Continental bills of credit. The incident induced the Board of War to transfer the exiles to the more remote Staunton, Virginia, and take away their writing materials. In his effort to help, Timothy talked to a Pennsylvania delegate in Congress; presented a petition in Council; and sent letters to influential men such as Samuel Allinson, J.B. Smith and General Roberdeau. He told Jones Jr., "Your present application to me, I esteem a mark of your friendship, and shall retain a just sense of it."

Negotiations for the release of the Quaker men had accelerated following the deaths of John Hunt and Thomas Gilpin. Hunt had died after the painful amputation of his leg, above the knee, "a fever having fallen into it."[37] Now Edward Pennington, said to be very ill, was threatening to become the third man lost. The Supreme Executive Council wanted to release the men but would not acquiesce without a stubborn display of power. On April 1, 1778, Matlack wrote Allinson: "The case of the prisoners in Virginia has been very often mentioned in council within a few weeks past; tomorrow is appointed for a full consideration of their case." But, Matlack warned, the outcome of the session could be serious: "Their situation will not excite envy in the minds of any considerate person, and they *must* decide on a question ... of very important consequence to them and their families." His ominous news was: "A law has passed this day requiring all persons to take an oath of affirmation of allegiance to the state within a short time: The penalties in case of refusal or neglect are very heavy."[38] But everyone knew the Quakers would not sign an oath. The Pennsylvania authorities were blustering their way out of the affair.

The Quaker wives met with President Wharton. Afterwards, Elizabeth Drinker wrote, the group "returned to Webb's by moonlight, where we lodged. Timothy Matlack paid us a visit this evening." The next morning the wives visited members of Council and followed up with a letter requesting the prisoners' release. Elizabeth Drinker recorded the progress of the women's two week visit during which Timothy acted as a liaison to the Supreme Executive Council:

> April 10, 1778: We were this day waited upon by T. Matlack, who undertook to advise us, and perhaps with sincerity. We paid a visit to 3 of ye Councillors [members of the Supreme Executive Council].... We were at Timothy's, where one of them lives; Nelly seemed pleased to see us.... T. M. came for our address, which was signed by all ye women concerned.
>
> April 11, 1778: T.M. read to S.J.(Sarah Jones) a copy of ye orders ... which was

favorable.... After consulting our friends here, we heard of one John Musser, a Mennonist, who ... was willing to go on our errand [to Virginia] — We packed up ye things in his Saddlebags, and he set off before dinner with a Pass ... signed by T Wharton and T Matlack.

April 13, 1778: Stopped at Tim Matlacks, who told us if we would stay and drink tea with his wife, he would hurry Council on their business.... When he was gone, we went over to Christopher Marshall Sen ... then came back with Nelly Matlack and drank tea. Timothy on his return informed us the G.B. (George Bryan) had no inclination to see us.

April 18, 1778: James Webb ... brought 2 letters, one from O. Jones Jr. to his Parents, ye other from T. Matlack, informing that our dear Friends were generally well.... Our Hearts feel rather lighter this evening than usual.

April 20, 1778: John Musser returned from Winchester with letters from our Husbands.... After we had read our letters over and over, we went with Becky Parke and drank tea with O. Biddle and wife.... T. Afflick, Tim Matlack and I. Morris were also there.

April 21, 1778: While we were at Whitlocks, T. Matlack came with our dear Friends sham release.

April 24, 1778: We went to Town after Breakfast, and drove directly to ye Court-House, where we met with George Bryan and Tim Matlack going up to Council. We presented our second address.... G. B. said that all was granted that could be — he would not feed us up with false Hopes.... We had more talk with Timothy at ye Door.[39]

The "sham" release did allow the exiles to return as far as Lancaster. In the Council journal Matlack gave the wives credit for winning their husbands' release: "The Council resuming the consideration of the case of the Prisoners which are ordered to this borough from Winchester agreeable to the request of Mrs. Jones, Mrs. Pemberton, Mrs. Pleasants and Mrs. Drinker." Their husbands arrived in Lancaster four days later. Elizabeth Drinker was surprised to find her Henry "much hartier than I expected, he looked fat and well." All were back in Philadelphia by the end of the month. Sarah Fisher said her beloved husband returned "with health of body & peace of mind, which unspeakable favor I earnestly wish I may ever keep in grateful remembrance."

* * *

Timothy labored on in an increasingly secretive environment. His Lancaster neighbor, Christopher Marshall, was a friend but also a member of the opposition party. On one occasion Marshall said he was "visited by Timothy Matlack to enquire for news, but as he never communicates or tells me any, I am grown as saucy, for I never ask him for any, he being too great a man." In May 1778, Matlack told Marshall the United States and France had signed a treaty of alliance and Britain had declared war on France. Marshall wrote

Eight. The British Occupation

of his source, "It's to be remembered that the above news was freely communicated to me by Timothy Matlack, which being so contrary to his constant practice, I make this memorandum in order that I may not forget this singular act of his friendship."

The treaty between France and the United States meant England was facing an alliance between her traditional nemesis and her breakaway colonies. The King and his ministers would have to take steps to protect England's interests around the world. American leaders saw that Philadelphia would no longer be a tenable position: the British army would have to withdraw to New York. London did order this move, and an evacuation was put in motion, but General Howe's officers were too proud, and too well supplied, to pack up and go without a display of arrogance. Major John Andre took charge of plans for a fete-to-end-all-fetes: an all-day, all-night festival, pageant, and dance to dazzle the womenfolk and set the stage for the army's honorable departure.

General Howe's send-off, following his resignation, became the pretext for this big event, the Meschianza. Held on May 18, 1778, the party included a parade, regatta (complete with floating bands and booming cannon), knight's tournament, carousel, and elaborate feast served by twenty-four slaves in Turkish costumes. All this was capped off by a grand ball and "Sky-Rockets and other Fireworks ... exhibited after Night." The invited women, including the beautiful Peggy Shippen, wore towering hairstyles which became symbolic of the "Scenes of Folly and Vanity." Elizabeth Drinker, for one, was appalled by the display: "How insensible do these people appear," she wrote, "while our land is so greatly desolated and Death and sore destruction ... impends over so many."[40]

In Lancaster, Pennsylvania, authorities were increasingly incensed by the occupation's legacy of excess and devastation. An angry Supreme Executive Council wanted to punish those who had collaborated with the enemy or profited excessively during the occupation. In March the Assembly passed an Act of Attainder: a law which allowed for the cancellation of civil rights in cases of treason. The law said individual traitors named by Council would forfeit their estates upon failure to stand trial. But everyone knew the thousands of loyalists who had fled to New York, Nova Scotia and England were not about to appear in Pennsylvania courts.

In late May Timothy Matlack was given the job of executing the new law as Keeper of the Register of Persons Attainted for High Treason. Matlack's forty-four agents were authorized to "vest in the Commonwealth" and lease out loyalist properties. This force was to be compensated with commissions on rents and fees from the sale of personal property.

Some Pennsylvanians considered the new law proof that a new tyrant had already replaced the one they were trying to evict. The edict was hard to square with the Pennsylvania Constitution, which said the right to acquire, possess and protect property was natural, inherent and unalienable. The Supreme Executive Council defended the new measure as necessitated by a state of war. But only seven months earlier, in response to a similar ordinance by the Board of War, Council had warned "intrusion upon the private property of individuals" would be viewed as "a grievance arising from the Constitution" and would "greatly weaken & disable the Council from performing essential services."[41] This earlier statement was now seized upon by Anticonstitutionalists. But Council's desire to punish enemy collaborators trumped all other concerns. In May, Council issued a list of fifty traitors, including numerous Quakers, said to have actively worked for the British.[42] Sarah Fisher worried "another severe trial" was coming: "The English, who we had hoped & expected would have stayed & kept possession of the city, are leaving us ... we may expect some great suffering when the Americans again get possession."[43]

By late May British sailors were busy loading the army's baggage while loyalists made hurried preparations to leave with their protectors. The arrival of the Earl of Carlisle and his peace commission delayed General Clinton's departure, but by 6:00 A.M. on June 18, 1778, the last of the grenadiers and light horse pulled out, and "there was not one Redcoat to be seen in town." Control of the city changed hands immediately: "In less than a quarter of an hour the Americans were in the city."[44] Washington pursued Clinton across the Delaware, and their armies fought at Crosswicks on June 23 and Monmouth on June 28.

A few days after the evacuation Timothy Matlack and one of his daughters joined other people returning to Philadelphia. On the road they found "houses ruined and destroyed." In the city itself they were shocked by the scenes of desolation, "dirt, filth, stench and flies ... scarcely credible." Marshall said "grief seized me in beholding the ruins, viz., houses quite demolished." On July 4, Secretary Matlack published, by order of Council, a bitter condemnation of the Crown troops:

> The indiscriminate destruction of whig and tory property to be seen in the neighborhood of the city strongly mark the character of those British savages. They have increased the resentment of their old enemies and turned the hearts of their friends: Many ... followed them with the bitterest execrations.

Matlack reserved a parting shot for the Hessians, who he predicted would now be drawn off to Great Britain or the West Indies: "We leave it to our readers to determine, whether those military 'dogs of war' have done anything but bark ever since they came to America."[45]

Elizabeth Drinker, for one, agreed the conduct of the British officers and their lady friends had been reprehensible. Local women who had consorted with officers became the target of ridicule. On July 4, 1778, a crowd parading a local prostitute topped with a massive wig mocked these ladies and their ridiculous hairstyles. Drinker agreed with the message, if not the medium: "A very high Head dress was exhibited thro the Streets, this Afternoon on a very dirty Woman with a mob after her, with Drums &c by way of ridiculing that very foolish fashion."[46]

A reduced Congress returned to Philadelphia in time to join a tepid July 4 celebration. A published report claimed Congressmen, civil officials, and military officers had gathered for a "grand festival" at City Tavern. The event was, however, a subdued affair.

Festivities on the streets were also contained. Secretary Matlack requested residents refrain from illuminating their windows due to the "excessive heat of the weather, the present scarcity of candles, and other considerations." Among the latter was the realization it made no sense to light up the damaged city.

But in the midst of this gloomy occasion, some were exuberant about the future. The young inventor Robert Fulton reportedly traded in his candles for powder. He explained, "Our rulers have requested the citizens forebear illuminating their windows and streets: as good citizens we should respect their request; and I prefer illuminating the heavens with sky-rockets."[47]

* * *

The British were gone but the war continued in Pennsylvania. Word arrived of a battle in the frontier Wyoming Valley. On July 3 a regiment of loyalist fighters and their Seneca allies killed over three hundred Pennsylvania militia in the biggest of a series of attacks on settlements along the Allegheny and Susquehanna Rivers. Elizabeth Drinker heard an "account from Backwards ... that the Indians are committing great ravages there."[48]

In the militia call-out that followed, Quakers were among those pressured to serve. Charles Biddle had heard Friends were not excused from militia duty in Virginia. Even in Philadelphia, he said, Quakers were dragged up with the troops, though "nothing could be done to make them learn the manual exercise, much more make them fight." Biddle said it was cruel to force pacifists into the field.

As vice president of the Supreme Executive Council, Biddle was forced to deal with a corollary problem: false Quakers. These were men who joined the Meeting to avoid being drafted into the militia. Biddle called one group, from the Beaufort area, "the most profligate fellows in the country." Council said no one would be excused who did not belong to Meeting before the war.[49]

While faced with active combatants in the Wyoming Valley, the Supreme

Executive Council was preoccupied with its search for loyalists who collaborated with the British during the occupation. Informants were, however, few and far between. On July 9 Council reminded citizens the chief justice was hearing charges against Tories "accused of joining and assisting the British Army." The Court House would be open on Saturday.

Whigs guessed misinformation and intimidation were being used to stop people from making statements. In response they formed a new committee, called the Patriotic Society, to rally a reticent public and collect information. Timothy Matlack kept the committee's book. Its effectiveness was enhanced by bipartisanship: more than twenty of its members were Anticonstitutionalists.[50] The Patriotic Society published a "Coffee-House Declaration" on July 25 which encouraged people to come forward with evidence. The board wanted to hear about treasonous activity during the occupation and any "oppression or insult whatever." Individuals hesitant to appear at the Court House or State House could call on Secretary Matlack at his office on Fourth Street, a few doors south of Market Street. The secretary was available to fight Tories, and conduct normal business, between the hours of three and five in the afternoon.[51] Now people came forward.

On July 9 the Supreme Executive Council named the agents authorized to seize Tory real estate. One of them was Charles Willson Peale. Peale's primary target was Joseph Galloway, the delegate to the first Congress who'd switched sides to serve as General Howe's Superintendent of Police. Galloway had previously fled Philadelphia, but his wife had stayed behind to guard the family property.

When Grace Galloway received her eviction notice from Peale she summoned Timothy Matlack for help. Mrs. Galloway hoped for Matlack's assistance in light of his social visits to her estate. But this time Timothy's visit was not so pleasant. She wrote that "his behaviour Convinced me their is no dependence on him & threw Me into a state of Dejection."[52]

Mrs. Galloway *was* offered protection by the new commandant of Philadelphia, Benedict Arnold. But once advised against this Arnold changed his mind and told her there was nothing he could do.

On August 10 Peale returned to the Galloway residence with a prospective tenant, Don Juan Mirailles, ambassador of Spain. At the sight of the men the lady of the house fell ill and was taken upstairs to lie down. Undiscouraged, the visitors continued their tour downstairs. Mrs. Galloway said they sent up a note in which "ye Spaniard offer'd to let Me chuse My own bed chamber" and stay on as his guest.

Before ending their visit, the men opened a window in the parlor and locked the door to the room. Their ungraceful plan was to reenter the house by climbing in. A series of visitors, including Israel Pemberton, arrived to

Eight. The British Occupation

advise the worried owner. Concerned friends milled around trying to decide what to do. Grace Galloway wrote, "I sent for Tim Mattlack ... at Night he came & said I must go out of my house & Molly Craig told him she had a mind to get in at the window & take ye lock of[f] ye Door [and] fasten ye window he told her if she had she would be hung." Once calm was restored the discussion continued. Mrs. Galloway reported, "I coaxed him & he seem[ed] as if he was desirous I shou'd have my estate, but was Violent in respect to their laws & told me the Lawyers flatter'd Me for I must give up possession."[53]

General Arnold placed a guard at the open window, to prevent thieves from entering. When Peale and his men returned the next day they found the window locked. The men made their way around the back of the house to the kitchen door. Grace said, "They made repeated strokes at ye door & I think it was 8 or 10 minutes before they got it open.... When they came in ... they look'd very Mad." After arguing back and forth Peale finally took Mrs. Galloway by the arm and escorted her out.

Other women faced similar evictions. Among these was Rebecca Shoemaker, the wife of a prominent Quaker merchant. In Pennsylvania, one hundred eighteen loyalist families lost their homes for the duration of the war or longer.[54]

But prominent loyalists who did not evacuate with the British army exposed themselves to physical danger. Two individuals in this category were the Quakers Abraham Carlisle and John Roberts. Both were accused of treason and surrendered to authorities.

Nine

Benedict Arnold
Part One (Illicit Affairs)

In early September 1778, the *Pennsylvania Packet* reported that a London gentleman meeting with congressmen was in fact a British agent. The publisher had discovered this visitor's covert ties to the failed Carlisle Peace Commission. The Earl of Carlisle's official negotiators, who had arrived in June, were dismissed by Congress soon thereafter.

Dr. John Berkenhout had used his acquaintance with Arthur Lee, with whom he had studied medicine, as a pretext for an introduction to his brother, Congressman Richard Henry Lee. R. H. Lee had subsequently introduced Berkenhout to John Adams and others. The congressmen were embarrassed by the item in the *Packet*, which called attention to its earlier references to the gentleman. One of these was a reprint of a London notice announcing Berkenhout's departure for America: "supposed to be sent on a private embassy to the Congress." Another mentioned his arrival in New York, behind enemy lines. Lee demanded Pennsylvania authorities investigate, and Sheriff Nicola escorted Berkenhout to the Supreme Executive Council for questioning. The councilmen looked through his papers before confining him to jail.

While incarcerated Berkenhout said he was "frequently visited by Matlack, Secretary to the Executive Council." On these calls Matlack "affected great openness, and ingenuous conversation." Matlack assured the doctor:

> If I had anything to propose, I might safely speak to him, without reserve; if I wanted any information, he would frankly answer my questions; or, if there was any other person, any man of letters with whom I wished to converse, he should be immediately sent to me.

The men talked about the success of the American army at Trenton. Berkenhout did not hide his disdain for General Howe's "retreat from the Delaware when he was almost in sight of Philadelphia." In view of what he had heard of the condition of Washington's forces, the doctor was convinced "the British troops might have marched triumphantly into Philadelphia without ... hindrance or molestation!" Cued by this outburst, Matlack may have shared a fable about George Washington. According to the story, on the morning the British army was expected to cross into Pennsylvania, Washington had lamented over breakfast, "Well, 'tis a noble cause lost!" The general supposedly said of himself: "For my own part, I will retire to the banks of the Ohio, where I hope, the English will not think it worth their while to molest me." Washington, it was said, sent a message to Congress informing them that his next letter would probably announce the breakup of the Continental army.

Matlack might have fed Berkenhout this tale to fuel his frustration. He hoped the doctor would respond with something of interest. But the storyteller may have been Dr. Benjamin Rush, who also called on Dr. Berkenhout in jail. Rush, the detainee said, expected "to make some important discovery concerning the nature of my commission." Berkenhout presumed Rush's "uncommon loquacious plausibility" had been "a mask of sympathetic feeling for my situation." Dr. Rush would have been very familiar with the Washington anecdote since he was involved in the Conway Cabal.

To extract information, Berkenhout wrote, Matlack tried the effect of fear. The secretary ordered the jailor to place the prisoner in confinement. The doctor was "separated from the other English prisoners" and denied "visits from any person whatsoever."

But by September 14 Pennsylvania authorities were ready to send Berkenhout away. Matlack presented him with a release which read:

> I John Berkenhout Doctor of Physic, do declare upon my honour, that I will immediately proceed, by the usual rout, to Elizabeth-town in the State of New-Jersey, and from thence within the British lines, and that I will not, from this time, untill my arrival there, do, or say anything, which can, by any means, be construed, or understood to be injurious to the states of North America.

Berkenhout signed, and Matlack told him to be ready to leave by two o'clock. At the appointed hour the secretary escorted the prisoner down to the river and put him on a sloop sailing for Trenton. Matlack gave him a pass that read: "The above mentioned Doctor John Berkenhout is ordered to return to the city of New York after having been some days past confined in this city, by order of the supreme Executive Council of the Commonwealth of Pennsylvania."

In his diary Berkenhout called the Supreme Executive Council "seven or nine of the lowest, most contemptible fellows I ever saw assembled, except at the Robin Hood [a liberal club in London]." "From their appearance and capacity they seemed such a club of tradesmen as commonly assembly at an Ale-House, in the borough of Southwark."

The doctor peppered his written account with criticism of Howe, Cornwallis, the Hessian commander Rall, Washington, and Congress itself. The latter he called "unpolished, illiterate, poor and of no character." Berkenhout reserved a special assessment for Timothy Matlack: "His character is that of a deep, shrewd fellow." The British agent speculated, "This Matlack, I think, might be bribed, and I believe it not impossible to open a secret correspondence with him."

Benedict Arnold commanded the provincial troops against Quebec, through the wilderness of Canada, and was wounded in storming that city, under General Montgomery. Mezzotint print. London: Thos. Hart, March 26, 1776. Library of Congress, Prints and Photographs Division.

But Timothy's commitment to the American cause, and his hatred of the King, had only been reinforced by the death of his son. The British had destroyed his city. Berkenhout's characterization was likely motivated by his own desire for financial reward. The doctor hoped his journal would be enjoyed by a very specific audience: his sponsors in the British ministry. The identification of corruptible authorities, however inaccurate, was something his patrons would value. Berkenhout did find an eager reader in Lord Germain, who granted him a comfortable pension.[1]

* * *

One man who would have listened to bribe offers was Benedict Arnold, the officer Washington sent to secure Philadelphia following the British evacuation. Washington took this step in response to Congress' request that he "prevent the operations of ill-disposed persons" by preventing "the removal, transfer, or sale of any goods, wares, or merchandise" in the wake of the enemy's departure. In naming Major General Arnold Commandant of Philadelphia, General Washington instructed him to "take every prudent step

Nine. Benedict Arnold Part One (Illicit Affairs)

in your power to preserve tranquility and order ... restraining, as far as possible, till the restoration of civil government, every species of persecution, insult, or abuse."[2]

While this delicate assignment called for impeccably restrained personal conduct, Arnold was soon calling attention to himself by driving around town in a chariot and hosting lavish entertainments for the same pretty women who had paraded in the company of British officers. In early November 1778, Joseph Reed asked General Greene, "Do you not think it extraordinary," that at a party Arnold had given the night before, "not only common Tory ladies, but the wives and daughters of persons proscribed by the State, and now with the enemy in New York, formed a very considerable number. The fact is literally true."[3] Among these women was one who had attracted Benedict's romantic attention. For Arnold, loyalty to King George III was no impediment to love. Arnold threw expensive parties to please the object of his desire: the beautiful Peggy Shippen.

Local authorities learned to despise Arnold's presence. In early October 1778, preparations for another party triggered a dispute between the major general and Secretary Matlack. Matlack sent Arnold a letter complaining that a militia sergeant, on duty at Arnold's headquarters, had been ill-used by a staff member. Matlack said Arnold's aide, Major David Franks, had ordered the sergeant to fetch his barber. The sentry, Matlack told Arnold, had been hurt "*by the order itself* and by the *manner of it.*" As if addressing a child Matlack asked Arnold, "What would have been *your* feelings, had an Aid to *your* commanding officer, ordered *you* to call *his barber*?" Matlack proceeded to lecture Arnold on the need to make militia duty as comfortable as possible, with relaxed military discipline, since freemen would not submit to indignities. The soldier in question, he mentioned, happened to be his son William.

Benedict Arnold replied that no man has a higher sense of the rights of a freeman than himself. But, Arnold said, when a civilian joins the militia his situation changes: "the respect due to a citizen is by no means to be paid to the soldier, any farther than his rank intitles him to it."

With elections looming and verdicts due in two major trials, Matlack was under severe pressure. After four days he responded that situations could justify an officer's commands which expose a citizen to certain death; but none may warrant an order to clean his shoes.

In the eyes of Pennsylvania's radical leaders, traditional military discipline conflicted with democracy. Their value system extended citizenship "beyond the political sphere and into the military sphere."[4] In both realms the inherent conflict in question was that of class. In the barber incident Arnold's aristocratic aide-de-camp, David Franks, had insulted a common citizen, Timothy's son Billy. The order to find Major Franks' barber was, Matlack scolded, "the office of a menial servant, not the duty of a soldier." Such commands could not be mistaken for "the orders of a wise and prudent general." Soldiers in battle, he said, would not respond with the necessary "implicit obedience" unless officers commanded with "great prudence and discretion." He added, ominously, that "Commanders who destroy [trust] ... will be accountable for the consequences." Matlack told Arnold he was "not a little mortified to find the order, of which I complained, so fully justified and supported by you." Matlack also informed his adversary he had decided to withdraw his son from the service and explain his reasons publicly.

If Matlack hoped to aggravate his correspondent, he was successful. Arnold answered, "If the declaration, that you will withdraw your son from the service, and publish the reasons, is intended as a threat, you have mistaken your object." But, he said, "being earnestly desirous of closing this correspondence," he was willing to agree the officer's "haughty, imperious or insolent manner" was improper. But the affair, Arnold claimed, was out of his hands. If the major "behaved amiss, it was his duty to make reparation." In closing Arnold reminded Matlack that disputes between civilian and military authorities could hold serious consequences: "Let me add, that disputes, as to the rights of citizens and soldiers, in conjunctures like the present, may be fatal to both."

Had this warning come from, say, George Washington, Matlack would have understood it in the broader context: divided we fall. But Benedict Arnold was not a messenger Matlack could hear on that subject. What he read was a suggestion his son William seek reparation in a duel. Matlack responded forcefully, "Whereas the order being *your order*, and my son *several years under age*, I conceive [the dispute] to lie between yourself and me." Timothy made it clear that if there were to be a contest, he himself would be meeting Benedict Arnold on an open field.

Days later Matlack made good on his promise to go public. He published the protest of "one of those mean and insignificant people called Militia Men." Matlack's Militia Man found it "humiliating and absurd," after serving in battle, "to stand at the door of any man, be he ever so great, and when there liable, not only to his orders, but at the whim and caprice of any of his suite to be ordered on the most menial services." Matlack's Militia Man took a parting shot at the well-coiffed commander with the observation that he had no reason to fear the British or Tories as "they are all remarkably fond of him."[5]

* * *

In the summer of 1778 the British sloop *Active,* loaded with a cargo of rum, waited in Jamaica. Captain Underwood needed more sailors for a run

Nine. Benedict Arnold Part One (Illicit Affairs)

up to New York. A press gang brought him four Connecticut mariners, and the *Active* started her trip. But somewhere off the mid–Atlantic coast the Americans mutinied. In an attempt to take control of the ship the Connecticut men heaped "a cable and other incumbrances over the stair-way between the deck and the cabbin," trapping the Captain, his first mate, and the passengers below. The Captain and his mate, the report said, fired their pistols "through such openings as they were able" and threatened to blow up the quarterdeck. The sailors had control of the two three-pound cannons but were unable to subdue their prisoners because the British "possessed the stock of victuals, water and ammunition."

The standoff went further adrift when Captain Underwood succeeded in wedging the rudder. "Under this embarrassment the ship was disabled, and could not be steered." Finally the two sides agreed the Americans would row off near the coast. But as the *Active* neared the New Jersey coast a Pennsylvania brigantine, *Convention,* appeared, with the privateer *Gerard* in support. The *Active* was captured.[6]

In Philadelphia a battle for the sloop and her cargo ensued. The fight pitted Captain Houston of the *Convention* and Gideon Olmstead, representing the Connecticut sailors. In the Court of Admiralty, Olmstead argued that his men had had control of the *Active* before the *Convention* took her prisoner. But, favoring Pennsylvania's interests, the court awarded Olmstead and his party just a quarter of the prize. Unhappy with the ruling, the men appealed to Congress.

On November 12, 1778, another Connecticut man, Major General Benedict Arnold, was displeased to find the following anonymous paragraph in his copy of the *Pennsylvania* Packet:

> It is whispered, that some Gentlemen of high rank, now in this city, have introduced new specie of champerty, by interesting themselves in the claim of the sloop *Active*. If this be so, there can be no doubt but that the contract is in itself void; and that the seamen are not bound to fulfill it.

While Arnold was not directly named, the identifiers "high rank" and "now in this city" left no doubt he was the officer in question. Arnold had been accused of champerty: the crime of buying into a lawsuit, punishable by imprisonment. Arnold demanded that the publisher, John Dunlap, identify the penman. Dunlap responded by asking for Arnold's written comments, to be published with the name of the accuser. Two days later Dunlap printed Arnold's letter. Benedict said the piece had been "slander thrown out against him" and that he knew how to "despise anonymous calumny." Timothy Matlack identified himself as the author of the *Packet* rumor: "If ... General Arnold demands the author of [the paragraph], and he can derive any advantage to those of the claimants of the sloop *Active*, who he has undertaken to support, by knowing that I wrote and sent it to the press, he is welcome to that knowledge."

Matlack had suspected an arrangement when Arnold appeared before a committee of Congress hearing the Olmstead appeal. His inquiry uncovered evidence Arnold had "furnished his countrymen with money to support their claim."[7] Documents found at a later date confirmed he was to receive half the prize if he could convince Congress to award it to the Connecticut men in its entirety.

Now Congress made a decision on Olmstead's appeal. To Arnold's great pleasure, the delegates "not only reversed the sentence of the Court below, but made a new adjudication, awarding the whole to Gideon Umpsted, &c the claimants."[8] But the Supreme Executive Council made sure Arnold received no financial reward. In a mockery of the congressional injunction, Pennsylvania sold off the *Active* and her cargo and retained the proceeds. Faced with this direct challenge, Congress' lame response was to name a committee and table its report.

A newspaper writer signing "An American" criticized Pennsylvania for humiliating Congress in the *Active* affair. The piece warned America's enemies not to take comfort in "the symptoms of discontent, lately exhibited by the Executive Council of Pennsylvania."

> And depend on it ... the Whigs of Pennsylvania will not engage in any dispute with the representative body of America to the prejudice either of the acknowledged rights of that body, or of the privileges of those brave citizens who have drawn their swords in the cause of Freedom.[9]

Timothy Matlack identified New York Congressman Governeur Morris as the author of this "truly Machiavellian" piece. He fired back, "But to those who know, that your favorite objects are, to disgrace Pennsylvania, insult the President of its Council, and to support General Arnold, the design stands naked and detested."

Pennsylvania authorities did not back off the hated Arnold. In December 1778, the Council's president and its secretary said they had collected incriminating evidence of transactions involving illegal passes and the improper use of army wagons. The Pennsylvania leaders now insisted Congress strip the general of his command and detain him pending further investigation. Congress, not relishing another fight with the powerful state authorities, said it would cooperate with their investigation.

By early February 1779, Arnold was ready to get out of Pennsylvania. His friends in New York were prepared to offer an estate and a safe haven. Arnold left town, but Reed and Matlack sent a rider galloping after him with a formal list of charges. A few days later a rumor regarding Arnold's sudden departure spread to Lancaster. Christopher Marshall wrote, "News of the day is that Gen. Arnold has left Philad and gone over to the English."[10]

* * *

Earlier in the fall of 1778 the Whig coalition known as the Patriotic Society disintegrated ahead of Assembly elections. Constitutionalists continued to meet as the Patriotic Association, but the board now served as a campaign committee. Their drive for seats was, however, unsuccessful: on election day Philadelphia voters picked four Anticonstitutionalists.

That month the two sides also faced each other in the Supreme Court. The Quaker loyalists Carlisle and Roberts were being tried for treason. Abraham Carlisle was defended by James Wilson and two other conservative lawyers. For the prosecution Pennsylvania had hired the increasingly radical Joseph Reed. Reed had resigned from Congress with the understanding he would become president of the Supreme Executive Council after the trials. In the weeks leading up to the hearings Philadelphia juries acquitted at least eleven men charged with treason. Reed said the juries had succumbed to "popular Humanity," itself "a species of Treason & not the least dangerous Kind." While unhappy with the string of decisions he'd lost, he conceded they were "an error on the favourable side."[11] On September 26 Reed finally won a conviction. A jury found Carlisle guilty of having worked as a gatekeeper for the British army, and Chief Justice Thomas McKean handed down the death sentence.

In the Roberts trial, witnesses recalled he had offered to lead a troop of cavalry to Virginia to rescue the Quaker exiles. Chief Justice McKean called this "a strange piece of conduct in one who pretended that he was conscientiously scrupulous of bearing arms in any case."[12] Roberts was also found guilty and given the death sentence. The news of the verdicts stunned some Pennsylvanians. Elizabeth Drinker wrote: "John Robarts, miller, condem'd to die, Shocking doings!"

The sentences triggered a flood of petitions for clemency. Appeals for mercy were signed by citizens, jurors, judges and the prisoners of war Roberts had once aided. Among the signers was Timothy's brother, Josiah, a grand juror. The petitioners said the Quakers had earned compassion with philanthropy. The Chief Justice himself acknowledged their "acts of humanity, charity, and benevolence."[13]

As secretary of Council, Timothy Matlack was unable to support the men publicly. But behind the scenes Timothy likely expedited the submission of petitions to Council, as he had in the case of the Quaker exiles. Joseph Reed told the members of the Supreme Executive Council, who had constitutional authority to grant pardons, "the Voice of the People will certainly justify Council in any Act of Mercy." But, he said, "Neither Clamour, Fear of Offense, or Hope of Favour ought to influence the judgment of the Patriotick Senator."

Public support for Carlisle and Roberts was undoubtedly heartfelt, but Reed considered the rigorous campaign part of a "settled fixed system to subvert the Whig interest." Reed suspected the Revolution was being undermined by a partnership between the government's opponents and loyalists. One motive he saw was business interest: money linked Anticonstitutionalists and Tories. Radicals also suspected men like James Wilson maintained friendly relations with loyalists as a hedge: these contacts could get them pardons if America lost the war. True Whigs, those with everything staked on independence, feared amnesty had been prearranged in some cases. These suspicions explain why George Bryan called Anticonstitutionalists the "patrons of Tories."[14]

A newspaper writer using the name Sully said "the men of the greatest property in the state are in the opposition." He predicted the elite would win control of government because "power will always go hand in hand with wealth." The great achievement of the radicals in 1776 was to break this equation and put power in the hands of the people. Now, two years later, state officials felt they had a mandate to defend a Constitution that had reordered society. In the cases of Carlisle and Roberts, wealth became part of the logic for a refusal of clemency. Reed said, "These being rich and powerful [men], we could not for shame have made an example of some poor rogue after forgiving the rich."[15] Radicals saw it as no coincidence that John Roberts, the wealthier of the two defendants, received the greater support from petitioners. The radical government felt it needed to show its resolve, and hanging these wealthy Quakers became the means to that end. Chief Justice McKean told Roberts in his summary: "Your junction gave encouragement to the invaders of your country; your example occasioned the defection of others; and you exerted yourself in forwarding their arbitrary designs." His sentence was severe. "You shall be taken back to the place from whence you came, and from thence to the place of execution, and there to be hanged by the neck until dead. May God be merciful unto your soul."[16] Carlisle was also put to death.

In Pennsylvania only five of the approximately one hundred forty-two men attainted for treason during the war were executed. Carlisle and Roberts were the only two who voluntarily surrendered after being charged.[17]

* * *

After gaining strength in the fall elections, Anticonstitutionalists issued their third major challenge to the Pennsylvania Constitution. Unfazed, Constitutionalists held a wild celebration in honor of Joseph Reed, the new president of the Supreme Executive Council. On December 1 Elizabeth Drinker noted "great rejoicing all day; on choosing a President, Josh. Read is said to be the man; ringing of Bells and fireing of cannon." At a banquet at City Tavern two hundred seventy guests consumed five hundred twenty-two bottles of Madeira, twenty-four of port, one hundred sixteen bowls of punch, nine of toddy, and six of "sangaree." The revelers broke ninety-six glasses, five decanters and one large inkstand.[18]

Constitutionalists had good reason for confidence. The response to the Assembly's convention call was overwhelming negative. Christopher Marshall wrote:

> Last night came Robert Whitehill; stayed some time in political conversation; said that the people in Cumberland and York counties were generally displeased with our Assembly for their taking upon them to call a Convention at this time, and are preparing a Memorial that will be signed by some one thousand ... in opposition to their proceeding.

The Assembly was flooded with petitions in support of Reed's government. Close to fourteen thousand Pennsylvanians signed sheets; the largest number, Matlack reported, ever collected.[19] On February 27, 1779, in a vote of forty-seven to seven, the Assembly canceled its convention plebiscite. To Timothy Matlack's pleasure, his Constitution had survived another challenge.

A month later the Republican Society responded. Society Chairman Richard Bache complained his party had been vilified in the petition drive as a "junto of gentlemen in Philadelphia, who wished to trample upon the farmers and mechanics, to establish a wicked Aristocracy, and to introduce a House of Lords, hoping to become members of it." Fourteen thousand signatures were not definitive, said Bache, because fifty or sixty thousand men were qualified to vote.

Bache listed his group's objections to the Constitution. The first, as always, was unicameralism. The charter's system for appointing judges left them exposed to "every veering gale of politics." The Council of Censors review board, scheduled to meet in 1783, would be "a jubilee of tyranny." Bache asked: "Have the citizens of Pennsylvania ever given their consent to the Constitution framed by the late Convention?" He wondered why officials were so anxious to prevent a referendum they insisted they would win. Why did they deny themselves, he asked, such "well founded joy?"[20] Bache warned his readers: "The charms of Power may bewitch [Constitutionalists]; but they ought not to blind you." Bache's essay was endorsed by eighty-one members of the Republican Society, including James Wilson, Whitehead Humphreys, Charles Thomson, Benjamin Rush, Robert Morris, Thomas Mifflin, Francis

Hopkinson, John Cadwalader and Jacob Hiltzheimer. But Bache made the mistake of criticizing pro-constitution writings by "persons high in office in the present government, and from some whose daily bread depends on their office." Timothy Matlack pounced:

> When I consider how many of the brave officers of our army, who have nobly defended our common country and the cause of liberty, depend, honorably depend, on the commission and office which they have bravely earned ... I am astonished that such a sentiment should have been obtruded on the world by the Republican Society.

He concluded: "I think it an honor to any man to earn, by a faithful discharge of his duty, the bread he eats, and it is particularly so in a Republican government."[21]

Matlack reminded Bache that his own father-in-law, Benjamin Franklin, had been president of the 1776 Constitutional Convention. The Convention, Matlack said, had asked Franklin for his thinking on one key question: "Doctor Franklin was requested by the Convention to give his opinion on the point — and he declared it to be clearly and fully in favor of a legislature to consist of a single branch, as being much the safest and best." Matlack asked Bache: "Whose opinion, among the members of your Club, would have equal weight in the political world?" Matlack then brought up the subject of a recent portrait of Franklin. He asked Bache to "look at the elegant print of that good old man, which you have lately received from Paris, — observe the cheerful dignity of his countenance, justly copied — a picture of patriotism and philosophy, of virtue and of truth — look steadily, recollect the original." Now Matlack pointed Bache's attention to a document, "lying open on the globe at his right hand," labeled "the Constitution of the government of Pennsylvania."

The new portrait was in fact prettily painted publicity. The artwork was a new Franklin endorsement of the Pennsylvania Constitution. Had the old politician conspired to ensnare his son-in-law? Matlack forgot to mention that the portrait artist was Charles Willson Peale, chairman of the new Constitutional Society. Peale must have secured Franklin's agreement to this oil-on-canvas seal of approval.

Bache's copy of the painting was a Trojan horse. Matlack imagined how he had come to own it: "This print must have been intended for some friend of the Patriot and Philosopher, and have been handed to you by mistake; or, perhaps, his piercing and prophetic spirit foresaw your conduct, and sent it to you as a just and a needful reproof."

In his newspaper piece, Matlack didn't bother to address the opposition's well-known objections to the Constitution. His tactic was to prick Bache him-

Nine. Benedict Arnold Part One (Illicit Affairs)

self. Matlack reminded the Republican Society chairman he had become prominent thanks to his connection to Franklin, not "any extraordinary exertions in favour of our American cause, or from the possession of more than common abilities." Matlack said Bache's "want of consequence," a condition he claimed to share, had its benefits: "That neither of us are in danger of being bribed, or of being suspected to have been bribed by the enemies of America." This solace, he offered, was in reach of "a respectable part of the Republican Society."

With the mention of bribes, Matlack was changing the subject. Dr. Berkenhout's diary had been published and his impromptu evaluation of Matlack's ethics had become public knowledge. Timothy was the subject of innuendo regarding pecuniary corruption. Responding to malicious rumors, Matlack said it was the fate of more important men than he, those with "extensive connexions, great riches, great abilities, and who are supposed to have great influence, to be the peculiar objects of such suspicions."

An official member of the Carlisle Commission did try to bribe the congressmen Joseph Reed and Robert Morris. In the spring of 1778 George Johnstone sent both of these men letters with references to emoluments. A few days after the British evacuation in June, Reed was summoned by a "married lady of character" with connections to the British army. This emissary told Reed that if he promoted "the objects of their commission, viz., a reunion between the two countries ... he (Mr. Reed) might have ten thousand pounds sterling and any office in the Colonies (meaning these United States) in his Majesty's gift." Reed reported the incident, and Congress told Carlisle it felt "pointed indignation against such daring and atrocious attempts to corrupt their integrity."[22] Matlack now hinted that others were also offered "British gold."

Matlack concluded his piece with a warning that whether or not his opponents had taken bribe money, the prominent lawyers and merchants of the Republican Society were at risk of appearing to "divide, distract and weaken" the state of Pennsylvania during a war. Their actions could earn them the label of "Conspirators."

* * *

Benedict Arnold's response to Pennsylvania's charges, which included treason, was published on February 13, 1779. Arnold informed the public he had requested a court-martial to defend his conduct. The major general said he had served his country faithfully for almost four years without once "having my public conduct impeached." But two weeks later a newspaper writer signing Tiberius Gracchus was more than happy to remind the general, "who's memory seems to have failed him," of the charges leveled against him in

December 1776. Gracchus said he had received a copy of the complaint, which listed thirteen indictments, from the accuser himself. This was Lieutenant Colonel John Brown, an officer who served with Arnold in Canada. Brown's most serious charges were that Arnold had been involved in the theft of goods in Montreal and "a treasonable attempt to make his escape ... to the enemy at St. John's."[23]

Brown's accusations were read in Congress in May 1777. Arnold, who was present, received strong support from the signer Charles Carroll. Congress' report absolved Arnold of Brown's "imputations" while lamenting that the general's "character and conduct" had been "so cruelly and groundlessly dispersed."[24] Brown was not notified of the proceeding. Now in March 1779, Tiberius Gracchus said, "It will require that some faith be exercised by the next generation, before they can believe that Congress really acquitted you of those charges upon hearing such evidence as you could produce in your own favour, and without hearing the evidence against you." In fact, he said, Congress separately confirmed at least one charge by nullifying Arnold's demotion of Brown and restoring his rank. Gracchus went so far as to claim circumstantial evidence supported Brown's charge of theft:

> When I meet your carriage in the street, and think of the splendor in which you live and revel ... and of the purchases you have made, and compare these things with the decent frugality necessarily used by other officers in the army, it is impossible to avoid the question — From whence have these riches flowed, if you did not plunder Montreal?[25]

Benedict Arnold responded to Gracchus, complaining "It is ungenerous and unjust to attack my character in anonymous publications, the authors of which are equally unknown to me and to the public."

As Arnold should have realized, Tiberius Gracchus was Timothy Matlack. Matlack's enemies were bitterly amused he had the gall to sign articles with the name of a Roman politician who fought to distribute public land to the poor. Matlack's opponents came up with their own sobriquet for the secretary: Tim Gaff. "Gaffs" were the spurs Timothy once attached to the legs of game fowls, while "gaffes" were the social blunders they claimed he was prone to make.

Lending credence to the second charge were Timothy's emotional outbursts. These eruptions were the manifestation of irritability. By the spring of 1779 twelve months had passed since Matlack first complained of fatigue and stress. Even as he wielded a sharp pen as the defender of his government, the years of relentless conflict were taking their toll. An eruption at the end of March was a blunt demonstration of the mental strain he was suffering. Elizabeth Drinker reported, "Tommy Fisher and John James, who were this

Nine. Benedict Arnold Part One (Illicit Affairs)

The old prison on the southwest corner of Third and Market Street. Samuel Fisher was confined here, as was Timothy Matlack. Print. Library of Congress, Prints and Photographs Division.

Morning at Timy. Matlacks on a visit to his Son, were beat by Timothy with a Cane, in his Entry and in the Street — until he broke the stick."

Quaker Meetings customarily sent representatives to speak with members who strayed from their teachings. During the War of Independence numerous young men were visited for violating the rule of pacifism. Some mended their ways, others were disowned. The two Quakers in question had been sent to speak with Billy Matlack "on account of his having taken Arms under some of the present usurpers against the King & Government." The men had had a polite conversation with the young man and were preparing to leave when Timothy walked in. Encountering the emissaries he asked the nature of their visit and, "upon being told it, he gave them some little very abusive language & immediately taking up a Hickory Walking Stick, way lay'd them in the passage, gave them many hard blows over the head & shoulders, following them some distance in the street till he had broken his stick."[26]

Matlack viewed the visit as a personal challenge and reacted with violence. Now he was forced to defend his behavior. In the *Pennsylvania Packet*, two days later, he explained that when he returned home that day he found Thomas Fisher and John James sitting in his parlor with his son. Matlack reminded the public that Fisher was a former exile, "another of the men removed from the city by desire of Congress." He was also the brother of

Samuel R. Fisher, "now under arrest upon a charge of having written a treasonable letter ... which was intercepted at Elizabeth Town." John James, Matlack said, had also been named on the 1777 proscription list but had avoided arrest. Matlack wrote: "*This* Thomas Fisher and *this* John James, I found, upon enquiry, came to "'deal with'" *my* son for bearing arms in the defence of his country!" Matlack confirmed that he "turned them both out of my house and gave them in the open street, in full measure, but not without mercy, the chastisement which their audacious impudence demanded and thus extorted from me." Timothy denied the claim the stick he had wielded "was a very heavy one, and a mere cudgel." In fact, he said, the uninvited visitors were lucky that "my horse whip being out of place, I was obliged to use a smallish middle-sized walking stick, which I have usually carried in my hand for several years past." He had taken the precaution of leaving a piece of the broken cane at the printer's office for public inspection. It measured, at its "thickest end," a mere "six-tenths of one inch in diameter." In closing Matlack offered no apology for his outburst, this being the first time he had been provoked "to strike a man by anything less than a blow." But he was ready to accept the public's verdict: "To my country I appeal for a judgment in this case; and by their judgment I will stand or fall."

But Timothy had not been entirely candid about the incident. He left out the detail that he himself had ordered the arrest of Samuel Fisher in retaliation for the house call. Immediately after the beating incident this Fisher had been summoned to appear before Chief Justice McKean to explain the traitorous letter. The accused appeared the next day and told Judge McKean he had "never written any Letter for which I was ashamed to acknowledge, nor had ever conveyed any Intelligence to the British Army, neither meddled in any warlike Affairs in any shape, that I was principled against any such thing...." Judge McKean exposed the link between the beating incident and the arrest by summoning Timothy Matlack and Thomas Fisher to the hearing. But Matlack said he was too busy to attend and Thomas Fisher said he "was unwell of the wounds given him by Timothy & had not been out since." Judge McKean told Fisher "the whole tenor of my letter carried an Air of disaffection & clearly shewed that I held myself a Brittish Subject..." McKean ordered him to jail but the sheriff simply escorted him a few blocks in that direction before sending him home.

Fisher was detained again on April 3. The reason for this second arrest, he said, was that Timothy Matlack had seen him coming and going at his ease: "Timothy having observed me riding out was much displeased with it." Fisher said Matlack sent an urgent note to the Sheriff, who was in Germantown, "charging him with Neglecting to put the Laws [into] Execution and directing him to come to Town and put me to Gaol." The sheriff's deputy,

John O'Kelly, showed Fisher this new demand, "upon which I washed myself & Before I could get away James Claypoole appeared, seemingly very anxious for my being put in Gaol." Claypoole and O'Kelly may have feared the secretary but they did not consider Fisher a public enemy. The merchant was treated respectfully. He said: "I was put in a Room of the Gaolers without the prison & I was neither locked, barr'd nor bolted, but used to go without the Gaol Door in the Evening & OKelly came and asked whether I had been to see my father he being ill & confined during most of my three weeks imprisonment." Fisher was released on April 24 only to be detained once again, in late July, on a charge of treason.

Ten

The Fort Wilson Riot

Rapid inflation, first seen in the summer of 1778, shocked Philadelphians the following winter. A newspaper writer signing Mobility said the scarcity and high price of flour were the deliberate work of "Monopolizers and Forestallers." He warned that hunger would trigger food riots. "We can live without sugar, molasses and rum — but we cannot live without bread.— Hunger will break through stone walls." Mobility informed the presumed culprits— predatory merchants— their stores would be appropriated by the people or, worse, they would find themselves "hung up ... without judge or jury."

In January 1779, the Supreme Executive Council threatened to punish forestallers of basic necessities (merchants who bought up goods to profit from higher prices at a later date). In February large purchases of bread and flour by the French Navy aggravated shortages.[1] Miserable conditions suffered by the hungry poor that winter did not improve in the spring, and merchants were blamed. What followed was another season of confusion and tension caused by hunger. Conditions were so bad people were ready to take action.

On Saturday May 22, 1779, Elizabeth Drinker worried about a crowd action: "Many are apprehensive of a Mob rising on second day [Monday] next — with a view of discovering monopolizers &c." The following night a notice posted on street corners announced the people had reached their breaking point. The populace was furious that "in the midst of money we are in poverty, and exposed to want in a land of plenty." The people warned: "We have turned out against the enemy and we will not be eaten up by monopolizers and forestallers."

On Monday incidents of scattered violence preceded militia exercises in the afternoon. The next day "a great concorse of people assembled at the State House.... Men with clubbs &c have been to several Stores, obliging the people to lower their prices." The angry men who gathered for a town meeting resolved to investigate suspect merchants and force prices down from their "enormous heights." The people were incensed that after the arrival of shipments, "prices of dry goods have arisen when they ought to have decreased." In their opinion, the failure of prices to follow the law of supply and demand proved there had been interference.

The town meeting was supported by the authorities. Officials adhered to Thomas Paine's theory that prices should be set by government because self-regulating markets ultimately failed. Timothy Matlack, however, publicly opposed price fixing. His preference was for free markets. At the town meeting Matlack rose to speak in opposition to the "mad project" of price fixing in a scene described by the loyalist poet Joseph Stansbury:

> Sagacious *Matlack* strove in vain
>   To pour his sense in Dutchmen's brain,
> With ev'ry art to please:
> Observ'd "that as their Money fell.
> "Like Lucifer to lowest Hell,
> "Tho' swift, yet by degrees—
> "So should it rise and goods should fall
> "Month after month, and one and all
> "Would buy as cheap as ever;
>
> But thoughtful Rush, and artful Gaff,
> And Bryan, too much vexed to laugh,
> Were filled with grief and pity;
> And soon dismiss'd the Rabble Rout:
> Concluding what they were about
> With chusing a Committee.[2]

Matlack lost the argument. The town meeting named a price-fixing committee, which published a list of acceptable rates in a broadside titled "Committee-Room."

Matlack later wrote, "When the impossible project of regulating prices was attempted the infatuation seemed to be general and a large committee was elected to enforce it." Matlack said he had stood alone in opposition to "the dangerous measure" and was attacked for his independent stance: "The insults which were offered to me on that occasion from every quarter are known to very few; but the event is known to all."[3] In this break from his party, Matlack showed he was not afraid to stand on his own. He proved, by thinking and acting independently, he was no demagogue. In so doing he earned an unwanted compliment from a Tory (Stansbury) and the ire of his supporters. Nonetheless Matlack was named to two other committees that summer. Radicals felt he had betrayed them, but they were in desperate need of his leadership.

In a tense environment, Whigs and Tories clashed on the third anniversary of independence. In 1779, with Independence Day falling on the Sabbath, Whigs scheduled their celebrations for Monday, July 5. In Lancaster Christopher Marshall led a parade of militia, with "colors flying, drums, fifes and band of music, we went in procession down Queen street to a spacious piece of woodland, adjoining Conestoga Creek, with a fine spring, where, after some time was spent in social cheerfulness, the men having grounded their arms, then they formed in order, whereupon ... healths were drank, I being Toast Master." But this pleasant occasion turned ugly when a group of Tories came in "about a half hour after ours broke up, behaved themselves like drunken madmen, cursed the Committee, called them rebels.... Some of our people got angry.... Though some were struck at, they returned the compliment, so that a few blows passed...."

* * *

The May town meeting had named a committee to investigate the trading activity of one merchant: the powerful Robert Morris. The men assigned to this committee were David Rittenhouse, Thomas Paine, Charles Willson Peale, J.B. Smith and Timothy Matlack. In a letter to Henry Laurens, Richard Henry Lee said: "I have a very high opinion of our friend T.M. and as bad a one of H — — r and company. The former has already done much good to the cause of America, the latter essential evil."

"H —-r" was John Holker, an agent-general for the French Navy and Robert Morris's trading partner. Holker was considered persona non grata in Philadelphia. In 1781 the French government demanded he desist from his private trade activity or resign. Holker choose the latter. Morris, the high profile merchant who had absented himself from Congress on July 2, 1776, was the heavyweight behind the Holker trade syndicate. The Matlack committee's investigation was politically charged because Congress, the French, the Spanish, the Portuguese, and a handful of American states were all interested parties in the various transactions under investigation.

In response to a committee inquiry Morris claimed flour purchased in one particular transaction had gone to the French fleet.[4] But Matlack and Lee agreed that at least part of this stock was bound for the West Indies, where it would be sold at "amazingly" high prices. The American public back home would receive "the prime cost in paper money, which by that time may be depreciated a thousand per cent."

Another Morris controversy involved the illegal capture of a Portuguese snow, *Nostra Senhora de Carmo*, by a privateer in which he had an ownership interest. Captain Juan Garcia Duarte was in Philadelphia that summer appealing to Congress for a settlement of four thousand half Johannas, or seventy-one hundred pounds sterling. But Morris simply declined to appear before a congressional committee headed by his rivals Henry Laurens and James Searle. Congress paid the ship's owner $18,000 in 1781.

In Philadelphia it was thought the questionable commercial activities of Morris and Holker were driving both runaway inflation and the rapid depreciation of paper money. Richard Henry Lee feared, "They are capable of and will undoubtedly execute every villany in the world to obtain ... enormous wealth." Lee considered the men as "artful as they are wicked." He was sure that "under cover of high office" they would "pervert every thing to private emolument."[5] Lee hoped Matlack would be the man to stop Morris and Holker: "They will require such a guard as our friend T.M. whose universal acquaintance, sound sense and penetration, with indefatigable perseverance can alone detect them and unravel their subtlety otherwise protected as they are by hitherto successful plunders of the public, they will again escape with impunity." To finally expose Morris and his partners, Lee told Laurens:

> Infinite pains and the best information both here and in the West Indies will be necessary to detect these bad men. If our friend T.M. accomplishes this, (as I really believe he will, when once firmly engaged in it) he shall be my Magnus Apollo, and he will undoubtedly, by breaking up a nest that will otherwise disgrace and ruin America, deserves the thanks of every good man in the U.S.[6]

The Matlack committee also investigated Morris's role in the purchase and resale of the cargo belonging to a ship named *Victorious*. The committee's report, probably written by Thomas Paine, speculated the ship's secret owner was Silas Deane. That Morris and Deane had business connections, Paine wrote, was known thanks to an account published by Morris himself. Deane's involvement was no minor detail because questions about his conduct while serving as commissioner to France had entangled Congress since December. Thomas Paine had asked of Deane, "Would anybody have supposed that a gentleman in the character of a commercial agent, and afterwards in that of a public minister, would return home after seeing himself both recalled and superseded, and not bring with him his papers and vouchers?" In December 1778, Morris accused Paine of revealing congressional secrets in his newspaper attacks and moved to discharge him from his position as secretary of the Committee of Foreign Affairs. Paine resigned his post a week later.[7]

Now in the summer of 1779 a writer using the name Cato attacked both Thomas Paine and Timothy Matlack. Matlack had defended his friend in the Deane imbroglio. Richard Henry Lee wrote to Henry Laurens, "I observe that Mr. T.M. and Mr. P-n-e are both attacked by a scribbler in your Evening Post, of July 9th under the signature of Cato, — a wretch who is as much their inferior in every worthy respect as virtue is superior to the dregs of vice."

This writer abused Paine with such nasty lines as, "Go, wretch, hide thy pitiful head in oblivion." Stung by the attack, Paine demanded publisher Benjamin Towne identify the penman. Towne initially refused but changed his mind when a group of men led by Charles Willson Peale, Colonel John Bull, and Major Alexander Boyd brandished a noose in front of his print shop. Towne revealed the offensive penman was Republican Society member Whitehead Humphreys.[8] That evening an unruly crowd convened at Humphreys' house and in his absence, he claimed, "dangerously wounded" his sister. Upon his return Humphreys managed to bring up a small company of Continental soldiers. A series of threats and insults ended with the two sides agreeing to a meeting the next morning at the London Coffee House. The episode was over but Matlack, for one, was not about to forgive this new enemy.

The purchase and resale of the *Victorious* cargo was dubious business, but the committee's investigation uncovered nothing strictly illegal. Nor could the committee confirm Silas Deane's interest. Matlack's board did, however, accuse Morris of dishonest behavior. Thomas Paine said that "however unwilling Mr. Morris may be to acknowledge the term engrossing or monopolizing ... we are at a loss to find any other name." Paine said that "as a merchant, (Mr. Morris) may be strictly within rules, yet when he considers the many public and honorary stations he has filled and the times he lives in, he must feel himself somewhat out of character."[9]

* * *

Meanwhile the price-fixing committee was struggling to make headway. On June 28 a militia company issued an ominous warning to merchants. The militia thought "designing and interested persons," who tried to elude the committee's efforts to reduce prices, might be brought to reason with "something more *poignant* and *striking*."[10] The militia reminded merchants they had arms and knew how to use them.

At the end of August the committee tacked up a notice calling on citizens to "Rouse! Rouse! Rouse and COME ON WARMLY." Its members said it was time "to humble and prove by this days conduct, that any person whatever, though puffed like a Toad, with a sense of his own consequence, shall dare to violate the least resolves of our Committee." But the board was dealt a death blow when cordwainers, tanners, and curriers rebelled against price fixing. In mid-September the price fixers' last gasp was a petition asking the Assembly to stop monopolizers. A week later the committee members conceded defeat and suspended their activities.[11]

With the failure of their popular intervention, some Philadelphians were losing hope. Amid rampant inflation and scarce supplies the city's poor found themselves without decent food. In May Sarah Bache had told her husband, "You can't think how much worse the money is since you left this [city]....

Many families yesterday went without bread; not a bit to be bought."[12] By early September people were eating bread made from "musty English Flour, which formerly would have been given to the cattle."[13]

President Joseph Reed told the Assembly that his "apprehensions of great distress among poor house-keepers in this city, from the high price of Flour" compelled him to ask for the distribution of one hundred barrels. He wanted preference given to "Families as have performed Militia duty." The Assembly agreed but limited the food benefit to the families of men who turned out for the militia call-up in progress. By this false act of charity the authorities acknowledged the militia and the poor were one and the same. The injustice of it all was obvious to the men being victimized. It was they who were sent to fight the war while others avoided serving by paying absentee fines they could easily afford.

The poor were also upset that families of departed loyalists were thriving in cohabitation with the patriotic population. In September 1779, the Supreme Executive Council tried to appease the militia by arresting a loyalist named Joseph Wirt. Not satisfied with this scapegoat, a group of angry militia met at Mrs. Burns' tavern. The men, ready to vent, asked Charles Willson Peale to lead them in a move to evict the wives and children of absent loyalists. This ill-advised scheme had its origins in the May 24 price-fixing town meeting. That mass rally decided not to allow individuals "inimical to the interest and independence of the United States ... to remain among us." Stansbury mocked meeting chairman Daniel Roberdeau's "humane" declaration that "Tories, with their brats and wives, Should fly to save their wretched lives." In June the Philadelphia Grand Jury had likewise complained that "the wives of ... the most notorious of the British emissaries [i.e., those who defected to the British] remain among us." These women were said to be spreading "poisonous, erroneous, wicked falsehoods."[14] But Peale told the militiamen that "the taking of women and children from their homes would cause much affliction and grief, that, when seen, the humanity of their fellow-citizens would be roused into an opposition."[15] With this advice Peale put a stop to the militia's imprudent plan.

In a confluence of events, the Quaker Yearly Meeting now opened in Philadelphia. A rumor went around that the government was considering arresting Quakers to stop their annual gathering. It was thought the authorities would send the militia to "take up all the Tories & Quakers." But the Supreme Executive Council apparently ordered the militia *not* to disturb the Yearly Meeting. The Council did this to give a pro-independence faction time to advance the cause internally. These independence Quakers were clearly formidable: a town crier "publicly cried in some parts of the city that the Quakers had agreed in the Yearly Meeting to acknowledge & accede to the

Independence of America."[16] But this news, which panicked Tories, was erroneous. The conservative and loyal leadership of the Society of Friends did not acquiesce.

On Saturday, October 2, the militia was infuriated to learn James Wilson had won Joseph Wirt's acquittal. Two days later Charles Willson Peale was again summoned to Mrs. Burns' tavern "where great numbers of the militia had already assembled." This time the men asked Peale to lead them in carting Tories and Quakers. Peale refused to head this roundup but the men were ready to take action on their own.

Now the militia went out in search of Wirt. Unable to find their target, they took up the Quakers Buckridge Sims, Thomas Story, Matthew Johns and John Drinker. Drinker, brother of the former exile Henry Drinker, was abducted as he was leaving Pine Street Meeting House. The gentleman was allowed to "go home and eat his Dinner" before his cart ride.

While fife and drums played "The Rogue's March," the militia paraded the prisoners up to the commons and back down Arch Street to the Delaware. From there the demonstrators, about two hundred in number, headed for Second Street. A party of "between twenty and forty gentlemen," including Sharp Delaney, had gathered at City Tavern. But when the marchers drew close the men dispersed.[17] James Wilson, who lived a block away, was watching the street through closed shutters. Now he was joined by "Delany and the rest." All armed themselves with muskets and pistols.

After stopping in front of the tavern for three cheers, the militia rounded the corner onto Walnut Street. Wilson's house was on the next corner. As the militia was walking past the house, a Captain Campbell called out a challenge from an upper window. Perhaps someone threw stones at the residence. This confrontation escalated into a violent battle. Muskets were fired. Men trying to force their way into the house with iron bars and hammers were repelled in hand-to-hand fighting. As the riot raged on, Joseph Reed, Timothy Matlack, the sheriff, and his deputy came galloping down Third Street. These officials were followed closely by members of the City Light Horse and Baylor's Continental Dragoons. Someone cried out: "The President! The President!" Reed, Matlack and their "sundry assistants" dispersed the crowd before turning their attention to the men rolling two field pieces down Market Street. Reed, Matlack and their police force took control of this artillery with "many strokes of their Swords." From there the authorities hurried on to Center Square, where the militia was regrouping. Here they chased away the crowd. Hiltzheimer said he and his family encountered "a part of the militia running from the Commons toward the city, pursued by the President and militia light horse." More than two dozen marchers were arrested. Also incarcerated, for their protection, were the four hostages. Samuel Fisher shared his room with his fellow Quakers that night. These five were kept awake by the "very noisy and turbulent ... 27 Militia Men" jailed in a room downstairs.

* * *

On the street outside Fort Wilson, as the riot house became known, five to seven men were reported killed. Fourteen people were wounded, including bystanders. Inside the house Campbell was killed and three others wounded. Hiltzheimer said the next day, "Two men was buried which was killed by yesterday's riot."[18]

The next morning incensed militia officers assembled outside the courthouse. Meanwhile the Germantown militia was ready to march to the city in protest of the prior day's events. Before leaving to deal with the situation in Germantown, President Reed told Matlack to control the scene at the courthouse.

Matlack faced a tense situation. The militia officers insisted Wilson's party had played an equal role in the fight and should be sent to jail in tit for tat. Matlack refused, Charles Willson Peale reported, but the officers "appeared to be ripe for undertaking the release of the prisoners." Worried that "all Mr. Matlack's arguments, perhaps, would have been insufficient," Peale suggested "taking bail for the persons, and let them be released by the magistrates then present." Matlack agreed to this and the militiamen were freed. "As soon as they got into the Street," they "drew up in a line, gave three very loud Huzzas & then walked home." Now President Reed, having convinced the Germantown militia to call off their march, returned to the city. Upon learning what had happened he "was not a little mortified to find that Mr. Matlack could not do as he was ordered." Reed "publicly harangued" his subordinate for allowing the release. As Matlack burned with humiliation, Peale stepped up and admitted to Reed, "Mr. Matlack ought not to suffer blame, for if the measure was wrong, that he was the unlucky person who had proposed [it]."[19] That afternoon feelings of discontent simmered. One observer wrote, "It is not over. [The militiamen] will have blood for blood."[20]

James Wilson was now hiding out at Robert Morris's country estate. Two days later Morris warned him that if he valued his life he should stay there. The following day Morris told Wilson search parties were out looking for him and suggested he go to New Jersey: "Retreat until the ferment is over."[21] Wilson said he wanted the Republican Society to organize a show of strength but Morris told him to cross the river and wait until Reed restored order.[22]

Two days after the riot, perhaps with Reed's tacit approval, the militia attacked Benedict Arnold in the street. The outraged major general complained, "Your President has raised a mob, and now he cannot quell it."[23] Dr. Benjamin Rush, for one, agreed. He said, "My country I have long ago left to the care of Timothy Matlack, Charles Willson Peale, and co.... They call it a Democracy — a mobocracy in my opinion would be more proper."

But Reed and Matlack had put the *militia* in jail. It was the militia that felt betrayed by the government. In quelling the riot Reed and Matlack had effectively saved their political opponent, James Wilson. Washington's aide-de-camp, Arthur St. Clair, told Reed he was pleased "you were happy enough to rescue that gentleman" despite the fact "his opposition to the constitution of Pennsylvania has been perhaps too warm."[24] And so Reed and Matlack were caught in the middle. On the one hand they were accused of mob rule and on the other of betraying the people.

President Reed may have "encouraged [the militia] to take up [Quakers] & the tories." If so he underestimated the panic and distress of scared and angry men going home to hungry families.[25] Witnesses said the marchers were provoked by the heckler Campbell. With that aggression a routine demonstration devolved into a deadly fight. When Philadelphians started killing each other in the street Reed and Matlack had had no choice but to ride in with force.

Timothy Matlack's high profile role in arresting the militia came at an especially bad time for him. His opposition to price fixing had recently exposed him to accusations of disloyalty. From the people's point of view, this was their tribune's second deception. Timothy Matlack felt himself unfairly misunderstood and unappreciated. He had ridden in to stop a riot, not to rescue one side and arrest the other. Matlack was also humiliated when he released the militia only to be dressed down by his superior.

But, as in predicting the failure of price fixing, Matlack could soon consider himself vindicated. Constitutionalists won a complete victory on election day a month later and gained full control of government. Anticonstitutionalists were stunned. Benjamin Rush wrote: "Poor Pennsylvania has become the most miserable spot upon the surface of the globe."

Eleven

Benedict Arnold Part Two (Court-martial)

In March 1779, Timothy Matlack wrote to Benedict Arnold once again: "It appears to me proper to communicate to you, that I shall, on Saturday evening next, lay before a respectable number of citizens, the several letters which have passed between you and myself, relating to the order delivered by one of your aides to my son."

Two weeks after Matlack's meeting Congress ordered Washington to convene a court-martial. Arnold and his accusers would be facing each other before a panel of officers. George Washington scheduled this hearing for the first week of June 1779. On June 2, Timothy Matlack arrived at camp in Middlebrook, New Jersey, for the start of the trial. The dispute between the powerful state of Pennsylvania and the still-respected major general was a powder keg for all involved. General Nathanael Greene, for one, was well aware of the delicacy of the situation. In a letter to President Joseph Reed he took care to explain why Arnold was staying with him and Matlack was not: "I urged Col. Matlack to take lodging with me for General Arnold was at my quarters and he from regard to the General's feelings declined it."[1]

Wherever Matlack stayed, he was gone by daylight. The trial had opened that afternoon, but, Greene informed Reed, "The enemy having made a movement up the North River the Court Martial is adjourned and the Col. will return in the morning to Philadelphia."

Details of the one session emerged. As the proceeding got under way General Arnold had objected to certain officers on the panel. General Arnold had "at the same time expressing great respect for them, declaring he did not think it proper to assign the reasons on which his objections were founded, and repeatedly desiring they would not consider his objections as being personal." The officers in question were General Irwin, Colonel Butler and Lt. Colonel Hammer: all three Pennsylvanians. Unsure of what to do, the Judge-

Advocate had asked for an adjournment: "A peremptory challenge of this kind being new, the Judge-Advocate laid the case before his Excellency George Washington, who referred it to a board of General Officers." Washington told Matlack he convened a meeting of his officers "to consider of some points, which I judged it material to submit to them respecting the trial, in consequence of a letter from the Judge Advocate." At this meeting Washington and his staff decided to move the army and postpone the trial. Washington explained to Matlack, "The movement of the Enemy make it indispensibly necessary, that the Army should at least advance towards the North [Hudson] river, with all practicable expedition." The officers on the panel would be leaving with their several commands, he said, and the court-martial was adjourned.[2]

A few weeks earlier Arnold's liaison, Joseph Stansbury, had communicated with the enemy on his behalf. Through Stansbury, Major John Andre had informed Arnold that his commander, Sir Henry Clinton, would be willing to pay twelve thousand guineas for a corps of six thousand men. Clinton was offering Arnold a large reward for two divisions. To receive the money the major general need only set up the American army for defeat.

* * *

Now, near the end of the year, Matlack was on his way to army headquarters for the continuation of the court-martial. The proceeding reconvened on December 23, 1779, at Norris's tavern, in Morristown, New Jersey. The three Pennsylvania officers Arnold had "peremptorily" objected to in May were excluded from the new twelve-member board. As per the orders of Congress, the court was to review four of the Supreme Executive Council's charges. Among these was the accusation of the mistreatment of Sergeant William Matlack in the barber incident. Billy, now present, was called to testify. Now he described the series of orders that, perhaps at his father's urging, he had objected to the next morning. At this meeting, Major General Arnold had informed him "that it was customary for sergeants to do such duty and that if I did not like such duty, I should not have come there." Billy said the general told him, "if Major Franks had insulted me at the time he gave me the order, it was wrong and he did not approve of that." Facing a board of Continental officers, Billy was questioned directly by Arnold: "Was any menial office imposed on you, or upon any orderly sergeant, to your knowledge?" According to a published report, Billy replied:

> I considered the office that was imposed on me as menial; and the orderly sergeant who stood at the same time with me, belonging to the continental troops, complained of major Franks giving him a small bundle of paper in his hand, bidding him follow him, which he did; and upon his coming to a house a small

distance off, bid him give him the bundle of papers and return; which the man complained to me, when he returned, as an insult.

While Major Franks' display of arrogance on these occasions was stunning, the court was not impressed by the charge. In hindsight, if Matlack had posted his son as a spy, he should have ignored this insult and kept his observer in place. But Timothy did uncover wrongdoing from other sources. The court considered the next charge much more serious.

While at Valley Forge, Pennsylvania, it said, Arnold had written a pass for a Tory-owned vessel, *Charming Nancy*. In June 1778, ahead of the British army's evacuation of Philadelphia, loyalist merchants scrambled to ship their goods to other markets. But out at sea their transports faced the threat of seizure by American vessels. Arnold's pass announced that the *Charming Nancy* was "hereby permitted to sail into any ports of the united states of America ... without umbrage or molestation."[3] Arnold now claimed the ship's owners, Robert Shewell and his partners, were "friends to their country," but the judge advocate's first witness, Timothy Matlack, countered that Shewell was a well-known Tory. Congress had previously ordered the seizure of his property at a port in Virginia. And, more dramatically, in a confrontation at Valley Forge, Baron von Steuben had allowed his men to manhandle the merchant. Undeterred by the rough treatment, Shewell returned to camp and came away with Major General Arnold's signed pass. Upon learning of the permit, the Supreme Executive Council assumed Arnold had been promised a share of the *Nancy* and her cargo in exchange for his protection. This supposition was confirmed at a later date.

While the subject of the *Charming Nancy* would come up again, the court now moved on to the third charge. This one stated that following the British evacuation of Philadelphia, after ordering the closure of city shops, Arnold had made purchases for personal gain. A witness, Colonel John Fitzgerald, stated that he had seen, lying on a desk, unsigned instructions to Arnold's aide-de-camp, Major Franks, to purchase any amount of European or East-India goods. Fitzgerald had observed, by comparison with signed documents he found there, that the order was in Major General Arnold's hand. Arnold asked the court why Fitzgerald, lodging in the same house as Franks, had thought to examine his aide's papers: "When he stumbled upon a secret to big to keep?" The implication was that Fitzgerald had been encouraged to snoop around.

Arnold now asked Timothy Matlack, "Is the deposition of colonel Fitzgerald in your hand writing?" Matlack answered that yes, the statement signed by Judge Plunket Fleeson, had been dictated to him by the officer. As Arnold was well aware, Fitzgerald's original deposition had been revised by Matlack at Fitzgerald's request. Addressing Arnold, Matlack said Fitzgerald "informed me he had seen you, in consequence of your request; that there was one or two alterations he wished to make, in consequence of the conversation with you." Matlack denied any anterior involvement in Fitzgerald's discovery. He claimed Colonel Fitzgerald had been "a perfect stranger to me, having to the best of my knowledge never seen him before."

At this point the judge advocate produced Major Franks as a witness. Franks admitted his superior *had* given him the purchase order. Franks explained he and Arnold had discussed his desire to find business opportunities. Arnold had promised his assistance, assuming his participation in the profits. But, Franks claimed, nothing had come of their arrangement.

But there was a second element to the charge which the court did not review. Upon placing Arnold in command at Philadelphia, following the British evacuation, Washington told him he would send officers representing the quartermaster general, commissary general, and clothier general to take possession of stores left by the British. These goods were to be seized for the use of the American army.

But Arnold's proclamation, closing city shops, subverted Washington's plan in two stages. The first part of Arnold's order directed all persons having "European or West-India goods, iron, leather, shoes, wines and provisions of every kind, beyond the use of a private family" to provide a complete inventory by *noon the next day* for review by agents. These officials, he said, "may contract for such goods as are wanted for the use of the army." In this part of his order Arnold was threatening to requisition American-owned goods; not the British stores Washington had in mind. Arnold's illicit motive for this directive was his secret arrangement with Clothier General James Mease and his deputy. The three men had a signed agreement to resell goods purchased for the army for the "joint equal benefit" of themselves.[4]

The second part of Arnold's order said anyone holding stores or property belonging to British or Tories had *three days* to make a similar report. Arnold was giving loyalists more time to get their contraband out of town. Benedict's scheme ensured that the only windfall Washington's soldiers would enjoy, after their brutal winter at Valley Forge, was an apple under a tree.

Following an adjournment the court reconvened on December 28 to hear the final charge. This one said Arnold had used a wagon brigade on duty in the public service for private business. In October this team had arrived in Philadelphia and reported to Deputy Quartermaster General Mitchell for army duty. Mitchell, acting under an arrangement with Arnold, ordered the wagon master to report to the major general. Arnold commanded: "YOU will proceed immediately with your teams to Eggharbour or the Forks, take the orders and directions of Captain Moore, whom you will obey in every particular." Moore was, not coincidentally, captain of the *Charming Nancy*.

Events had placed his ship in a dangerous situation. The New Jersey privateer *Xantippe*, ignoring Arnold's pass, had taken the *Nancy* as a prize. But in September 1778, a New Jersey judge of admiralty upheld the pass and released the vessel back to her owners. Soon after this ruling a British squadron had come down from New York to attack Egg Harbor, a haven for privateers. Houses and ships were burned. This attack prompted Arnold to retrieve the *Nancy*'s cargo. The twelve wagons completed their trip in late October and delivered the salvaged goods to an agent in Philadelphia. This broker promptly sold the stock and paid half the proceeds directly to Arnold himself.

Timothy Matlack was now called again to testify. Matlack told the court he had received a full account of Arnold's private errand from wagon master Jordan. In his investigation Matlack discovered that Deputy Quartermaster General Mitchell had altered his account book. He did so to cover up the fact he had not charged Arnold for the use of the transports. When Matlack asked to see his book, Mitchell had replied he was "unable to lay his hand on the book at that time, and some reasons of that kind." Matlack pressed him for the accounts, saying the excuse was trifling. Finally a clerk brought it in and Mitchell "looked over the book in such a manner, as if he found some difficulty in recurring to the entry." "I mentioned, it was made the twenty-second of October, and he would find it, if he turned to that date." Finally Mitchell turned to the correct page. Matlack said, "We were sitting close together at the time, face to face, when he read the entry." From where he sat the alteration was clearly visible. The original book entry, dated October 22, had indicated Jordan's team had "Gone to Egg-harbour, by order." The revised version read, "Went to Egg-harbour, by the direction of general Arnold." Mitchell had also obliterated the notation discharging the wagon team on October 30. With these changes Mitchell hoped to support the claim he intended to charge Arnold. But Matlack produced the contradictory payroll submitted by Jordan to his boss. As was clear to all, Arnold had compensated Mitchell for the use of the army wagons.

In January 1779, Arnold was surprised to receive a large bill from the attorney general. In cross-examination Arnold asked Matlack: "Did not the president and council advise Mr. Jordan to charge eighty pounds for the hire of each waggon, and to send the account to the attorney general to prosecute?" Matlack confirmed this fact.

On December 29 General Arnold began his defense by calling Major Franks. On cross examination the judge advocate asked Franks: "Do you know whether general Arnold purchased any part of the *Charming Nancy* or her cargo?" Franks answered: "I do not of my own knowledge; but have heard general Arnold say he did, and I have also heard Mr. Seagrove say he did."

Franks claimed the ownership interest was acquired subsequent to the granting of the pass. On the subject of the wagons, Franks said, "I understood that general Arnold was to pay for the waggons; that he got them as a favour, and that they were not to transport public stores, but private property for himself and friends, and that he did not order them officially." Deputy Quartermaster Mitchell's clerk, John Hall, took the stand and claimed that he had taken it upon himself to change the account book, to "assist my memory," and because "I thought it was not good English." This ended court proceedings for the month of December.

After a delay the court reconvened on January 19, 1780. Arnold now produced Colonel Mitchell, but his witness did not help his case. On cross-examination Mitchell testified that Arnold and his staff had repeatedly pressured him for wagons. These demands presumably came with no offer of payment, except for his consideration.

In his closing statement Arnold said he would allow his conduct to be judged "in the cool hour of reflection." He presented earlier testimonials which, he said, Congress and the commander in chief "have been pleased to give of my conduct." Arnold made his motive in these affairs very clear. In answering the call to duty, he said, "I sacrificed domestic ease and happiness to the service of my country, and in her service have I sacrificed a great part of a handsome fortune." While determined to replace the latter, he complained, "the presses of Philadelphia have groaned with libels against me." This he blamed on the "phrenzy of party."

Arnold reserved parting shots for the two men who had led the campaign against him. Timothy Matlack's letters, he said, had been "an insult and indignity." And Joseph Reed, Arnold claimed, had once plotted treason. Arnold said that during Washington's 1776 retreat through New Jersey a "ruling member of the council" had suggested to other officers that they quit the American army and go over to the British. Whether or not this was true, Arnold was projecting his own plans. He attributed the following words to Reed, but he himself was the one prepared to "sacrifice the cause of my country to my personal safety, by going over to the enemy, and making my peace."[5]

On January 26, 1780, the court-martial announced its ruling. The officers said the charge that Arnold made "considerable purchases" after shutting Philadelphia's shops was "unsupported." It also dismissed, without comment, the accusation that his staff officer had insulted Sergeant Matlack. In the use of public wagons, the court felt Arnold had intended to pay, but that his actions had been "imprudent and improper" considering "the delicacy attending the high station in which he acted ... that requests from him might operate as commands." On the charge of writing a pass for the *Charming Nancy*, the officers found that Arnold had had no right to give a vessel permission to leave a port in possession of the enemy. The court sentenced the major general to be reprimanded by the commander in chief. Congress confirmed the verdict two weeks later.

On April 6 Washington issued a formal reprimand and a statement of his personal disappointment. Washington said a "sense of duty and a regard to candor oblige him to declare that he considers his conduct in the instance of the permit as peculiarly reprehensible, both in a civil and a military view, and in the affair of the wagons as 'imprudent and improper.'" Here was the moment of triumph for Timothy Matlack. His investigation of the unscrupulous commander had ended decisively with this severe rebuke from Washington. The conclusion of the Arnold affair was another boost to Matlack's authority.

George Washington probably disliked Pennsylvania's pursuit of his officer. He still considered Arnold a valuable field commander. But the commander in chief had come to disapprove of the man's contemptible profit quest and vile character. Arnold's despicable conduct in Philadelphia was the same behavior Colonel Brown had observed in Canada.

Ignoring both of these episodes, the New York politicians who supported the major general were stunned by the scheme their hero came up with next. So too was Washington. It was the commander in chief who gave Arnold a command in that state.

* * *

While still in Morristown, Timothy Matlack learned he had been made a member of the American Philosophical Society, the intellectual fellowship started by Benjamin Franklin many years earlier. The Pennsylvania Assembly had recently incorporated and "enlarged the Powers" of the Society.

Also selected for membership in 1780 were George Washington, Thomas Jefferson, John Adams, John Jay, Henry Laurens and fifteen other luminaries. In a letter to Jefferson, Matlack made it clear why the Society's members felt it important to carry on meeting during these difficult times:

> The members of this society flatter themselves that the benevolent and liberal objects of it will ... enable them to show to posterity that in the midst of a bloody and unparalled war, when every moment was indeed precious, men of the first imminence in America cherished the arts and science and dedicated a part of their time to philosophy.

When war broke out the Society had been forced to suspend its annual oration. Now its members decided to revive that tradition. Two weeks after returning to Philadelphia Matlack learned that Dr. John Ewing, provost of the new university, had declined the address due to pressing duties. Others had likewise passed on the honor to protect their "literary character." Timothy Matlack was chosen to give the speech as a last minute replacement.

On the day of the oration Matlack was exuberant in describing the members and invited guests in attendance, "as respectable an Audience as ever collected within the same Compass in any Country." One attendee said the audience included "the French Ambassador and all the Principal Officers of Government, House of Assembly &c."[6]

David Rittenhouse had delivered the last address, on astronomy, in 1775. The year before Dr. Rush had presented a discourse on Native American diseases. Matlack was following two respected scientists. Now he stood before his audience. While not "unpracticed in the Art of Speaking," Timothy had prepared his speech on short notice. He admitted to the collected dignitaries: "When a few Days ago you appointed me to the Duty of this Evening, entirely unprepared for the Discharge of it, I had not even thought of a Subject on which to speak." Sitting down to consider, he had noticed the state seal lying on his desk. However unexciting at first glance, Matlack's topic offered hope for an interesting afternoon. On one side of the seal was the figure of Liberty, her face set in an animated and determined countenance, a drawn dagger in her right hand, ready to defeat the "huge, grim, furious" lion trying to rise up and devour her: "How just a Picture of the Contest between these United States and prostrate *Britain*, still haughty, desperate and furious in her Fall!"

Matlack was confident America would be victorious on the battlefield, but he feared England's naval power. Captain Biddle had "too boldly dared the unequal Combat." Biddle had died on the *Randolph*, as had his son. Now he broke down with emotion. He asked his audience to forgive his "falling Tear." His son, he had planned to say, was a young man who never expressed fear and never complained. Mordecai had "lived and died unconquered." Timothy consoled himself: "But wherefore do I weep?—' Tis my Glory that I had such a Son to fall in such a Cause."

Once recovered from this breakdown, Matlack turned to his theme: his vision for America. Matlack imagined the country's prosperous future as an agrarian, democratic republic. Agriculture, he said, strengthens the bonds of a civil society and increases a nation's wealth and happiness. He thought that as long as "the Owners of our widely extensive Fields cultivate them with their own Hands," America would thrive. With foresight, Matlack was anticipating the Jeffersonian era. In 1814 Jefferson reported: "Most of the laboring class possess property, cultivate their own lands ... and from the demand for their labor are ... fed abundantly, clothed above mere decency, to labor moderately and raise their families." Matlack was proud to tell his audience his own ancestors "were all of them Husbandmen." Matlack's heroes were farmers and their families. In his speech he would have a lot to say about their lives and their future. American farmers, he said, were blessed with good fortune.

After the hard work of the summer harvest, Matlack said, the plowman and his "industrious, healthful Sons" are rewarded with a bountiful meal. The men are served by "the careful Wife and the attentive dutiful Daughter ... so much and so deservedly beloved." At the abundant table the family is joined by assisting neighbors and their sons. These young men can't help admiring the sensible daughter. With a flourish of alliteration Matlack described how the boys had come to their senses after misspent days as idle "foplings."

> Our young Men, to while away an idle Hour, may toy and frolick with some tawdy, fluttering Thing, flounced off with foreign Frippery; but whenever their Sober Thoughts lead them to settle in the World, they turn their Eye upon the prudent homespun Lass — with her they hope for Happiness — Her industry has already shown that she is worthy of their Love —

All eyes are on the young woman, who can't hide her pleasure in her homemade dress. This garment, Matlack thought, would soon improve. While "we have clothed ourselves in Wool," he had no doubt that within a few years "the Farmer's Wife and Daughter will clothe themselves in Silk." Timothy considered this reasonable because the family would plant Italian mulberry and feed the silkworms themselves.

Surveying this idyllic scene, Matlack even had a suggestion for the main dish: "Let it be remembered that a savory sirloin, served up at the Harvest Board, deserves a distinguished place at the well earned feast."

But on the subject of meat Matlack also had a serious concern. He had been told the people of Pennsylvania and New Jersey ate more of it than those of any other nation. Timothy blamed an increase in fatal diseases on this aspect of the local diet. The best preventive and remedy, he said, was to eat more ripe fruit. The problem, he said, was that local farmers were far behind in the cultivation of fruit trees. He blamed the poor quality of American fruit, which was often sour, on a lack of knowledge in "Graffing and Inoculating." Immediate attention, he said, must be paid to the propagation of fruiters. America, he said, should take inspiration from France and "her Cherries — the great variety of rich melting pears, her delicious Plums, — her blushing Nectarins, — and above all her delicious Peaches."

America's fields, Matlack said, would one day be covered by fruit trees and vineyards. The country's wines, he predicted, would someday "vie with the best the World can afford." America's "strong Desire" to drink wine was not a problem, economically speaking, because "we have no real need for foreign wines."

Another local product with a limitless future, he said, was beer. The prospects for this beverage were bright because "our Fields produce hops and barley in abundance." And beer, he thought, offered health benefits. Those who drank it, "well tinctured with the Hop," did not suffer the shaking chills and fevers associated with spirits.

Matlack told his audience that science was the key to the success of American agriculture: "In forming a System for Agriculture for these States, we must depend on Experiments made in this Country." In one example he said experiments were needed to combat a mischievous destructive insect which was havocking wheat fields. He thought kilns should be erected to dry the grains: "A few Experiments with a Thermometer will point out the Degree of Heat necessary to destroy the Insect and her Eggs." Another area needing study was fertilization: "The Time is fast advancing in which Manures will be of great Importance — indeed they are already so in the older settled Counties."

Timothy Matlack shown with a printed copy of the 1776 Pennsylvania Constitution; a Council proclamation with his signature and attached state seal; law books; and his old militia rifle and power horn in the background. Painting. Philadelphia: Charles Willson Peale, 1790. Photograph © 2013. Museum of Fine Arts, Boston.

Matlack also had ideas about breeding horses for farm work. Since "a stallion to breed good Plow-Horses for this hot Climate, must have sound Lungs," Matlack thought "long Races with heavy Riders" would be a good way to identify the strongest animals. Unfortunately, the former track aficionado lamented, "Racing is disgraced by its Connection with Gaming." Timothy Matlack's America was a place where citizens joined together to feed themselves, clothe themselves, defend themselves, and govern themselves. The people used education to steer their children to a better future. To this end Matlack's government had endowed a new university. Educating the "Husbandman, Patriot and Statesman in one" was important because

Their Voice will long be the Law of the Land: Their Knowledge and Virtue must fix among the Nations the Reputation of the State: Their Industry and Skill in Agriculture will determine the Value and Extent of our Commerce — the Importance and Worth of our Alliance [with France]. When Husbandmen are liberally educated, Agriculture and the State, will flourish together.

In Timothy's America, farmers and political leaders were one and the same. Matlack said he hoped the new University of the State of Pennsylvania (later the University of Pennsylvania) would prepare young men for the future with a curriculum strong in science.

Matlack's government had recently replaced the College of Philadelphia, which it considered a loyalist hotbed, with the new university. The provost of the college had been the Reverend Doctor William Smith. Writing as Cato, Smith had strongly opposed *Common Sense* in 1776. Several of the college's trustees had subsequently gone over to the British, and three who stayed were considered Tories.[7] Near the end of 1779 the Assembly said the college had shown "an Evident Hostility to the present Government and Constitution of this State, and ... Enmity to the common Cause." The legislators revoked its charter.[8]

The Assembly named Joseph Reed president of the new university's board of trustees. When six clergymen — Episcopal, Presbyterian, Lutheran, Calvinist, Baptist and Roman — were named trustees, there was no overlooking the fact Quakers had been unceremoniously left off the list. Benjamin Franklin and Timothy Matlack were two of the prominent citizens named as third division trustees.

On December 3 the Supreme Executive Council reserved certain confiscated property as a fund for the support of the new provost and other officers of the University. On December 16 the trustees elected the Reverend Dr. John Ewing — a strong supporter of the Revolution — provost and professor of philosophy. David Rittenhouse was named vice provost and professor of astronomy.

* * *

While most of the dignitaries sitting in Matlack's audience assumed white males would fill the university's classrooms, Matlack's government had taken the first step toward the enrollment of African-American students. (The University of Pennsylvania accepted its first black students one hundred years later.) This crucial first step was a law which said the grandchildren of Pennsylvania's slaves would be born free.

On March 1, 1780, Pennsylvania's Assembly passed an Act for the Gradual Abolition of Slavery, the first law of its kind in the Western Hemisphere. Thomas Paine wrote the preamble, which said, "We esteem it a peculiar blessing granted to us, that we are enabled this day to add one more step to universal civilization, by removing, as much as possible, the sorrows of those who have lived in undeserved bondage."[9] In crediting the Assembly for its achievement, Matlack told his audience:

> In the Midst of a ... distressing War, and the Hurry, Confusion and great Difficulties which attend it, we have seen the same Patriotic Legislature ... attending to the Cries of our Fellow Men, though differing in Color from us, though dishonored and disgraced by Slavery — we have seen them loosing the Bands of Oppression.

Paine, as clerk of the Assembly, and Matlack, as secretary of the Commonwealth, probably worked together on winning passage of the Act for Gradual Abolition. Three other men principally involved were George Bryan, vice president of the Supreme Executive Council; Charles W. Peale, assemblyman; and Anthony Benezet, the Quaker abolitionist who had likely been Timothy's schoolteacher.[10]

All of these men were inspired by the work of another Quaker abolitionist, John Woolman. John was a son of Timothy's aunt Elizabeth (Elizabeth Burr was his mother Martha's sister). In 1756 Woolman said he opposed slavery because "I believe that liberty is the natural right of all men equally."[11]

In 1778 Vice President George Bryan and the Supreme Executive Council began pushing the Assembly for an emancipation law. The state's executive branch went as far as to draft a sample bill. Bryan called slavery "disgraceful to any people, and more especially to those ... contending in the great cause of liberty themselves." As a member of the radical Assembly of 1779, Bryan led the committee that wrote the bill that passed into law by a vote of thirty-one Yeas to twenty-one Nays. George Bryan was a primary force behind the passage of the law. Timothy Matlack, according to one account, was Bryan's benefactor. The writer of this account, in attacking Bryan for opportunism, said:

> As to your patriotism, you were unknown in the town meetings and Committees that laid the foundation for the present revolution. You kept yourself quiet in your office as Justice of the Peace, 'till the new government was made, and then you threw yourself into the way of Timothy Matlack, who brought you in to be the Vice-President of the State. This office supplied the place of the one that dropped, by the declaration of Independence and supported your family for three years.[12]

Thomas Paine had a strong influence on Bryan, Matlack and the rest. In March 1775, Paine published an essay entitled *African Slavery in America*. He wrote: "If the slavery of the parents be unjust, much more is their children's."[13] The practice of transporting kidnapped free blacks to the southern colonies, where they were sold into slavery, led Paine, Benezet and others to form the Society for the Relief of Free Negroes unlawfully held in Bondage. This was first association of its kind in America. The year after this group was organized some Philadelphians were ready to move to the next step: the abolition of slavery. In early April 1776, the Assembly received "several petitions from a number of the inhabitants of the City of Philadelphia relative to the setting Negro Slaves at Liberty."[14] The Society of Friends banned slave ownership among its members that year.

While the Assembly's Act for Gradual Abolition failed to free any living slaves outright, it did say existing slaves not registered by November 1, 1780, would be legally free. In 1781 slave owners and their supporters in the Assembly tried to extend this registration deadline to January 1, 1782. Their plan was to reclaim slaves freed under the clause. The radical newspaper *Freeman's Journal* campaigned against the extension. A letter appearing in the *Journal*, signed Cato, offered a former slave's plea not to be returned to captivity. Another writer said of the freed slaves: "I take them by the hand as brethren, and boldly declare to the world, we are equally free, and the moment their liberty is wrested from them, the moment my own is departed."[15] A petition presented by "Divers Negroes" said slavery or liberty was "the momentous question of our lives." If returned to their former state of bondage they would lose the right to speak out; "if we are silent this day, we may be silent forever."

Act for Gradual Abolition declared children born to enslaved mothers after March 1, 1780, would serve as indentured servants until the age of twenty-eight. These servants would be entitled to "relief in case he or she be evilly treated" by his or her master or mistress, as well as to freedom dues and other minor privileges. It was the children of these indentured servants, the grandchildren of slaves, who would be born free. While the act was a compromise measure, it did allow people held in bondage to envision a better future for their descendants.

According to Bryan, the new law thrilled the Society of Friends. He told Samuel Adams, "Our bill astonished and pleases the Quakers. They looked for no such benevolent issue of our new government, exercised by Presbyterians."[16] While the ruling faction of the Society opposed the government, here was a cause the two sides could agree on.

Matlack's role in the passage of Act for Gradual Abolition could not have gone unnoticed by Quakers. In a love-hate relationship dating back twenty years, this was a moment to pause and make peace. Friends were, after all, Timothy's family and lifelong friends. But a temporary thaw in the surface did not crack the permafrost: the war was not over and the Society was considered a haven for Tories. One Quaker merchant, Samuel Fisher, was still in jail thanks to Timothy himself. And the founding of the Free Quakers was about to trigger a new wave of conflict.

Matlack published his oration and sent a copy to Benjamin Franklin in Paris. Matlack told Franklin he accepted the assignment "as I had no wish to appear anything more than I am, the task was very easy to me, and an apology for so crude a performance is only necessary on account of the society, not on my account."

* * *

Timothy Matlack now took some time to rest. One Friday afternoon he and Jacob Hiltzheimer joined Terrance Palmer for a ride down to William Jones' meadow. On the way home, Jacob said, "We stopped at the Sign of the Buck and had a bowl of punch." On another occasion he and Timothy measured his "brown colt by Wilson's Hunt's horse called Washington, — very near 15 hands and one inch high and only two years old last May." In early March 1780, Jacob's assistant, George Nelson, mentioned that the details of their latest livestock weighing had been printed in the newspaper: "Mr. Dunlap published an Acct of the weight of the big cow that I gave him last Thursday as drawn up by Mr. Matlack." This Hiltzheimer cow weighed one thousand seven hundred sixty-three pounds and was slaughtered by McCutcheon & Company. Matlack wrote:

> It is acknowledged by all, that this cow was the fattiest as well as the largest ever kill'd in Pennsylvania, the fat on the ribs measured full three inches in thickness, the clear fat on the brisket measured full seven inches through — the rump is not to be described and what is almost incredible, the skin was covered with near an Inch of clear fat.

The patriotic weighing of prize cows was a social activity the men enjoyed from the earliest days of their friendship. Nelson noted that Hiltzheimer had penned some lines in honor of the current occasion that arrived too late to be included in the newspaper article. Jacob's couplet read:

> Above is the weight of a famous Whig Cow
>   Who fled from the tyrants Cornwallis & How
>   But freely did bleed to give speedy relief;
>   To Great Washington, our Commander in Chief [17]

* * *

In May, Timothy's brother White described the intimate scene of a medical procedure performed on his daughter Betsy. In preparation for this eye operation White had helped make the lid speculum himself. The device impressed the doctor because it fit the patient's eye so exactly. But the doctor was worried. He said "he could not reconcile it to his mind to undertake it without repeated tryals (upon so young a subject) to see whether she had resolution to bear it." Gathered in the family sitting room were family members and friends, including Dan Wister's daughter Sally. White said the patient was seated in "Brother Timothy's lap, he held her Head steady against his Breast, Jonah held her right Hand, I held her left hand & held her eye lid open ... all was still not the least interruption." When the doctor introduced the needle, the child seemed agitated, and looked like she wanted to cry, "but upon our joint promises of rewards for her good behavior, she held as still as a lamb." A small amount of liquid spurted out and the "pupil or black spot of her eye became perfectly Black & Shining to my great Joy & Admiration." The doctor closed the eye, applied a poultice, tied a bandage over both eyes, and gave the girl an anodyne. The doctor said that the "catarach was completely depressed" and the operation had succeeded beyond his greatest expectation. Betsey, he said, was to be kept perfectly quiet and constantly watched.

White Matlack and the doctor had more than one patient to worry about that day. He wrote: "My poor wife is sorely afflicted with Dissiness & pain — in her Head & Bones which Obstinately resists Bleeding & Blisters."[18]

Twelve

A Brief Term in Congress

Matlack had amassed power and influence since first being elected a committeeman in 1775. Now he was sent to Congress "with loud huzzas."[1] On May 31, 1780, the Assembly appointed Timothy Matlack and Jared Ingersoll to Pennsylvania's delegation in the Second Continental Congress. Matlack was now a member of the same body he had served as a clerk.

Whitehead Humphreys, the man who told Thomas Paine to "hide thy pitiful head in oblivion," was none too pleased by Matlack's promotion. Humphreys went to the trouble and expense of printing a sixty-line satire entitled *An Epistle from Titus to Timothy*. In this production, which appeared later in the year, Whitehead reminded his eager audience that Matlack had been "wretched poor" and "idled time with Negroes." His readers needed no reminding that Timothy had been a cockfighter, or that he was one of the radicals who reduced Pennsylvania's government in 1776. "ALTHO,' dear *Tim*, you've rose so great, From trimming Cocks to *trim* the State." The implication of the verb "trim" did not escape Whitehead's partisans. He was accusing Matlack of having adapted his views to the prevailing political current for personal gain. In Humphrey's retelling Timothy and his cohorts had taken power by ruling the mob: "With Paine and Peale, you mounted the stage, To work the people into a rage." Matlack, he said, "bade them seize ev'ry man, Who disapproved your *quixote* plan ... to trample on the laws." Humphreys was also critical of his subject's more recent behavior. Timothy's appearance and behavior at a Fourth of July banquet, he said, was that of an upstart:

> At such a time you judg'd it best,
>   To have yourself superbly drest;
>   You were so greas'd and puff'd with powder,
>   No coxcomb sure cou'd e'er look prouder;
>   Until the festive board was laid,
>   Then knife and fork *you* briskly play'd.
>   Your auk'ard grandeur deserves a check.[2]

Twelve. A Brief Term in Congress

Matlack's fellow congressman, Ezekiel Cornell, likewise observed: "He hath a great notion of being a courtier; perhaps in some countries he would appear a coarse courtier."[3] Another critic mocked his "modern courtly breeding." These men accused Matlack of a lack of refinement and unseemly overeagerness.

Timothy *was* pleased by his promotion. He felt, perhaps, a bit stunned to find himself among his nation's leaders. Certainly he hoped to earn the regard of men like Richard Henry Lee and Thomas Jefferson. But the opinion of such tertiary figures as Cornell and Humphries was of little concern.

In the spring of 1780 Timothy Matlack was one of the most powerful men in Philadelphia. He was at the pinnacle of his revolutionary career. Matlack was the last of the original radicals still in office and one of the most visible members of his wartime administration. He was the public face of a government that continued to advance a radical program. Now his enemies looked for an opportunity to crush him.

* * *

On September 25, 1780, General Nathanael Greene reported, "TREASON of the blackest dye was yesterday discovered.... Arnold the traitor has made his escape to the enemy." General Washington, Greene said, was now at West Point taking steps to unravel so "hellish a plot."[4] The commander in chief had given Major General Arnold command of the garrison on the Hudson River, fifty miles north of New York City, less than two months earlier.

The previous day, near the British lines at Tarrytown, three armed men had stopped a rider traveling along the road. Forcing him to dismount they discovered that under his coat he was wearing the uniform of a British officer. Their search of his person uncovered papers which were plans of the fortifications at West Point. The three captors, sensing a big reward, turned their prisoner over to Colonel John Jameson at Continental headquarters in Westchester. Jameson sent a dispatch to Arnold notifying him of the detention and forwarded the incriminating papers to General Washington. Washington was on his way to a stopover at Arnold's residence at West Point.

When Arnold received Jameson's notice he realized the British officer he had just met with did not make it back to New York: their plan for an attack on West Point had been discovered. Arnold rushed to break the news to his wife Peggy, his accomplice in the treachery. Leaving her in a state of shock, Arnold mounted his horse and rode down to his river barge. Benedict made his escape by ordering his bargemen to row him out to the *Vulture*, the British ship anchored in a broad expanse of the Hudson River called Haverstraw Bay. The British officer captured on the road, Major John Andre, was hung a week later.

When the news reached Philadelphia the people were quick to burn Benedict Arnold in effigy. This was a spontaneous celebration of America's salvation, taken as a sign of the new nation's hallowed destiny. A second, more elaborate, Arnold dummy was burned on Saturday, September 30, in an official ceremony organized by the government. A procession of gentlemen and officers, Timothy Matlack presumably near the front, led a "numerous concourse of people" through town while drums and fife played the "Rogue's March."[5] Elizabeth Drinker said: "Several hundred men and Boys with candles in their hands" paraded a "ridiculous figure of Gen. Arnold with two faces; and the Devil standing behind him pushing him with a pitch-fork."[6] *The Packet* reported the Arnold effigy was dressed in regimentals. The dummy's two faces were "emblematical of his traitorous conduct." Behind the model, a figure of the Devil dressed in black robes, shook a purse of money at its left ear. With the pitchfork in his other hand, the Devil was "ready to drive him into hell as the reward due for the many crimes which his thirst for gold had made him commit." In front of the effigy hung a large lantern made of transparent paper. Displayed on the float were two drawings by Charles Willson Peale: one depicting the hanging of Major Andre and the other Arnold being pulled into the flames by the Devil. A text pronounced the people's sentence: "The effigy of this ingrate is therefore hanged (for want of his body) as a Traitor to his native country, and a Betrayer of the laws of honor."[7]

A subsequent search of the papers Arnold had left in Philadelphia uncovered documents which proved his financial interest in the *Active*. These records also revealed two previously unknown Arnold schemes: his arrangement with Clothier General James Mease and another with John R. Livingston, to seek profits in New York. Timothy Matlack laid these papers before his fellow congressmen on September 28.

The discovery of Arnold's treason was a moment of glory for an exuberant Timothy Matlack. While Americans celebrated their divine protection, Matlack and Reed were once again vindicated for their relentless pursuit of the major general. The stunning turn of events capped the earlier court-martial and Washington's reprimand. George Washington, in fact, owed the two Pennsylvania leaders a debt of gratitude. The court proceeding and reprimand proved he had not been completely in the dark about his officer. Timothy Matlack enjoyed the *Packet's* prophetic epitaph: "And odious for the blackest Crimes. Arnold shall sink to latest Times."

* * *

But if Pennsylvania officials hoped their villain's parade would distract voters ahead of fall elections, they were badly mistaken. The long war had continued to inflict pain and suffering on the people. Continental paper money, which traded at eight-to-one (dollars to pounds) in early 1779, had fallen to as low as one-hundred-to-one by the autumn of 1780. Now the incumbent party took the blame. In the October election Constitutionalists were turned out of the Assembly in large numbers and replaced by Republicans.

In November the Assembly and the Supreme Executive Council retained Joseph Reed as president, but his party was in no mood to celebrate. Samuel Fisher reported "some firing of Cannon & parade on this occasion tho I am ready to believe not so much as usual." The *Packet* claimed the bad economy was the reason for a subdued reception at City Tavern: a "cold collation was provided, consistent with that frugality and economy which the present situation of our public affairs not only renders necessary but honorable." But in truth, Constitutionalists were feeling mistreated. A bitter Joseph Reed said his government had been the victim of unfair attacks:

> Events have justified the government of this state in many measures, which for a season were the subject of the greatest complaint, and in which the most laudable actions, were ascribed to the most ungenerous motives, and yet the torrent of calumny, public and personal, does not cease to flow.[8]

Reed argued that considering the level of conflict in Pennsylvania, "It is to be admired that we have preserved any government, much more that it should have grown to the vigor and strength it now has."[9] The president warned Republicans in the Assembly against strong countermeasures since "in the course of such frequent elections, we shall soon be in the like situation ourselves."

Conservatives did not launch an immediate assault on the Constitution, but they did move to punish their rivals. On November 23 the Assembly named five new delegates to Congress. Among these were two returning members: S. J. Atlee and Henry Wynkoop. Constitutionalists had removed this pair for their votes in the Silas Deane affair. Now it was Timothy Matlack's turn to be replaced. His brief term in Congress was over.[10] Matlack went back to his office of secretary of the Commonwealth. Having debated America's finances at the State House, he was relegated to more mundane tasks. One of these was chasing down a counterfeiting ring. Fisher reported, "It has been a constant practice of the thieves &c in this house [the jail] for about 3 months past to sell such pewter as real dollars & I conclude that its being generally known and talked of in town, Timothy had come here to know the truth of it."

On New Year's Day, 1781, the man who described Matlack as "greas'd and puff'd with powder" got a sense of his frustration. Timothy Matlack and Whitehead Humphreys crossed paths on Market Street, between Fifth and Sixth Streets, "when after some fine words got to blows."

If Timothy felt any better after this fistfight, Republicans made sure his good humor did not last. In December the Assembly had proposed cutting the salaries of the president, Supreme Court justices, secretary and other posts held by radicals. Now in March the Assembly proposed a second bill to reduce salaries. Matlack's party complained these cuts would force their secretary out of office. While this bill did not come up for a final vote, the message was clear: five years after the radical takeover of Pennsylvania, Republicans had seen enough of the powerful secretary.[11]

As the Supreme Executive Council had no constitutional power to fight the Assembly, Reed and Matlack vented their frustration with another Tory roundup. Joseph Stansbury and five others were charged with trading goods across enemy lines. Stansbury—whose role in Arnold's treachery was not known—was safe in New York, but the other men were arrested. These individuals "were each separately examined by Joseph Reed & Timothy Matlack & demanded to confess on every matter to them, if they expected Mercy."

If this looked like a government that had run out of ideas, Matlack did make a serious effort to address the source of voter distress: the country's financial mess. In a lengthy newspaper essay entitled "Paper Money, Trade and Finance" Matlack identified depreciated paper money as the obvious culprit. Printed currency was, in fact, another political battleground. Radicals wanted to save continental and state issues while Republicans wanted them eliminated.

In another show of moderation, Matlack said the merchant class was not the enemy of the people in the case of paper money: "The importer has no interest in depreciating the paper money ... on the contrary, what the retailer gains by depreciation, during the credit allowed him by the importer, is in every instance the precise loss of the importer." Matlack's defense of merchants exposed him to fresh accusations of having abandoned his constituency. But Timothy also said any plan for redeeming paper money, to keep it in circulation, would depend on the people:

> That a faithful execution of the plan ... does not depend on the will and pleasure of assemblies or of Congress, but that so long as the people retain the right of electing annually their own representatives in those assemblies, the people have the right and power to see that those plans are faithfully executed.

Early in 1781, Congress named Robert Morris Superintendent of Finance. His job was to save the country from financial disaster. In May, Morris presented a plan for a bank. Congress drew up a provisional list of directors who would serve "until a choice of a new direction should be made by the stockholders."[12] On November 1, at City Tavern, the Bank of North America's directors and stockholders named Thomas Willing president. Congress confirmed incorporation, and the bank opened for business on January 7, 1782.

The new bank's directors, as chosen by Congress, were mostly prominent conservatives such as Cadwalader Morris and James Wilson. But one appointee was not like the others. That was Timothy Matlack.

For the conservative bank interest, which faced a fight for *state* incorporation, Matlack represented a useful advocate. But for Timothy, the directorship risked political death. He later claimed he told a friend at this time, "It is indeed an honor ... but remember that I tell you, it will prove also the greatest injury." Republicans may have had a second, more sinister, motive in choosing the secretary. They knew Matlack's acceptance of their offer would cost him the support of his party: they were setting him up for his downfall.

At a later time Timothy Matlack tried to explain his decision to accept a prominent role in the bank. He said although the institution was "opposed by the leading men of that party to which it was supposed I leaned," and although he could see its "tendency to favor the monied and trading interest of the state," he had considered it "the best means of defence left us." That a bank was needed to save America from financial ruin was an opinion he had formed in the months he spent in Congress. Now, despite the serious political risk, Matlack stood by this conviction. For Constitutionalists, Timothy Matlack was persona non grata.

Constitutionalists were anti-bank and pro-paper money while Republicans were pro-bank and anti-paper money. Matlack, pro-bank and pro-paper money, was somewhere in the middle. Constitutionalists did not want to grant official status to a financial institution that would be perpetually dominated by aristocrats. They feared elites would use the bank to create wealth and power for themselves. Radicals especially despised Thomas Willing, one of the two Pennsylvania delegates who voted against independence. Giving him the honor of the bank presidency, they said, would be "a discouragement to the whigs, is a wound to the cause of patriotism, and is trampling on the blood of those heroes and martyrs who have fallen in the defense of our liberty."[13] Anger and bitterness filled the air. Matlack said of the acerbic tone, "The contentions and resentments between parties and among individuals were at the highest." With the head start Congress had given the bank, passage of the state charter was inevitable. Radicals wanted to limit the charter to seven years or vest power in the Assembly to amend or repeal it in 1789. Both of these measures were defeated.

* * *

On Thursday, March 1, 1781, Philadelphia celebrated the ratification of the Articles of Confederation: the United States' first constitution. The *Penn-*

sylvania Packet reported, "The Ariel frigate, commanded by the gallant [John] Paul Jones, fired a feu-de-joy, and was beautifully decorated with a variety of streamers in the day, and ornamented with a brilliant appearance of lights in the night."[14]

By mutual consent, the Society of Friends did not participate in these festivities. As always, Quakers were under pressure for their pacifism and Anglophilia. In the *Pennsylvania Packet* a writer said he was offended by Quaker "impudence and Toryism." The writer asked why the government allowed the members of this faith to "remain among us?"

During the war years, the Society of Friends methodically disowned members who participated in the conflict or supported the wartime government. Among the growing ranks of the disowned was Nelly Matlack's brother-in-law, Samuel Wetherill Jr. Wetherill was married to Nelly's sister Sarah. In supporting the American cause, Wetherill believed he was following in the footsteps of the seventeenth century Quakers who had backed Oliver Cromwell.

In February a group of disowned Quakers began meeting at Wetherill's home. Their object was to "consider the propriety of establishing a religious Society, Separate from the Society of Friends."[15] Among the eight men who attended the first meetings were Timothy's brother, White, and Owen Biddle. Timothy joined in early April, and the first public meeting of the Free Quakers, as the group became known, was held in his home. In their first public address the members said although they had been forced from their religious home, they considered themselves Quakers. It was their "scattered and distressed situation" as men without a church that had induced them to come together. The address said:

> We have no new doctrines to teach, nor any design for promoting schisms in religion. We wish only to be freed from every species of ecclesiastical tyranny, and mean to pay a due regard to the principles of our forefathers.

The members invited others to "partake with us in the blessings we seek and hope to obtain."

Unlike the Society of Friends, the Free Quakers were committed to an independent America. It members complained they had been disowned for no other cause than "the faithful discharge of those duties we owe to our country." By saying they would conduct their affairs under the same liberal democratic principles adopted by Pennsylvania the members of the new Society made their politics clear: they supported the 1776 Constitution. The Free Quakers said the government lacking resources to defend freedom of religion, they themselves would take up the challenge: "governments established upon those liberal, just, and truly christian principles, and wisely confined to the great objects of ascertaining and defending civil rights ... must unavoidably leaves some cases unprovided for, which come properly under the care of religious societies."

A second Free Quaker address, written by Timothy Matlack and Christopher Marshall, spelled out claims the group planned to file against the Society of Friends. The address said, "The property of that society of which we and you were once joint members, is far from being inconsiderable, and we have done nothing which ... forfeited our right therein." The Free Quakers wanted the use of a meeting house and the burial ground. The group promised the Society of Friends that if it gained the use of a meeting house, it "would not seclude you in a joint participation with us in the use of it." A legal inquiry, it said, gave the men confidence in their pursuit, but they promised not to take the matter to the courts "unless you by your conduct compel us to it."

Quakers reacted with outrage. Timothy's brother-in-law David Cooper complained, "They call themselves Quakers, but their mode of faith was just what Satan would wish it; as, that every Christian had a religious liberty to do whatever was right in his own eyes."

Timothy Matlack, thought to be the group's "principal projector," had earned the Quakers' renewed ire.[16] For a man in a tenuous political position, Matlack's decision to pick this fight was a serious risk: Quakers had close ties to the Republicans in control of the Assembly.

Matlack also had to be concerned about irreparable damage to personal relationships. Perhaps with this in mind he found a case Free Quakers could champion: the jailed Quaker merchant Samuel Fisher Jr. Fisher wrote, "My Sisters Esther & Lydia went to Timothy Matlack and asserted my innocence in clear & strong Terms ... Timothy they thought, seemed uneasy on my account & was desirous of my release..." Matlack told two other visitors the Free Quakers would send a petition to the Supreme Executive Council on Fisher's behalf. While Fisher assumed "*Timothy is the father of this Petition,*" he was not exactly grateful. Matlack was the man who had had him arrested in the first place. But Fisher now hoped "the hearts of the most hardened men may be secretly reached ... to alter those purposes which to all human appearances have been so fixed as if nothing would move them." Samuel Fisher was released soon thereafter. Timothy lost no time promoting his role in obtaining the merchant's freedom, which was like setting a house on fire and taking credit for leading the bucket brigade that put it out. Fisher reported: "I have been frequently told that Timothy Matlack assumes to himself the merit of obtaining my release, to use his own words & it was confirmed to me by Samuel Allenson of Burlington a near Relation to Timothy." The paradox of this claim was not lost on the former prisoner: "I mention this because Timothy was the instrument of my first being taken up & confined."[17]

* * *

On October 24, 1781, Philadelphia celebrated the stunning news of Lieutenant General Lord Cornwallis' surrender at Yorktown. Cornwallis' capitulation ended the last major battle of the Revolutionary War. At Yorktown, American and French forces, led by Washington and Rochambeau on land and the Comte de Grasse in the Chesapeake, surrounded the British army. After successful attacks broke British defenses at two key redoubts, the enemy was forced to yield. Eight thousand British troops were captured.

Celebrations in Philadelphia were marred by more violence targeting Quakers. Hiltzheimer said, "The city was handsomely illuminated ... but am sorry to have to add that so many door and windows have been destroyed by a set of people that have no name." The damage suffered by the Drinkers was typical. Elizabeth wrote, "We had near 70 panes of glass broken the sash lights and two panels of the front parlor broke in pieces—the Door crack'd and Violently burst open, when they threw stones into the House for some time."

In early May 1782, the *Pennsylvania Journal* published the news of Parliament's decision to stop fighting in America. Elizabeth Drinker said, "A report prevails at present, that independence is granted: believed by many." For Timothy Matlack it was time to celebrate. He had dedicated seven years of his life to winning the war. With the aide of France and Spain, America had triumphed over Great Britain. Independence was won.

On Sunday, July 14, Jacob Hiltzheimer recorded in his diary, "His Excellency General Washington, from the northward, and the Commander of the French army, from the southward arrived today." The following day the two leaders joined eleven hundred guests at a banquet hosted by the French Ambassador. Drinker reported, "Great doings at the French Ambassadors (who lives at John Dickinsons house up Chestnut Street) on account of the birth of the Dauphine of France—feasting Fire-Works &c, for which they have been preparing for some weeks." At this feast, despite the allies he had lost, Timothy Matlack loomed as a powerful figure. He was still Secretary of the Supreme Executive Council, a secretary of the American Philosophical Society and a trustee of the university. By circulating through the large gathering of luminaries he reminded people he was still formidable.

* * *

The current chapter in Pennsylvania's political battle was the fight started by the Free Quakers. In late August the group's leaders sent the Assembly an address which spoke of the obligations of government and the rights of citizens. Though signed by Isaac Howell and White Matlack, the author of the piece may have been Timothy Matlack. Matlack and the Free Quakers said religious societies did not have the right to disown members for complying

Twelve. A Brief Term in Congress

with the laws of their country. Numerous Quakers had been disowned, they said, for swearing allegiance, holding public office, paying taxes, or bearing arms, all of which were required by the state. In one particularly grievous case, they said, Cadwallader Dickinson had been disowned for sitting on the John Roberts and Abraham Carlisle juries. The address stated religious societies did not have the right to withhold the use of the places of worship and the burial grounds provided by shared ancestors. A petition, signed by sixty-two Free Quakers, asked the Assembly to bring in a bill which would recognize their right to hold in common the meeting houses, schoolhouses, burying grounds, lots of lands and estates of the Society of Friends. They also asked for access to birth, marriage and death records.[18]

Once again Quakers reacted with anger. James Pemberton told his brother, "TM and his associates have presented their long laboured performance to the assembly and we are told it is very scurrilous and inflammatory."[19] The Society of Friends told the Assembly the Free Quaker petition was "artfully designed to impress your minds with unfavorable sentiments, by misrepresentations and injurious charges against us." In addressing the Free Quakers directly, the Society of Friends advised the group not to break the commandment, which said "Thou shalt not covet thy neighbour's house, nor any thing that is thy neighbour's."[20]

On Monday, September 16, 1782, a large contingent of Quakers met their Free Quaker adversaries at a hearing at the State House. Elizabeth Drinker reported, "T Matlack takes it upon him to be speaker for the Apostates." Waiting outside in the yard was an "exceedingly great throng of people." But there was little for the crowd to see that day. After three hours the Assembly adjourned. Two days later the body gave notice it would not proceed on the matter but refer it to the next legislature.

The Free Quakers had no chance of winning a fight against a Society of Friends that enjoyed great influence in the current Assembly. A week later the Society demonstrated just how powerful it still was. The established Quakers were tired of being attacked, and their leaders wanted revenge. If the Society encouraged the Assembly to examine Secretary Matlack's books, the conservative majority in the house did not need much encouragement. James Pemberton reported that following the hearing in the Assembly on September 16 "T.M. has since been required by the Assembly to account for the public money which has come into his hands as Secretary arising from marriage and tavern licenses, which is likely to furnish him with other employment than to abuse & calumniate those who have done him no injustice."

A newspaper writer identifying himself as "A Friend of Just Government and honest Men" turned up the heat on the secretary. This writer claimed the whereabouts of tavern license fees—amounting to several thousand pounds a year — was the subject of speculation. The public was convinced, he claimed, the money had disappeared:

> In general it was said, there had not been a single farthing of tavern license money paid into the public treasury (at least for a considerable part of the state) since the revolution commenced, but that the money was engrossed and embezzled. It would be of great satisfaction to the public, whose right it is, to know how the matters stands; because a variety of suspicions are daily getting abroad, and the reputation of government is nicely concerned therein, the circumstances happening within their own doors.

Two years had passed since the opposition had taken control of the Assembly and removed Matlack from Congress. Since then Republicans had tried to force him out of the secretary's office by cutting his salary. More recently they had launched an inquiry into his accounting practices and started rumors of embezzlement.

Now in November, in a close vote of the members of the Republican-held Assembly and the Supreme Executive Council, John Dickinson was named the new Council president. Dickinson immediately took control of the Matlack vendetta. At Dickinson's direction, the comptroller general — a powerful desk created by Republicans earlier in the year — added his piece to the Assembly's probe. The officeholder, John Nicholson, submitted a letter to the Assembly accusing the secretary of charging the state "a very considerable and altogether inadmissible sum." The next day the Assembly heard a motion of censure, which was postponed pending a committee report.[21]

Under intense pressure, Timothy Matlack did not languish or droop. Pemberton observed that by December he had recovered his "spirits and natural effrontery."[22] But on March 5, 1783, the Assembly said it was its "indispensable duty ... to discountenance, as far as lies in their power, all public defaulters; and it appearing to this House that the Secretary of the Supreme Executive Council hath neglected to keep accounts of money received by him on behalf of the public, and also to pay the same into the treasury, according to Law."[23] Branding Timothy Matlack "unworthy of public trust and confidence" the Assembly voted *unanimously* to sanction him. The one-sided decision meant at least twenty-five radicals voted against their secretary. Matlack's party had turned completely against him. Radicals held him responsible for a three-part deception: opposing price fixing, defending merchants, and joining the bank. Timothy had in fact already lost his bank directorship. In November trustees had reelected all of the original directors, *except* Matlack.[24] Having won their state charter, the trustees had tossed their advocate aside. Nonetheless, the damage was done. Now Timothy was paying the price for his independent streak. He was his own man and he was all alone.

Twelve. A Brief Term in Congress

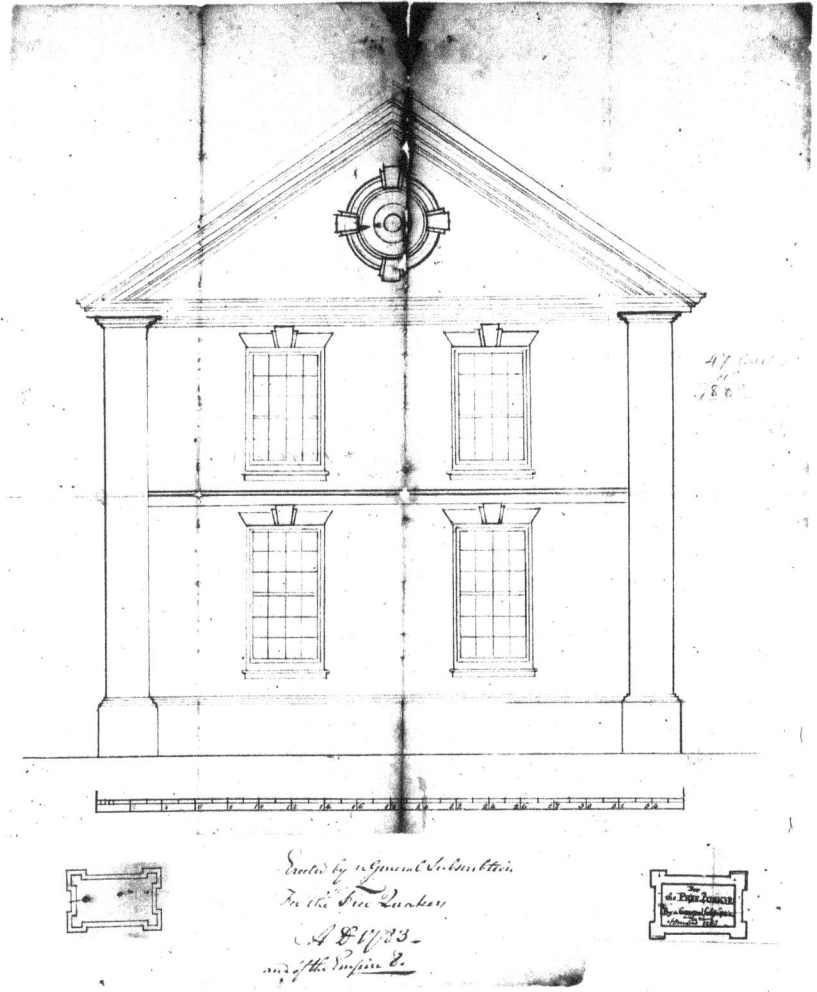

Plan for the Free Quaker Meeting House by Timothy Matlack. Dated AD 1783 and the Empire 8. Drawing. Philadelphia: Timothy Matlack, 1782. Library of Congress, Manuscripts Division.

Timothy Matlack fought back. He spent the next twelve days rendering his accounts and, as ordered by writ, submitted them to Comptroller General Nicholson on March 17. Then in a surprise turn of events, Matlack said Nicholson "admitted that the account of monies received by me is probably correct." Matlack quoted him as saying, "It is very improbable that there are any omissions."[25] Four days later the Supreme Executive Council said the secretary's request for a court hearing, to determine the question of right, was reasonable. A committee of the Assembly, however, recommended the comptroller General "prosecute the said Timothy Matlack Esq. in the Supreme Court in order to try the contested points by a jury." The accused was authorized to employ counsel.[26] Matlack later said that certain *other* objections raised by the Assembly were "questions of law." These were arguments about fees Matlack received as keeper of the great seal, payments made for militia commissions, and the timing of his salary reduction.[27]

On Saturday, March 22, 1783, the Supreme Executive Council asked Timothy Matlack to resign his office. Matlack agreed and was replaced on Monday.[28] Having received no support from his party, Matlack was hunted out of government without objection.

* * *

Eight long years had passed since Lexington and Concord. Timothy Matlack said he engaged in the American cause the day after news of that fight reached Philadelphia. Now, two days after he was terminated as secretary, Philadelphia received a report that preliminary articles of peace had been signed in Paris. While the Revolution and the war were over, Timothy Matlack faced a fight to save his political life. But the Supreme Court postponed his hearing and left him in limbo. So Timothy's friends sent him away from Philadelphia. In June he travelled to New England to visit the Quaker separatists Timothy Davis and Cornelius Wing. On this trip Timothy felt a letdown triggered by the end of his career in government. He felt angry and gloomy, unappreciated and abused.

But Timothy did not stay away very long. He was back in Philadelphia by early July. Christopher Marshall noted that he had been "visited by Timothy Matlack who gave satisfactory account of his taking & performing his journey to Rhode Island."

Upon his return Timothy was told the Free Quakers had suffered a setback. Owen Biddle had "offered a paper of acknowledgement of his transgressions" and returned to the Society of Friends. For Timothy, the news of Owen's defection was a personal blow. The two men had been friends for at least thirty years. They had co-owned a steel business and served together in the Convention of 1776. The Quaker John Pemberton wrote:

> I think the turn of O.B. must touch poor Timothy Matlack, and I wish it may profitably, and many others. May he be enabled to stand firm, for trials will attend him, and he may be perhaps powerfully attached by some of his connections. My dear Love to him, his wife and children. Tell him my concern is for his preservation in humility and watchful obedience; thus will he find hard things made easy, bitter things sweetened, and light and strength increase.[29]

Twelve. A Brief Term in Congress

The Free Quakers carried on without Biddle. The group had a project under way to establish their permanent home. With funds raised in a subscription drive they had acquired a lot at Fifth and Arch Streets. Now the Free Quakers prepared to build their own meeting house. The architectural plans for the new building were likely drawn by Timothy Matlack, who also served as construction manager. The meeting house was to have a vaulted cellar, to be rented out as storage space. David Rittenhouse approved Matlack's design for the underground arches. Matlack dated his diagrams: "AD 1783 — and of the Empire 8." The United States of America had entered its eighth year of existence.

Timothy's cost estimate for the project, £1,356, was approved, and on Tuesday, July 29, 1783, the first foundation stone was laid. Among the members present were Isaac Howell, Moses Bartram, Samuel Wetherill, White Matlack, Joseph Warner, "& his little son." Christopher Marshall said the foundation was laid "between the hours of nine and ten ... in the presence of a numerous body of spectators." Each workman received a dollar, and Timothy sent up "a dozen bottles of beer, 2 quarts of spirits, 8 loaves of bread & near half a cheese at noon."[30]

Construction got under way. White Matlack billed the Society £227 for the 113,800 bricks he delivered in the months of August, September and October. Work continued through the fall, winter, spring, and on into the next summer.

In later years Quakers liked to tell the story of the day Samuel Emlen walked by the construction site. Timothy Matlack, with complacency, expressed his regret that the meeting house had been planned on too small a scale. "Oh," responded Emlen, pointing to the mason's shed by the curb side, "in fifty years that lime house will hold you all."[31] But Quakers watching the rival meeting house go up were perhaps more worried than they admitted.

On June 6, 1784, the first two meetings for worship were held in the completed meeting house. Christopher Marshall reported two hundred people attended in the morning and another one hundred before noon. These numbers were well up from the thirty-five or so who attended meetings at the Academy in early March. Elizabeth Drinker said Jemima Wilkinson, a minister outcast by the Society of Friends, preached at the Free Quaker meeting house on August 15.

While enjoying the opening, Timothy was preoccupied with recovering his honorable name. In December 1782, the Assembly had branded him "unworthy of public trust and confidence." At that time Matlack had objected, in the third person, that a "heavy and exceedingly grievous censure has been passed upon him for a supposed neglect, not only without enquiry and open fair trial by his peers, but even without a specific charge made against him."[32]

Matlack said his rights as a citizen had been violated, and "it is a duty which he owes to the memory of his son, to himself, his family and country thus solemnly to remonstrate against the proceedings of this house." Matlack complained that "many strange and injurious falsehoods have been invented and spread abroad." One of these was that he had traded with public money. Matlack stated that while in office he had never been "concerned in the exportation or importation; purchase or sale of merchandize of any kind, directly or indirectly, other than such articles as were intended for the sole use of his family." He also said he had never at any time purchased or paid for a confiscated estate. He demanded a trial to clear his name.

Four months prior to the opening of the Free Quakers' new home, Jacob Hiltzheimer had gone to the State House, "being summoned as a juryman on a cause between the Commonwealth of Pennsylvania plaintiff and Timothy Matlack Esq. Defendant." But, Jacob wrote, "the counsel on both sides could not agree on the form this case should be tried therefore the court told the jury that they were discharged."

The state's attorneys, James Wilson and William Bradford Jr., told Assembly speaker George Gray the proceeding had been suspended because "the Defendant now refuses to join issue or to enter any plea unless we reduce the sum contained in the Declaration." The lawyers recommended an "*adversary* suit [be] commenced against Mr. Matlack for the sum supposed to be due."[33]

Matlack responded in his own letter to Gray that Wilson and Bradford had "artfully planned to Surprize and ensnare me." Matlack's adversaries, he said, had insisted on "filing a declaration against me for money had and received by me for the use of the State." Matlack was stunned to find the attorneys' statement said he had received ninety-seven thousand pounds, "a sum far beyond that stated by the Comptroller General and beyond what I had any imagination that I was ever suspected of receiving." Wilson and Bradford now exhibited a new account from the comptroller, "upon very different principles & for a much larger sum than that contained in his report." There was more. Matlack said the lawyers wanted to add charges "widely different from those which the house had ordered to be tried & which I came prepared to defend myself against." The new accusations were "ready to be brought forward at the very instant of trial, when material witnesses might be absent, records unsearched, papers and authentic documents out of my hands ... and my counsel totally uninstructed." The judge told the lawyers to conference but, Matlack reported, Wilson and Bradford began this meeting by stating their "fixed determination not to recede in the smallest degree from what they had before urged." "This very singular mode of accommodating the dispute which was entirely different from what was recommended by the court, broke off the treaty." Matlack told the speaker:

Twelve. A Brief Term in Congress

It is beneath the dignity of government to wish to ensnare an innocent man, & I cannot persuade myself that the legislature really desires it. The questions to be tried are fairly stated in the Comptroller Generals report. I am willing to submit those questions to court or a jury. I have no objections to the jury who were struck in the cause or to any other good men. [34]

Prior to his broken trial, Matlack had identified two adversaries in the Republican camp: Fredrick Muhlenberg and Jacob Rush. Matlack said the former claimed he "paid into the hands of the Secretary money which was not credited in his accounts." But the fact of the matter, Matlack said, as the books kept by his clerk would show, was that on October 20, 1780, Muhlenberg had received three hundred ninety-six pounds for thirty-six marriage licenses from the Rev. Mr. Van Buskirk. But by the time he turned the paper money over to the secretary's office, August of the following year, it had depreciated six-to-one. By buying and selling specie in the interval, Matlack said, Muhlenberg had retained five-sixths of the real value of the collected fees for himself. Matlack called this a "mercenary pitiful trick" by "the man that whispers negligence and fraud, concerning his neighbors."[35]

Matlack said Rush had written a piece, signed "An Assemblyman," which claimed affairs as "black as Matlack's" were turning up daily. More specifically Rush had accused the former secretary of having earned excessive sums on marriage license fees. Matlack now replied the fees he had received were worth less than "one penny farthing for each which is less than half the sum that the wafer under each seal actually cost me!" Matlack reminded Rush that his accounts had been on file at the comptroller's office, open to the public, for nine months. He said his clerk, who continued to serve under the new secretary, "perfectly independent of, and unconnected with me," had never suggested fraud or neglect. Matlack proposed that if Rush found any "juggling trick ... as that which I have stated of Mr. Muhlenberg's, I will consent to bear the brand of Fool and Knave upon my forehead forever."

But Rush's newspaper attack had come months earlier. Matlack claimed he bore the assault silently but now chose to defend himself because "my reputation is of infinitely more value than my life." But then he revealed the real reason for his delayed defense: "There has been a moment, sir, in which I confess I feared you. I heard that the president and council were about to appoint you a judge of the supreme court before which I expect to be heard." Now Matlack prayed, "Whether your proceedings against me have been the effect of malice, envy, avarice or ignorance, may that God ... preserve the people from such a judge." Jacob Rush, brother of Dr. Benjamin Rush, was in fact named to the Supreme Court, as the replacement for the deceased Judge Evans, a few weeks after Matlack's trial.

* * *

While power had shifted in Pennsylvania, Constitutionalists were able to block Republican measures which included another convention call. Republicans on the Council of Censors complained that while a majority of their board approved of a new convention, the Constitution required a two-thirds vote.

Republicans complained the Constitution had failed the people during the war and "the will of our Rulers became the only law." Radicals, they said, were now reneging on a promise, made seven years earlier, to allow changes to the Constitution once the enemy had been "driven from our Coasts." Republicans addressed the people: "What do these men fear from a Convention? Are they afraid to trust you with the exercise of the inestimable power of choosing a Government for yourselves?"[36] Radicals fought back by calling Republican proposals undemocratic and fanning fears of a mass influx of Tories.[37]

Republicans had overreached on their program: in the election of 1784 voters rejected their party in a major defeat. Constitutionalists regained control of the Assembly. In December 1784, Timothy Matlack became the beneficiary of this turn of events. Disapproval of his conduct from within his own party had subsided. Radicals had learned to despise the vendetta against their former leader more than his transgressions. Now the new Assembly said its predecessors had assumed undefined and arbitrary powers in his case, "powers that might be equally exerted to shelter a set of defaulters and peculators, and to destroy persons obnoxious to the predominant party." The Assembly said Mr. Matlack had been condemned with no "summons, hearing, charge or trial." Accusing the prior body of having acted improperly, legislatures voted to rescind the tag "unworthy of public trust and confidence" as unconstitutional. Forty-five Constitutionalists now voted in Matlack's favor against fourteen Republicans.

Timothy felt vindicated, but his troubles were not over. Two days after the favorable Assembly resolution John Dickinson requested the papers relating to his accounts be returned. The president of the Supreme Executive Council now arranged for an adversarial suit, as recommended by the lawyers Wilson and Bradford earlier in the year.

The Supreme Court, with Judge Jacob Rush sitting on the panel, heard this new challenge on April 17, 1785. The state's demand was for two thousand pounds specie. But after a hearing which "took up two days and a half, the jury found the common-wealth to be debtor to the defendant for £75 12 6."

The *Pennsylvania Packet* said the charge that Matlack had failed to account for public money was unsupported by "any evidence whatever." The paper turned the tables on the Republicans by demanding the guilt or innocence of individuals be left to "the dispassionate enquiries of the proper tribunals" since "large bodies of men too generally act like a mob!"[38]

Twelve. A Brief Term in Congress 157

Now Timothy Matlack was ready to celebrate. After two long years his name had finally been cleared. A few weeks later radicals held their annual picnic of the patriotic Sons of St. Tammany. Hiltzheimer reported "a large number of gentlemen collected with tickets in their hats which cost 8/4, but it afforded us plenty of victuals and drink. The first thing done was the gentlemen formed a ring and chose James Read Esq. their chief, Timothy Matlack is Secretary." And so he was forgiven. Matlack was honored by the newspaper that called him "*a whig in the darkest hour.*"

Thirteen
Savannah, Georgia

Immediately after his vindication Timothy Matlack made preparations for a trip to Savannah, Georgia. A request to represent the Meng family in court offered the opportunity for much needed time away. On May 6, 1785, Matlack paid thirty-three dollars for a "matrass," two sheets and a blanket. He also purchased sea stores, which included "bacon, eggs, butter, tea, chocolate, figgs, lemons, loaf of sugar, mustard, vinegar, wine, cyder, trunk, box of medicinal, paper, quills, and paper wax." Two days later he paid for a pig and also portage on the ship. On May 26 he arrived in Charleston, and two days later he was in Savannah. Here he stayed at the French Crown, where Mrs. Watts provided board, fruit, wine and washing. That summer Matlack took a trip to the onetime radical hotbed of Sunbury, Georgia, a town burned by the British in 1779. Here he likely visited the Declaration signer Lyman Hall.

In February of the following year, Matlack was still in the South. He wrote home to congratulate his daughter Patty and her husband Guy Bryan on the birth of their first child. (Timothy left Philadelphia a month prior to Martha's wedding, a ceremony which may have been planned on short notice.) Timothy mentioned that none of his friends "in the political line" had written during these months away. He thought, "Perhaps it's best so." But he felt "much obliged to my friends for their kind inquiries after me, and wish you to pay my respectful attentions to them all." Timothy reported he had visited Billy in Charleston, where he now lived, and spent eleven days with him. His son was in a "low state of health though cheerfull and tolerably free from pain." (Billy may have suffered from rheumatism.) Timothy said he would be returning to Philadelphia at the end of April and asked his son-in-law to "make my family as happy as you can, and divide a large share of the tender affection among them from a father who longs very earnestly to be with them again." Timothy sent his love to his daughters Kitty and Libby.[1]

But Timothy lingered in Georgia. In May he took a second trip to Sunbury. Timothy had been away from home for a full year but he needed more time. He had been forgiven by his own party but he was out of office. Matlack felt himself the victim of injustice.

In his mind Timothy reviewed all he had done. Ten years earlier he had stood before a massive town meeting in the State House yard and invoked the people's right to liberate themselves from the King of England and the Pennsylvania Assembly that derived its power from that ruler. Three weeks later he had asked his battalion "Whether they wished the province of Pennsylvania to be a free and independent State, and united with the other twelve colonies represented in Congress?" In the War of Independence he had "staked his life on the success of America, and repeatedly met the enemy in the field." He had "seen the blood of a brother and of a beloved son shed in her sacred cause." At the end of it all he had been treated with dishonor.

Finally in early June 1786, Timothy paid his bill for three hundred fifty-three days board ($353). By the end of the month he was back in Philadelphia. Jacob Hiltzheimer, now a conservative Assemblyman, said the two had met for breakfast. Timothy was pleased to be back in his own town, back among family and friends.

In March of the following year, 1787, Billy Matlack and his bride, Hannah Carmalt, were married at the First Baptist Church. On St. Patrick's Day, Timothy Matlack, Jacob Hiltzheimer, and a group of gentlemen gathered at Mr. Eberhart's slaughterhouse for the weighing of another giant steer. In Hiltzheimer's diary Matlack added the weight of the four quarters, thirteen hundred sixty-five pounds, and of the rest of the cow, four hundred six pounds, for a total of seventeen hundred seventy-one. Hiltzheimer's prize surpassed Marmaduke Cooper's, which was killed the same day and weighed seventy fewer pounds. After the event at Eberhart's, the men enjoyed a festive St. Patrick's Day dinner.

While these were enjoyable occasions, four years had passed since Matlack lost his office, and he was under financial stress. The politician could no longer afford the lifestyle he had acquired during his years in office. Timothy tried to find profitable ventures—including a partnership with the merchants Joseph Carson and William Bell—but nothing came of these efforts.

Matlack was also facing new legal problems. While in Savannah he had been told that new judgments had been filed against him. Here was another reason he had been in no hurry to return to Philadelphia. This time the pain was self-inflicted. Matlack was forced to admit his own requests for reimbursement had angered Republicans. The financially constrained Matlack had filed claims "to the amount of one thousand and five hundred pounds and upwards on one account only besides divers others."

On April 14, 1787, in a public notice, Attorney General J. B. Smith ordered

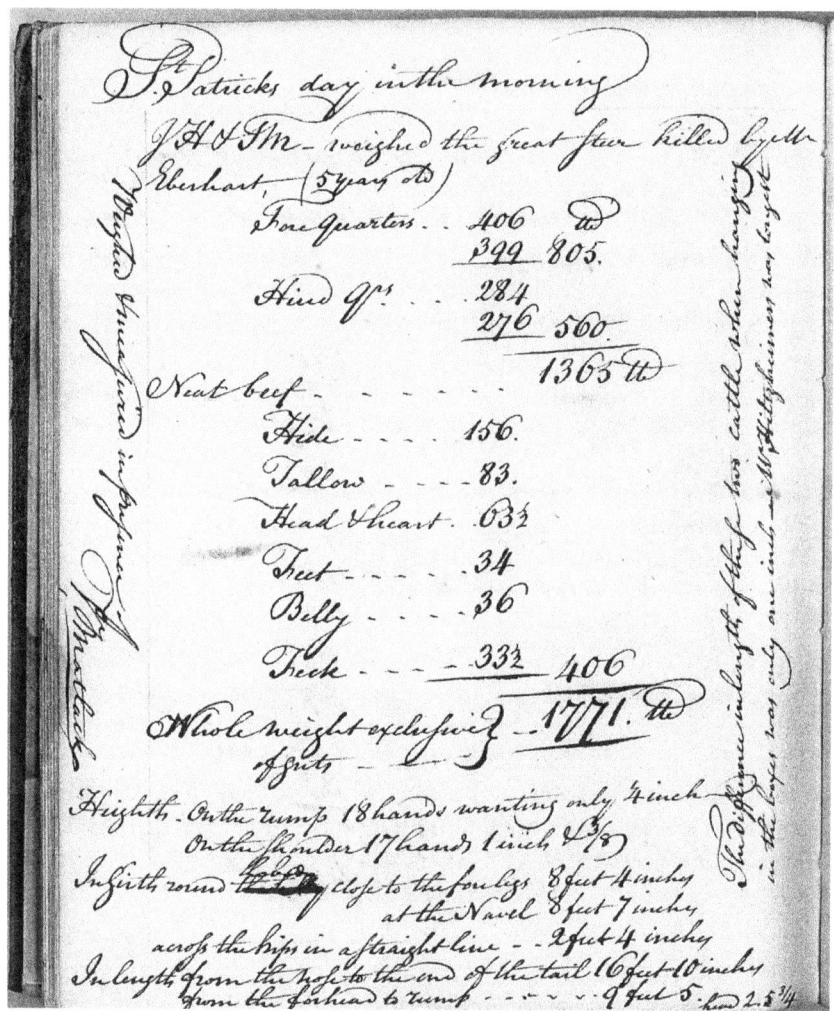

Above and opposite page: Pages from Jacob Hiltzheimer's diary in Timothy Matlack's hand records the weighing of a slaughtered steer on St. Patrick's Day, 1787. Philadelphia: Jacob Hiltzheimer, 1787. The American Philosophical Society, Philadelphia.

the seizure of Timothy Matlack's goods, chattels, lands and tenements, sufficient to discharge a debt of thirty-six pounds, thirteen shillings, and four pence. If this amount could not be raised in the sheriff's bailiwick, he had been ordered to "take the body of the said Timothy Matlack, and him safely keep in the goal of the county aforesaid." The amount named actually represented the smallest of four judgments issued by the comptroller general in Matlack's absence. The others were for £53.9.8, £300, and £1,058.15.22. Per-

Thirteen. Savannah, Georgia

haps the petty figure was published to maximize Matlack's embarrassment. The sheriff was not able to recover the amount in question, and Timothy Matlack was arrested on May 1. The timing of Matlack's arrest was likely planned to overlap with the start of the United States Constitutional Convention. By incarcerating him during the gathering of America's most prominent leaders his adversaries hoped to once again embarrass the former secretary.

Hiltzheimer wrote that George Washington arrived on Sunday, May 13: "The City Troop of Horse received him at Mr. Gray's Ferry. The artillery company saluted with firing the cannon." Washington's formal welcome was clearly audible to the men sitting in county jail.

Timothy Matlack now turned to the Supreme Executive Council for help. During his absence Benjamin Franklin had been elected president and the moderate Constitutionalist Charles Biddle, vice president. Timothy Matlack appealed to Franklin in a letter dated "Gaol of the City and County of Philadelphia, May 21, 1787." Matlack tried to explain why he was "encroaching on the time or attention of your excellency." The executions against him "were pretended to be founded on a judicial decision of the honorable executive body in which your excellency presides, which if made at all has been made in my absence without notice of any kind to me or to any person whatsoever on my behalf."

Matlack reminded Franklin the 1776 Pennsylvania Constitution held sacred the right to trial by jury. He lamented having been sentenced twice in violation of this right. Matlack asked, "What crime have I committed for which I alone may be compelled to ask as a favor what every other citizen may demand of right? There is none sir, even pretended against me." As a man "without connections of any kind with men in power; without any settled interest with either of the parties in which the people of the state are divided, and without any money," he said, the difficulty and danger of the situation was easy to perceive. Matlack admitted filling claims against the state was a mistake: "I may have erred in relying too confidently on public faith for reward of intended services."

Matlack pointed to his record of service. "No man has had more zeal in the common cause or exerted more fully ... the abilities God has given than I have done throughout the great contest for liberty." He had always followed his convictions "with the spirit of a freeman disdaining to be the tool of any man or party." In that spirit he had "aimed to surpress measures which appeared dangerous to the people, and support such as tended to their safety without regarding by whom they were suggested."

The two issues that had got him in trouble, he told Franklin, were price fixing and the bank. His opposition to the former had won him "insults from every quarter" and his directorship in the latter had, as prophesized, caused him the greatest injury. In the bank dispute, "I had offended both parties, one of them demanded and the other gave me up as a sacrifice." He did not mention these things to claim reward but as "evidence of the independence of my conduct on trying occasions."

Matlack's letter was dated the same day Judge Edward Shippen issued a writ of habeas corpus. The following day Matlack appeared before the judge with his counsel, William Murray Jr. and Peter S. Duponceau. In his opening remarks Murray said no parallel could be found "for the continued series of oppression and injustice" suffered by his client. In violation of the Pennsylvania Constitution Matlack had been "wantonly dragged from the enjoyment of what he has lawfully acquired." The judgments, he said, not warranted by any legal authority, were improper. The lawyer continued with a lengthy discourse on these issues before making closing arguments. Now Comptroller Nicholson responded. He produced a number of papers he said were Mr. Matlack's accounts, as settled by him and approved by Council. These procedures, he said, were "the same that are always practiced." Mr. Murray replied he "could not justify proceeding illegally or irregularly in Mr. Matlack's case, because he had proceeded illegally or irregularly in other cases." Mr. Murray observed that the question was not "what had been the comptroller general's practice, but what was legal?"

Judge Shippen asked what notice had been given of the executions. The comptroller general went to his office to retrieve a letter from General Wayne. "This he offered as evidence to prove that the notice was given, to Mr. Matlack, in Savannah, in the state of Georgia." Judge Shippen rejected the correspondence as proper evidence of notification. He said the matter had been determined on the first point and Matlack was discharged.

But the end of this trial was *still* not the end of Matlack's new ordeal. The state's claims were next reviewed by the Supreme Court. On May 30 Matlack appeared before a sympathetic magistrate, the former Council vice president, Judge George Bryan. Timothy offered security for an appeal of the judgments before the judge threw out the state's claims. Finally it was all over.

A writer signing LIBERTY complained that while Timothy Matlack was now free, "he has nevertheless suffered a long and ignominious imprisonment." This he saw as proof of the "evil consequences of vesting such enormous powers in the hands of a single man, under the title of Comptroller General, or any other title whatever." By abusing the law, LIBERTY said, the comptroller general had deprived a citizen of his freedom without the intervention of his peers.[2]

On June 4, 1787, Hiltzheimer and his wife "went down to market street gate to see the great and good man General Washington we had a full view of him, but the number of people that followed him on all sides was astonishing." A month later, Jacob was thrilled to meet "his Excellency General Washington taking a ride on horseback, his coachman Giles with him only."

On August 3 Washington paid a visit to the steel furnace owned by John Nancarrow and White Matlack. White's brother Timothy, who owned a furnace twenty-five years earlier, was an early advocate of the alloy. Timothy was out of jail in time to join his brother for Washington's visit. At least one of the Matlack brothers, if not both, attended a dinner at Washington's Philadelphia residence that month.[3]

* * *

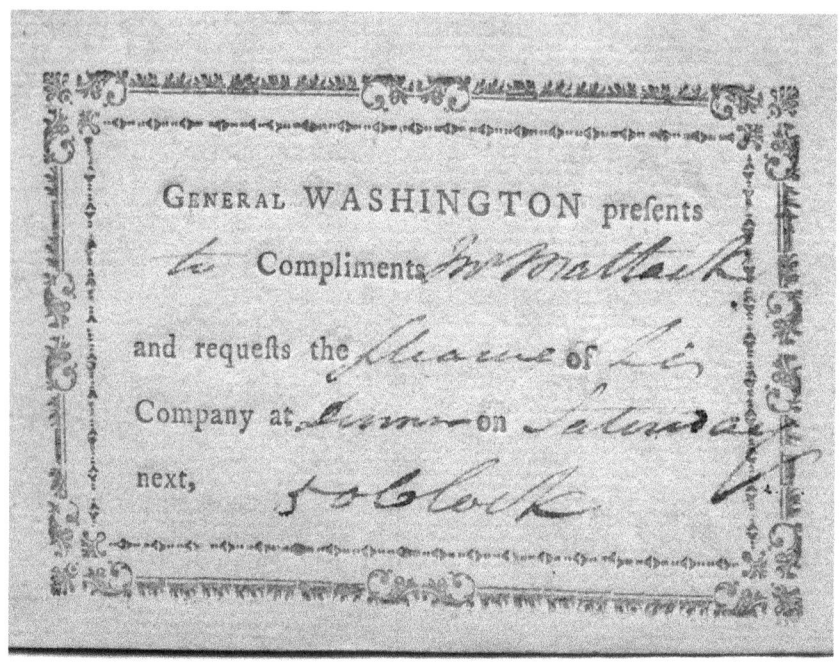

Mr. Matlack's dinner invitation from General Washington, circa 1787. The Rosenbach Museum & Library, Philadelphia, AMs 528/29.

In January 1788, Timothy wrote in Jacob's diary that the two men had "weighed Mr. Hiltzheimer's bull calf in the evening, he being now thirty days old and found his weight two hundred and twenty three pounds full weight having gained in twelve days sixty one pounds—that is five pounds per day and one pound over!" The friends weighed their beast three more times in the month of February. In late June Hiltzheimer wrote, "In the afternoon Timothy Matlack came to me and wanted to go with a country friend to my meadow to shew him my large calf. Took M. in my chair, his friend went on horse back down to said meadow." In March of the following year Matlack reported that the cattlemen "weighed the steer raised by JK 5 years old last August called St. Patrick's or Paddy."

On April 8, 1790, the Society of Free Quakers presented a congratulatory address to President-elect George Washington. The Free Quakers hoped the "Supreme Being which rules in Heaven and among men continue to pour his wisdom into thy heart, and so guide thy administration as to make the government a blessing to the people, and render it free, efficient and stable."

Benjamin Franklin, a man who dedicated most of his life to creating a free, efficient and stable society, died on Saturday, April 17, at the age of eighty-five. On Wednesday he was buried in the Christ Church yard opposite the Free Quaker Meeting House. Jacob Hiltzheimer wrote, "I think I never saw so many people collected together at any funeral whatsoever." In New York City George Washington was sworn in as president at the end of the month.

* * *

Far from the inaugural festivities in New York, a man named Samuel Maclay made his way to Lebanon, a town in Pennsylvania's Buffalo Valley. Maclay, a former officer in the Northumberland County militia and future senator, lived on a farm west of Derr's Town (Lewisburg).

On his way to Lebanon Maclay stopped at Mr. Fry's to buy bacon but was unable to eat it: he thought the hog "must have had the measels."[4] Later Maclay stopped at the Sign of the Boar in Millers Town and drank two quarts of cider. Mr. Maclay was on his way to meet Timothy Matlack and John Adlum. The three men were about to start an expedition to survey the rivers of western Pennsylvania.

In 1789 Matlack had linked himself to a new society dedicated to improving roads and inland navigation in the state. In September of that year, at this group's urging, the Assembly agreed to explore the state's navigable waterways, and Timothy Matlack was one of those assigned to study the Delaware. The following year the Assembly agreed to the current undertaking, to examine water routes to Pittsburgh and Lake Erie.

On April 30, the day before the scheduled rendezvous, Maclay arrived at the meeting point. But at the tavern on Quitte Creek he found no sign of his fellow "commissioners." Maclay was perplexed. On Saturday, May 1, a Captain Moore, arriving from Philadelphia, told him Colonel Matlack would either start out from Philadelphia on Thursday or arrive on that day: he was uncertain which. The weather had been so unfavorable the other commissioner had declined to appear on the appointment day. Maclay was not pleased:

> This Intelligence with the circumstances attending it Embrasses me much. Here I am with three hands at Expenses, 12 miles from our Boat, without any instrument proper for the Business I came on; among a number of People not overly Polite to strangers; near one Hundred miles from home; to return home, shameful; to stay disagreeable and altogether uncertain. Not a single line from my Colleagues either to apologize, or to assign a reason why they did not attend or to appoint another day.

When the two finally arrived, a week late, Timothy offered no apology. To make matters worse, from Maclay's perspective, he had the gall to ask for money for travel expenses. Matlack had been delayed, he explained, by his last-minute petition to the Supreme Executive Council "for a much Larger sum of Money than what was agreed on by the commissioners when the appointment was made to meet on the first of May at Lebanon." Matlack's bid for enhanced remuneration had been flatly rejected.

As the trip got under way Maclay's annoyance with his fellow commissioner only increased. In Northumberland he waited impatiently while "Colonel Matlack spent part of the after noon in cleaning and shooting his gun." In this town the men learned the Supreme Executive Council was sending instructions for a meeting with the Indians settled at the head of the Allegheny. The messenger, a Colonel Wilson, thought they should wait for the new orders. While Maclay agreed, Matlack said he would not wait a minute. He thought Council "might send an Express after us with their dispatches, if they thought Proper." Timothy said he would start out that afternoon and travel five or six miles up the west branch of the Susquehanna. His unilateral decision caused a rupture. Maclay said he would take time to visit his family, and Adlum said he would not go out that day. But despite his pronouncement, Matlack did not leave until the next morning. The reason, Maclay wrote, was that he had arranged to transport a load of goods to Derr's Town. Maclay could not object to this private enterprise because he too was sending up goods, which he asked to have unloaded at Rees' landing.

But later Maclay was stunned to learn his supplies had not been unloaded because Matlack would not suffer a delay. Maclay reported, "Mr. Rees told [Matlack] that he would send his Boy for Mr. Maclay & that he would come down Immediately, but he said he would not wait." Matlack insisted Maclay could send for his things at Derr's Town. There Matlack was again urged to wait for Maclay, as he had waited for him at Lebanon. Matlack snapped that Council was to blame for the original delay and that he would not wait "one hour on any man." Maclay was left stranded:

> I came to Darr's Town Expecting to meet the Boat and Get my Baggage on Board; but it was Gone, and the only account left for me was that they would push as far as possible. No alternative was Left; I was obliged to take my Baggage on my Back and follow the Boat, which I did and to ad to the Disagreeable situation in which the Boat left me to shift for my self it Began to Rain, and night came on before I could hear any certain acc't where the Boat had stopped. However, I continued to follow until about 10 o'clock at night, althow the Road was very Bad and the Night wet and Dark, and found them at James McLaughlin's nearly opposite the mouth of Warrior Run.

Timothy's behavior was perhaps a sign of lingering anger over his political evisceration. At fifty-four years of age he was in urgent need of work. And his bid to make the current trip more lucrative had been denied.

Thirteen. Savannah, Georgia

The expedition traveled up the West Branch of the Susquehanna from Sunbury. By the end of May the men were on the Sinnemahoning Creek. Maclay complained about painful rheumatism and steady rain. On the last day of the month, at an impassable shoal, the party decided to make canoes. During the delay Maclay and Matlack avoided each other. It was Maclay and Adlum who climbed a "verry high" mountain and it was Matlack and Adlum who walked up after dinner "to see how the canoe making came on." Maclay stayed behind and "assisted the boys at Baking Bread." This meal and "a dish of tea concluded the month of May."

When the canoes were ready the expedition continued up the Sinnemahoning and its northern branch, the Driftwood, while a team of pack horses followed with their equipment. The men fished, hunted, and caught a few beaver. At the end of the day they pitched their tents and prepared their meals. Maclay said he wanted it remembered he made a plum pudding in a bag, "as fine a one as I ever ate." One evening, Maclay complained, two men and two boys appeared in a canoe: "They discovered an inclination to stay all night at our fire, without either being invited or asking leave; their conversation was of hunting, and though in general fond of hearing hunting Feats, they in order to appear Singular made themselves Exceedingly disagreeable."

In mid–June Maclay took a party to survey the westerly Bennett branch of the Sinnemahoning and a fourteen-mile portage to Little Toby's Creek. But his mission failed when a man failed to return to camp. A cranky Maclay complained that "the creek falling, the favorable opportunity for which I had waited steeling away, and I by this accident totally prevented from prosecuting my intended journey." His generalized grievance was that making progress was becoming increasingly difficult. Provisions were running low and "I find myself much fatigued."

The meat supply was augmented one Thursday afternoon when the men shot at a "Doe Elk." A fawn appeared at the creek and Maclay "shot and killed it on the spot." A short time later a dog caught a second fawn. Maclay said, "I then ordered a fire and the Kettle to be put on and Determined to stay and feast for the night."

In the morning, having run out of flour, Maclay and his men got to work on a small supply of Indian meal. They made "some Dumplings and Boiled them in our Chocolate, and made with the addition of a slice of Bacon, a very hearty Breakfast."

The three leaders reconvened near the end of June at a twenty-three-mile portage between the Driftwood and the head of the Allegheny. When Matlack and Maclay took a walk up the river a heavy rain wet them to the skin. Maclay spent a very disagreeable night: he was suffering from a "most Violent Tooth ach" that lasted three days.

On July 2, at Potato Creek, two Indians arrived with a message. Their chief wanted to know if they were coming for a visit and when they would arrive. All traveled and camped together over the next two days. At one stop one of the Indians, Doctor Thomas, got a little drunk and decided to show off his horsemanship. But in attempting to ride up a steep bank, "him and his horse tumbled together into the River."

Arriving at the Indian town on Sunday the men learned Chief Con-ne-Shangon was away but that Captain John would make a speech in his stead. The Indian told the visitors the women and children were starving.

On July 7 the river commissioners met with the Seneca leader Cornplanter. Cornplanter was the son of a Dutch trader, Johannes Abeel, and a Seneca woman named Aliquipiso. The men were carrying a letter for Cornplanter, which was read and interpreted by a man named Mathews. The chief answered by saying he was glad to see the white men and they were welcome to anything they could catch in his country.

After Cornplanter's speech the men heard the discourse of the Seneca women, as delivered by an orator. The women said that as the "severst part of the labour of living fell to their Lot, they had a right to Speak and to be heard." The women thanked the men for the news that a good road was to be made. They thought once this was done they would be able to purchase the things they needed on better terms. The women said trade was "much worse than formerly," due to the scarcity of game, but it would be worthwhile for traders to come if there was a good road. They hoped a "Good Correspondence would still be cultivated between them and us untill we should become one people." Maclay said their speech was answered "verrey Properly by Col'l Matlack." Afterwards the visiting party departed in the rain. The following night they camped near "Capt'n Jno. Obeal's Town and had the honor of his Company at supper." This visitor was Cornplanter's father.

* * *

The Seneca returned the visit that fall. Matlack served as host to Cornplanter, Half Town and Great Tree during their four-month stay in Philadelphia. On October 24, 1790, Timothy Matlack and Assemblyman Jacob Hiltzheimer attended a reception for the Indian guests.

The attendees were probably unaware that two days earlier, in the Northwest Territory of the Ohio River, American forces under Brigadier General Josiah Harmar, the onetime member of the Quaker Blues, were crushed by Shawnee and Miami warriors in the Battle of the Pumpkin Fields.

On December 1, 1790, Matlack certified Cornplanter's written address to President George Washington, "the Great Counsellor of the Thirteen Fires." Cornplanter's paper appealed to the president for the protection of the lands left to the Six Nations by the treaty of Fort Stanwix, signed in October 1784. At Stanwix, Cornplanter said, American officials had demanded and taken a large tract in exchange for peace, "as if our want of strength had destroyed our rights." Since then, he said, the land left to the Six Nations had been impinged upon by all manner of commissioners, agents and swindlers. Cornplanter asked the president, "You have said that we are in your hand, and that, by closing it, you could crush us to nothing. Are you determined to crush us?" Cornplanter said solemnly, "The land we live on, our fathers received from God, and they transmitted it to us for our children, and we cannot part with it."[5]

Washington said he wished the miseries of the late war be forgotten and that in the future the United States and the Six Nations should be truly brothers. He said, "The President of the United States declares, that the general government considers itself bound to protect you in all the land secured to you by the treaty of fort Stanwix," not later sold to authorized persons. In conclusion he promised, "The sale of your lands in future will depend entirely upon yourselves," and "the United States will be true and faithful to their agreement."[6] In response Cornplanter made it clear the offer was inadequate and asked for the return of some of the Fort Stanwix land. Cornplanter wrote, "Father, Your speech, written on the great paper, is to us like the first light of morning to a sick man, whose pulse beats to strongly in his temples— he sees it and rejoices, but is not cured."[7] His request was denied by Washington that same month. Cornplanter, Half Town and Big Tree sent a farewell address thanking Washington for his pledges and said they planned to send nine Seneca boys to Philadelphia to be educated by the whites.

* * *

After visiting Cornplanter's village, Matlack and Maclay, having made their peace, traveled together down the Allegheny and up Conewango Creek to Chautauqua Lake. On Tuesday, July 13, Maclay wrote, the men "set off after breakfast; the morning perfectly calm and the whole face of the Lake as far as the Eye could see, as smooth as Glass; the country beyond the Lake Rose Gradually, and was covered entirely in Oak, now in Bloom." At the head of the lake they stopped to camp and caught a three-foot northern pike which they cooked and ate for dinner. The next morning the men set off to follow the old French road to Lake Erie. In many places cart ruts left by the French army were visible. "We walked in High Spirits untill Between Ten and Eleven O'clock when we were met by a Verrey heavy Rain, which lasted until near one o'clock." The men continued on in the rain and came to the lake just as the shower ended, "as wet as water could make us." That night they slept in an old Indian cabin.

On July 20 the party arrived at Fort Franklin on the Allegheny. Here they "dined and supped with the commanding officer who was exceedingly obliging and attentive." The party traveled up French Creek to LeBoeuf Creek where Maclay, not feeling well, decided to stay behind. That night Matlack and Adlum slept in an old fort. The next day they examined the long portage, which was part of an alternative route to Lake Erie. On August 5 the party camped at the juncture of the Allegheny and Toby's Creek (the Clarion River). Heavy rain fell that night. Matlack and Adlum explored this waterway while Maclay continued down to the Kiskiminetas. Matlack and Adlum rejoined an impatient Maclay on August 18. The party started up the Kiski but struggled to find fresh provisions. Rain continued to fall, and a tent fell off a pack horse. The men sent back to find the shelter had no luck; it was thought a man and a boy from the Jerseys, whom they had passed on the road, had picked it up. Maclay said he had no doubt "they played us a Jersey Trick." The end of the month was spent surveying the Conemaugh River on foot.

On September 1 the men came to a section of the road which would eventually link the Juniata and Conemaugh rivers. In this area, near Puzzletown and Blue Knob Mountain, the men surveyed a potential continuation through Poplar Gap, but their road hunting ended without success. On September 7 Matlack and Maclay stayed at Lowery's tavern in Frankstown, drinking late into the night. The next day Matlack bought mutton and a beat-up canoe from a Dutchman. In this vessel the men headed down the Juniata. On September 12, 1790, at a settlement called Water Street, the trip came to an end. The men arranged their business and made plans for their report. The next day Matlack got on a horse and headed for home.

On the rivers of western Pennsylvania Timothy Matlack made his peace. In April he had arrived in Lebanon in a foul mood. Now in September he was going home in high spirits. Sometime during those summer months, perhaps on that perfectly calm morning on Lake Chautauqua, he had come to terms with the past. Looking out on the face of the lake, as smooth as glass, he had felt the quiet of his own countenance, and the rain, later that day, washed his spirit clean.

It was the start of a new era. Washington was the country's first president. And near the end of the river trip Pennsylvania had adopted a new constitution. On September 2 Jacob Hiltzheimer had celebrated the adoption of the new frame at City Tavern. President Washington had come down from New York for the day's events. Ironically it was in the new state Senate that Timothy Matlack found his lifeline: he was named clerk of the Senate in December 1790.

Fourteen
The Revolution of 1800

Now that the War of Independence was over, friends and family hoped Timothy Matlack would rejoin the Society of Friends. In March 1791, Timothy made a visit to David Cooper, his sister Sybil's widower, in New Jersey. Cooper told his daughter Martha, "Thy uncle Timothy came on Seventh-day evening. His visit was very agreeable to us. I think he is more serious than in times past, but he would not go to meeting. What a shining instrument might he have been, had he kept to what he once knew."[1]

Friends and family who had returned to the Quaker fold included Owen Biddle and Timothy's brother-in-law, Peter Yarnall. Yarnall had been a surgeon's mate in the war. Alexander Graydon, a captain in the Continental Army, called him "a singular character and degenerate son of Mordecai Yarnall, a Quaker preacher." Graydon recalled Peter's talent for entertaining audiences with impersonations of Quaker ministers, especially his own father. Yarnall must have been acting out what was in his true heart because he later made his peace with the Society of Friends and became a curate.[2]

Ellen Yarnall Matlack, who had hoped and prayed for her husband's religious renewal, passed away on July 16, 1791. She was buried the next day, a clear and pleasant Sunday. Her body was taken from her home on Front Street, above Arch, to the Free Quaker graveyard on the west side of Fifth Street below Locust. Jacob Hiltzheimer said he walked in the procession with Andrew Geyer, a captain in Matlack's old battalion.

Nelly Matlack had lived to see the birth of Billy's second son, James, in February 1791. Billy lost his wife Hannah in 1793, the year a devastating yellow fever epidemic hit Philadelphia.

The yellow fever contagion was carried into the city by French refugees escaping the Haitian Revolution. It was not discovered until much later that mosquitoes spread the disease by transfusing the blood of sick people into healthy ones. The fever struck in early August, and more than 4,000 people were dead by early November. Cold weather finally killed off the mosquito population. Timothy's brother-in-law, Samuel Wetherill, chaired the first meeting of the Yellow Fever Committee on September 12 but stopped attending when the number of daily burials skyrocketed.[3]

The progression of the illness was rapid. Early fever-like symptoms often subsided before signs of jaundice appeared. From that point, Dr. William Currie wrote, the patient started a frightening downward spiral: "a vomiting of matter, resembling coffee grounds ... commonly called the black vomit ... succeeded by hemorrhages from the nose, [tonsils], gums and other parts of the body — a yellow purple colour, and putrescent appearance of the whole body ... comatose delirium and finally death." Richard Allen and Absalom Jones wrote, "Some lost their reason and raged with all the fury madness could produce, and died in strong convulsion."[4] The virus killed its victims very quickly — sometimes only days after the mosquito bite.

Those with strong religious views found just cause for the epidemic. In her dream a twelve-year-old girl named Tamar Roberts saw black wagons filled with human bodies "and the Screeches of Men, Women & Children terrifying to mine ears beyond Expression." Her guide told her the plague had been sent on to the people of the great City of Philadelphia for their "Pride, Deceit and other Backslidings."[5]

Yellow fever motivated wealthy Philadelphians to build houses away from the city. In 1794 Anthony Morris purchased land in Whitemarsh, and in June 1795 masons began construction of a manor house designed by T. Matlack, architect. Matlack also designed the estate's massive three-level stone barn and its two-story springhouse.[6]

In 1797 Timothy Matlack, now sixty-one, married Elizabeth Claypoole Cooper at Christ Church. Timothy's new wife was the widow of Captain Norris Cooper and the daughter of James Claypoole, the former sheriff, and Mary Chambers. Elizabeth's sister Mary was married to the artist James Peale, younger brother of Charles Willson Peale. Elizabeth's brother was the printer David Claypoole.

Yellow fever may have forced Timothy and his new bride to flee Philadelphia. Jacob Hiltzheimer wrote on August 17, their wedding day, "A malignant contagious fever has lately appeared in Pine street of which 10 or 12 persons have died. This is about the time the fever began in 1793 and continued to November 9 in which time 4042 died."[7]

Timothy lost his son William in 1797. Perhaps Billy finally succumbed to his long-term disease. Timothy Matlack's great lifelong friend, Jacob Hiltzheimer, was killed by the fever the following year.

After Jacob's death, in September 1798, Timothy sat down to read the diaries the stable owner had started keeping in the days of the Stamp Act. Timothy must have been pleased to find his own name on so many pages. He

Fourteen. The Revolution of 1800

also found his own meticulous entries, made at the slaughterhouses. At the last of these gatherings the men weighed their greatest cow of all, Hiltzheimer's twenty-one hundred-pound ox, Commodore Hawser Trunnion.

Hiltzheimer's diaries were records of pleasant days. The friends had supped at Mathias Slough's White Swan Tavern at Center Square; rode sleighs to Darby; and watched fireworks at the State House on the fifth anniversary of the Declaration. They had gone to see plays like *The Mourning Bride*; looked for a comet at four in the morning; and on Thursday, November 28, 1782, shared a day of Thanksgiving. They had seen Mr. Templeman "perform on the wire and flying down a rope." And Mr. Blanchard send up his balloon, "which carried up about a mile, his parachute wherein was a dog, a cat and a squirrel." On a cold day in late January 1774, they had seen hundreds of men and boys skating on the Delaware and in April 1783, watched boys ride a carousel. Not all the memories were happy ones, but Timothy was in the mood to remember the beef steaks and the beer, and the horse races and the cider.

* * *

In the spring of 1799, in the midst of an undeclared war with France, Timothy Matlack, Charles Biddle and other veterans made plans to form a militia company. Though excused from duty, these feisty old gentlemen resented "the infamous and menacing conduct of the French." They felt disgust for their "horrid cruelty to many of their own best citizens, particularly to a number of excellent females." The men held several meetings at Dunwoody's tavern, and Biddle said he was very pleased to see "such a number of hardy, jovial veterans as we mustered." He claimed many of them, though upwards of seventy, "were fit for almost any military duty, and would have fought as well as any men in the world had they been called into action." The men drew up articles of association in which they pledged to arm themselves with "a good musket, bayonet, cartridge box, and twenty-four charges of powder and ball." They talked of forming a cavalry troop, a more challenging endeavor. Biddle was reminded of the old City Troop, "very few of whom after the war could mount without going to a fence or horseblock."

It was another yellow fever outbreak that put a stop to these patriotic reunions. Biddle said the fever was so bad in town he was the only one who attended the last meeting at Dunwoody's.[8]

In the summer of 1799 Timothy and Elizabeth rented out their house in Mulberry Court, on Sixth Street near Market, and moved with the state government to Lancaster. Pennsylvania was entering a period of prosperity driven by agriculture and commerce. At the turn of the century, and even ten years later, Lancaster was one of only five towns in Pennsylvania with more than twenty-five hundred inhabitants (the others being Philadelphia, Pittsburgh, Reading and York). The overwhelming majority of the state's population lived in rural areas. Agriculture drove domestic exports, and Pennsylvania was also a leader in reexporting foreign goods. In the early nineteenth century Philadelphia was the country's financial center, and Pennsylvania led the country in producing manufactured goods.[9]

Matlack had been clerk of the Senate for more than eight years. The 1790 Constitution had installed a bicameral legislature and a governor with veto power. In conceding to these changes Constitutionalists negotiated direct election of all legislators and the governor. No property was required for office.[10]

One political opponent wrote that a "concurrence of fortuitous circumstances" had allowed Matlack to "rise out of insignificance" by gaining the office of clerk. This writer said the candidates for the office had been Samuel Bryan and three other men: none named Timothy Matlack. While Federalists held a slim majority in the Senate, the anti–Federalist Bryan, son of George Bryan, had been the frontrunner. The race was upended, according to the writer, when the Federalist leader William Lewis suggested Matlack as a last-minute candidate capable of defeating Bryan. Matlack won by two votes. The antagonistic writer claimed the senators who voted for him were "aristocrats, old tories or royalists." Any doubts Timothy may have had about playing spoiler for his old rivals were overcome by his need for employment. These unlikely sponsors had opened a door, and Matlack had walked through.

By the fall of 1799 Matlack was closely allied with the Democratic-Republican candidate for governor: Thomas McKean. Having used the Federalists to make his comeback, Matlack now joined the party that shared his ideology. The Democratic-Republicans were heirs to the Constitutionalists. Their core belief was in popular rule: they thought the people capable of self-government. This party emphasized the rights of man and liberty, while Federalists were obsessed with property rights and order.[11] William Duane, publisher of the Democratic-Republican *Aurora,* said his party was supported by the farmers on the land and the manufacturers in the cities and towns. He said Federalism was the party of the wealthy lawyers, merchants and physicians who thought themselves the nation's natural aristocracy.[12]

In the campaign McKean called the opposition "traitors, tories, refugees, French aristocrats, British friends and apostate whigs, together with all the officers of government, and expectants of office under the President of the United States [John Adams]."[13] McKean's victory was a triumph for Timothy Matlack, as a newspaper recalled with bitterness:

> The state resounded with the fame of your achievements, against the federalists and tories. The red cap of liberty was, on every public occasion, carried by you,

Fourteen. The Revolution of 1800

in pompous triumph, at the head of processions, through the streets of Lancaster! No strutting cock could look so wondrous big, in his own estimation, than you did, when acting as the champion of democracy.[14]

This newspaper claimed Matlack threw his support behind McKean when he learned Federalists planned to supersede him as clerk. Previously, the opponent insisted, Matlack had "almost lived at Slough's, the headquarters of federalism, and [Federalist gubernatorial candidate James] Ross's friends." This pungent political penman claimed that during the campaign Matlack had "bel-

Timothy Matlack in 1802. Painting. Philadelphia: Rembrandt Peale, 1802. Courtesy National Gallery of Art, Washington, DC.

lowed so loud in [McKean's] favor, that the governor, blinded to your selfish, interested views, believed you to be a genuine disinterested friend that would even sacrifice your life for him, if necessary!" The vehemence of the attack is a testament to Matlack's significance in this campaign. And so was the victory march that followed.

At the end of November the victorious McKean made a triumphant arrival in Lancaster. At a feast in his honor four hundred citizens took their seats around a three-hundred-foot table. Matlack offered one of the seventeen toasts that were each followed by a salute from a corps of militia. Later a parade of militia and dignitaries escorted the new governor to his lodgings ... at Timothy Matlack's house.

After the election the governor rewarded Matlack, who kept his position in the Senate, with a second office. This was master of the rolls, or state recorder.

Federalists, by contrast, were soon complaining about Governor McKean's energetic removal of their party members from office.[15] Federalists despised the appointees who replaced their people. Five of these, they said, were Timothy Matlack, Tench Coxe, William Barton, Frederick Muhlenberg and John Light. Calling these men the beneficiaries of cronyism, Federalists attacked their records. Coxe, they said, had joined the British in 1776 and performed as a knight in their infamous Meschianza. The Federalist press said he had appeared on horseback, dressed in black, carrying a sword and a shield painted with the inscription: "Nolumus leges Anglie mutar!" [The laws of England shall last forever!]. Coxe was attainted for treason but switched to the American side after the British evacuation of Philadelphia.[16] Federalist attacks on Timothy Matlack left out the relevant detail that his predecessor had died in office.

McKean's gubernatorial victory was a harbinger of the presidential election of 1800. Federal government under the Federalists had largely favored the commercial and moneyed classes. Farmers, mechanics, small tradesmen and laborers, although the greater part of the population, had received "less obvious benefits" than the elites. Democratic-Republicans denounced the control of government by aristocrats and the expansion of federal power at the expense of the states.

Pennsylvania had had firsthand experience with Alexander Hamilton's high-Federalist measures: Philadelphia had served as the nation's capital for almost ten years. In recent years Federalists had taken advantage of the threat of war with France to pass measures "of almost unparalled political stupidity." The ingrained Federalist belief that government served "the wealthy, the wise, and the good" made it impossible for them to initiate programs that would appeal to the common people.[17]

Now in the national election Matlack once again drew fire from the opposition. He was once again a man they feared. In the battle for electoral college seats his adversaries dusted off a revolution-era anecdote:

> The Cockfighter, Timothy Matlack having one day gaff'd himself, by putting on a long sword, was met by a friend [Quaker] who wished to know why he wore a Rapier — Tim replied, it was to defend his *liberty* and *property*. As to *property*, rejoined the friend, it is well known that thee never hadst any; and as to thy liberty, thou art now indebted to thy creditors for that.[18]

But this recycled attack was ineffective: Matlack won an electoral seat and cast the two votes on his ballot for Thomas Jefferson and Aaron Burr. Under Constitution rules the top vote-getter would be elected president and the second place finisher vice president.

The Democratic-Republican candidates defeated the Federalist incumbents, John Adams and Charles Cotesworth Pickney, but, in a voting snafu, Jefferson and Burr tied each other with seventy-three votes each. Neither had won the presidency. In the House of Representatives, Federalists now worked to deny their nemesis, Thomas Jefferson, the presidency. Their plan was to elevate Burr to the top office. Federalists succeeded in blocking the Virginian's ascension during a grueling sequence of thirty-five ballots, but Jefferson was finally named president on February 17, 1801.

Pennsylvania's Democratic-Republicans felt they had played the major role in Jefferson's victory: they considered their state the "key stone in the democratic arch." The Pennsylvanians felt Thomas McKean's victory had set the stage for Thomas Jefferson's. The election of 1800 triggered the decline of the party of the wealthy. Pennsylvania was a democratic cornerstone throughout the Jefferson era.

In Pennsylvania's state elections of 1803, a group of officeholders led by Timothy Matlack started a fledgling third-party movement in support of Governor McKean, who was losing popularity with core Democratic-Republicans. One critic said Matlack had made an earlier foray of this type: "He was connected with a party in Philadelphia which without going the whole lengths of the *third party,* contributed to encourage such a faction by their interested, temporasing, and affected moderation."

In the current campaign Matlack and his associates, who included James Hopkins, Charles Smith, William Barton and Andrew Ellicott, hoped to win seats in the legislature for their allies. The *Lancaster Intelligencer* said Matlack took a lead role in the campaign. The paper's unhappy editor addressed him directly: "The glare of patriotic professions had given you considerable popularity; and your brazen effrontery, it was calculated, would bear down all opposition from the discerning republicans." At a county meeting of the Democratic-Republican Party, Matlack stepped to the stage to propose a mixed ticket (combining Democratic-Republicans with certain Federalist allies) but, the *Intelligencer* reported with scorn, "before you had spoken 10 minutes, instead of 3 hours, as you said you intended to do, there was nearly a universal burst of indignation; and you were obliged to desist, and sit down." Matlack, the paper said, later requested permission to deliver his whole speech but was silenced by a "general hiss of contempt." The *Intelligencer* was more than pleased by what it said was Matlack's humiliation: "Never did inflated vanity experience a more unexpected, or more severe mortification. *Even your enemies pitied you!*"[19]

The Democratic-Republican *Aurora* found motive in this third-party movement beyond winning state offices. It accused McKean of aspiring to replace Thomas Jefferson as president and his "sycophant" Matlack of yearning to supplant Henry Dearborn as secretary of war.[20]

When the third party candidates lost the election, Matlack, the *Lancaster Intelligencer* claimed, was forced to backpedal. At a lightly attended dinner for legislators, "you took the occasion to give a pompous display of the *wonders* you had performed as a *statesman* and a *warrior,* for the good of your country; and denied, in terms of pointed and emphatic indignation, the charges made against you, of having joined the third party."

Matlack regained the authority he had lost in the Democratic-Republican Party in time for the national election of 1804. In December, Pennsylvania's electors chose Charles Thomson as chairman and Timothy Matlack as secretary.

Under the twelfth amendment to the Constitution electors now specified their choices for president and vice president. In Pennsylvania the electors' unanimous picks were Thomas Jefferson and George Clinton. President Jefferson and his running mate were the winners. In a letter to Thomson, Matlack raved about the new voting procedure: "The simplicity of the proceeding ... must astonish Europe, where such torrents of blood have been shed on such occasions; and one would think, would, of itself, recommend to every nation, the glorious elective principle on which our Republic is founded."[21]

In April 1805, in Pennsylvania, Democratic-Republicans broke completely from Governor McKean and nominated Samuel Snyder to replace him. The third party started by Matlack and his allies in 1803 — now called the Constitutional Republicans or Tertian Quids — regrouped to champion McKean's reelection. In the political battle that followed, which focused on constitutional reform, Matlack once again became a "prominent instrument to promote [the third party] views." In a print war the Quids were backed by the new *Freeman's Journal* while William Duane's *Aurora* continued as the powerful Democratic-Republican organ. The *Aurora* attacked Matlack: "Shameless man! you need not go from home, to produce the greatest phenomenon of effrontery, disingenuity, inconsistency, egotism, and folly; in short, of high sounding professions of public spirit, and pompous exhibitions of science and various merit, without any reality."[22] The paper added an unflattering review of Matlack's career:

> During the revolutionary war, when the ordinary restraints of law were suspended, you rendered yourself, in some degree, conspicuous, by an arrogant and turbulent disposition, which was particularly well adapted to a state of anarchy: Having no property to lose; and being indebted, for your *personal liberty, to the bounty of your creditors*; you roared very loud, in favor of liberty and property, as the means of rising into some consequence.[23]

Another critic said during the Revolution Matlack had led a party of "mercantile characters who wished to steer between the Scylla of politics and the Charybdis of the banks." The *Aurora* wished to remind Matlack that when "regular government" was reestablished, after the Revolution, he had been dispatched to anonymity. Now, from the lofty heights he had

Fourteen. The Revolution of 1800

again achieved, the editor told him, "you must soon descend, to your native level!"

But another writer defended Matlack as "a most active and staunch whig during the revolution." Timothy's temperament, the penman explained, pulled him into political storms. Conflict was a part of Matlack's nature: "he would perish in a calm, and prosper in a tempest." Timothy's mettle made him an effective politician: with his support McKean was reelected in 1805.

Matlack's political revival in this period was his vindication: his rise in the Revolution was no fluke. In both eras his opponents feared his political skills. Their constant vitriol was a testament to his value as an advocate for his candidate of choice. And while McKean and Jefferson were happy to have Matlack on their side, it was the farmers, craftsmen and laborers who made Pennsylvania "resound" with the "fame" of his "achievements."

The rise of Jeffersonian democracy was another vindication for Matlack. As one of Pennsylvania's 1776 radicals, Matlack had helped formulate a structure for a more equal society.

* * *

As nonvoters, women were not directly involved in the struggle for democratic rights. Their options in life were, of course, limited. While some ran taverns and shops, or worked as private tutors, the majority spent their lives serving men. Women served their husbands, and also bachelors and widowers: no decent man kept his own household. Women served men as indentured servants, family members, hired workers, and slaves.

When Timothy's first wife died he looked for help in a way that made the most economic sense. His circumstance, and financial motive, led to his moral failure.

Fifteen

Common Sense Revisited

In 1805 a visitor to Lancaster, Augustus Foster, observed that Timothy Matlack was living in "easy Circumstances." His government employment provided a comfortable income. Timothy took "great delight" in working in his garden, which was on the summit of the hill in the center of town. Matlack had carried the "Cultivation of Peach Trees to great Perfection" and had "28 different Sorts in his Orchard."[1] Foster said Matlack used

> the Horns and Hoofs of Cattle as Manure, preferring the Horns entire, or when he could not obtain them in that state, using Comb Makers Shavings. The Horns, he said, when laid under the Earth at the depth of 2 1/2 feet from the Surface became Receptacles for air, and gave Health to the Roots making the Plant thrive more vigorously.

In March 1807, President Jefferson wrote to thank Matlack for a shipment of fruit trees: "You have very much gratified me by the collection of choice fruit trees you have been so good as to forward me. It is gone on to Monticello to which I will follow it in a few days." These trees, Matlack had told Jefferson, would produce "the most juicy and highest flavoured of all the Clingstone peaches.... It retains more of the peach flavour in *brandy* than any other."[2]

But in October Jefferson wrote again to tell him the cart carrying the trees had been caught in severe weather. By the "impassableness of the roads & breaking down of the cart [the trees] were so long out that not a single one survived." Jefferson said he would not trouble Matlack for replacements until he went home for good. He expected to do so in March 1809. Jefferson asked Matlack to send "excellent pears, peaches, or grapes" a month before his retirement:

> I shall be able to carry & plant them myself at Monticello where I shall then begin to occupy myself according to my own natural inclinations, which have been so long kept down by the history of our times; and I shall bid a joyful adieu to politics and all the odious passions & vices of which they make us the object

in public life. I should be very much pleased to see you at Monticello & to prove to you that my heart has always been there, altho my body has been every where, except there, since our first acquaintance in 1775.³

In February 1807, Timothy Matlack — now seventy years old — published instructions for making a pumice press, a device he designed to crush fruit for wine, perry and hard cider. A Philadelphia newspaper said his contraption "consists of a combination of levers ... calculated to effect every advantage in the shortest time, and, being portable ... cannot fail to recommend itself to the use of distillers, cider-makers and vintners."⁴

In 1808 the Philadelphia Society for Promoting Agriculture published Matlack's guide to making hard cider. The apples recommended by the author, who had "tried very many for more than forty eight years back," were the Vandever, the Cooper's sweet russet, and the famous Virginia crab. Matlack had used the latter variety in 1777 to make an effervescent cider, which, a correspondent said, had been "so much approved by the French minister."⁵

With his press Matlack was also making wine from currants, blackberries, quinces and grapes. An article he wrote for the Agriculture Society, while "lame by an accident and confined," was a detailed how-to on viticulture. He was well aware of Burgundy, Morrillon and Tokay grapes, but his inherent preference was for local varieties from New Jersey, Virginia and the Carolinas. That the American continent was ideal for grape production, Matlack said, was made evident by the "spontaneous production of the vine in every part of the sea coast, from Georgia to Maine, and to the westward as far as we know." Had "General Washington lived to this day," he wrote, "I would have said to him ... that, after saving the world from a political deluge, thou hast not yet planted a vineyard."⁶

* * *

Timothy Matlack had held the office of master of the rolls for ten years. Covering for him during an illness, in February 1809, was his grandson Timothy Matlack. This Timothy Matlack was Billy's twenty-one-year-old son. But Governor McKean's term as governor had ended and Matlack's office was abolished in March.⁷

Timothy and his wife Elizabeth moved back to Philadelphia in June 1810. Matlack announced he had opened a shop at 65 North Second Street offering tea, wine, cider and ale. He invited his friends to join him in honoring the Fourth of July with a few demijohns "that shall *do honor to the day*."⁸

But the case of a woman named Hester exposed Matlack's evasion of a law his government had specifically linked to the cause of the American Revolution. In 1780 Paine said, "We conceive it is our duty, and we rejoice that it is in our power to extend a portion of that freedom to others, which hath been extended to us; and a release from that state of thralldom to which we ourselves were tyrannically doomed." The Assembly that passed Act for Gradual Abolition had added:

> It is not for us to enquire why, in the creation of mankind, the inhabitants of the several parts of the earth were distinguished by a difference in feature or complexion. It is sufficient to know that all are the work of an Almighty Hand.... He who hath placed them in their various situations, hath extended equally his care and protection to all, and that it is becometh not us to counteract his mercies.

Both John Woolman, the abolitionist, and Timothy Matlack were grandsons of Henry Burr, a man who freed a slave upon his death. While manumissions were rare in 1742, Burr may have been influenced by a hunch-backed, cave-dwelling, Quaker abolitionist named Benjamin Lay. Timothy remembered Lay's long white beard and a physical defect: "One of his legs was shorter than the other — and they were [both] extremely small."[9] In an antislavery demonstration Lay shocked the 1738 Quaker Yearly Meeting by spraying the audience with red juice he had stored inside a bible-like black case. If Lay moved Henry Burr to take action, his slave Maria was the beneficiary. Timothy remembered the day this free woman was introduced to one of his own sons: a boy who was in fact her former master's great grandson. Timothy was surprised to see "tears of affection flow from her aged eyes." Maria's display of humanity was something he never forgot. When Maria passed away Matlack wrote the epitaph for her gravestone, and in the years that followed he stayed in contract with her "industrious" family.

Having grown up amid progressive Quakers, Timothy Matlack acquired a special interest in the lives of people of African descent. Timothy said that when his uncle Peter White died, he set free a family of slaves. These people went on to own property, and one of them was Timothy's oldest acquaintance in life, in the years of their shared old age.

During the Revolution Matlack was repeatedly attacked for his tendency to consort with black people. One antagonist wrote:

> And yet, you know, with truth 'twas said,
> Your hapless babes oft' wanted bread;
> While *you*, unfeeling, idled time
> With Negroes— Cuff and Warner's PRIME[10]

Timothy had learned to respect the black people he knew as valuable citizens. One such person was a sailmaker who told Timothy he had received seven thousand dollars in orders from one mercantile house in a single year.[11]

Timothy Matlack later wrote a legalistic defense of the rights of slaves. In 1783 he published a plea for compassion in the case of five men, several of

Fifteen. Common Sense Revisited

whom were slaves, condemned to death for robbery. Led by a man named Kemble Stackhouse, the men had stolen a boat in an escape attempt. Matlack said that every man had a right by the law of nature to use every means in his power to effect his escape. He also asked: "Would he not have the right to make reprisals upon the state whose barbarous laws authorized that slavery; or even upon individuals of that state, so far as necessary to effect his escape?"[12] The idea that a slave had the right to sue his or her owner, or even the state, was clearly radical.

But however concerned for the fate of Africans held in slavery, Timothy Matlack was also susceptible to the general perception of black inferiority. In 1817, during the colonization debate, he wrote, "From what I have seen in the Mayor's Court of this city, of the conduct of the people of colour among us, much reason have I to doubt if they are much improved by their residence among us."[13]

In 1811, in Philadelphia's County Court of Common Pleas, Timothy Matlack found himself opposed by the Abolition Society in the case of "Negress Hester." Hester was a young slave Matlack purchased after the death of his first wife. Any moral concern about doing this was trumped by personal necessity and economic advantage: Timothy needed a housekeeper, and a slave could be sold at a later date to recover the cost.

After years of service in his household, Matlack "manumitted" his slave on her eighteenth birthday and bound her out to a man named Thomas Murgatroyd. Hester was required to serve ten more years, but she absconded from her new master. When she was recaptured, years later, a court sentenced her to five years additional servitude. At that point Matlack apparently repurchased her indenture and brought her back to serve in his household. But Hester escaped again. In September 1811, at the age of 31, she was *again* recaptured and sent back to prison. At this point the Abolition Society got involved in her case.

In the course of Hester's trial, held in the Philadelphia County Court of Common Pleas, Mr. Milnor, of the Abolition Society, made a crucial argument. He said that since her date of birth was August 17, 1780, she was actually born an indentured servant, not a slave. Moreover, she had never been registered. She was therefore a free woman.

The law that defined her legal status was Act for Gradual Abolition. Matlack's lawyer did not argue the fact of her status but countered that his client had purchased Hester's unserved time on the faith of the lower court's decision. If Hester was a free woman, he said, she should have made her defense before *that* court. Milnor countered that the question before this court had never been determined: "whether she was legally a slave at the time she was manumitted and bound to Murgatroyd, and whether she was lawfully bound to him."[14] Milnor added that since Hester was ignorant of the law and her rights, the decision of the lower court could not operate against her. The judge agreed and Hester was set free.

Hester's date of birth was apparently documented, as was her registration status. Matlack was either unaware of these biographical details or, more likely, chose to ignore them. Had Hester been registered as an indentured servant, she would have been forced to provide her unfree labor to the age of twenty-eight. By "manumitting" her at the age of eighteen, and binding her out for ten years, Matlack nominally complied with this age limit. But the law said her status changed when her first master, whoever that was, failed to register her as unfree. While still in infancy, she was, by law, released from servitude. She was a free woman.

Pennsylvania's abolition law was actively circumvented by President George Washington and many others. Washington, D.C., was conceived in part to avoid the inconvenience of state laws like this one. But as a man who came from a family of abolitionists, as a politician who sponsored Act for Gradual Abolition, Timothy Matlack should have done better. In the end he did not rise above his superiors on the question of slavery.

* * *

Timothy Matlack's great grandson Timothy C. Matlack was born on May 6, 1812. This Timothy's parents were James Matlack and Elizabeth Ristine. Elizabeth gave birth to seven more boys before her first daughter, Louisa, was born in 1835.

In the spring of 1812, Timothy C. Matlack's seventy-six-year-old great grandfather was looking for work. Matlack sent a letter to Thomas Jefferson to ask for a referral. The former president forwarded his letter, along with others, to President James Madison. Jefferson added his apologetic disclaimer:

> The difference between a communication & solicitation is too obvious to need suggestion. While the later adds to embarrassments, the former only enlarges the field of choice. The enclosed letters are merely communications.

But Jefferson also included his endorsement of the aged office seeker:

> Timothy Matlack I have known since the first Congress to which he was an assistant secretary. He has always been a good whig & being an active one has been abused by his opponents, but I have ever thought him an honest man. I think he must be known to yourself.

But President Madison was occupied with more urgent concerns. His predecessor offered his encouragement: "Your declaration of war is expected with perfect calmness."[15] The president declared war on Great Britain a week later.

Fifteen. Common Sense Revisited

In Philadelphia, in late June 1812, men who were too old for military service met at Oeller's tavern to plan for the defense of their city. Timothy Matlack was one of the "warmest Democrats" in the room. On July 1, at the Indian King, Republicans (formerly Federalists) joined the Democrats in a bipartisan assemblage of old gentlemen that drew up resolutions for the defense of the City and Liberties. But this bipartisan effort soon ran into trouble. While Democrats wanted to name their veterans' association "The Friend's of Government," Republicans preferred "Supporters of the Law." Attacks by the Society of American Republicans targeting Madison "gave great offense to some of the Democrats, and we were by no means as sociable as before." The men broke up without doing anything.[16]

Timothy Matlack was appointed a Philadelphia alderman in 1813. In 1817 the octogenarian was named prothonotary of the District Court of Philadelphia City and County. In June of that year he was on hand to welcome James Monroe, the fifth president of the United States. Five years later, in November 1822, Timothy Matlack was removed from office by Governor Heister. His career in politics had finally come to an end. At the age of eighty-six Timothy Matlack entered retirement. Timothy and Elizabeth gave up their house on Spruce Street soon thereafter.

* * *

It was about this time that a friend named Isaac R. Morris gave Timothy a gift: a worn copy of a pamphlet printed years earlier. Morris's present was well chosen. Matlack spent a few days rereading the small booklet, thinking about the things that happened to him nearly forty years back.

When Thomas Paine published *Common Sense* in January 1776, he set out to convince the North American colonists they were destined to leave the British Empire. Paine wanted the people to believe that after the rebellion they would live the rest of their lives as citizens of free and independent states. To this end he was completely successful.

Now Timothy took himself back to that eventful year. Perhaps in the morning light, when he could see best, he took a pen in hand and scratched through the pages, underlining words, writing comments and sketching little hands which pointed at undeniable truths. In Paine's introduction Matlack underlined, "The cause of America is in a great Measure the Cause *of all Mankind.*" After reading the writer's claim that "original sin and hereditary succession are parallels," Matlack scolded, "Tom. Thou hadst better have omitted this wicked comparison." Paine's economic plan for foreign commerce drew Matlack's ire: "No, Paine on no other occasion is so mistaken — the 'plan' of American —*Agriculture and Manufacture,* is the only rational plan of America proposed." Where Paine thought trade would offer America pro-

COMMON SENSE;

ADDRESSED TO THE

INHABITANTS

OF

AMERICA,

On the following interesting

SUBJECTS.

I. Of the Origin and Design of Government in general, with concise Remarks on the English Constitution.

II. Of Monarchy and Hereditary Succession.

III. Thoughts on the present State of American Affairs.

IV. Of the present Ability of America, with some miscellaneous Reflections.

Man knows no Master save creating HEAVEN,
Or those whom choice and common good ordain.
THOMSON.

PHILADELPHIA;
Printed, and Sold, by R. BELL, in Third-Street.
MDCCLXXVI.

Common Sense by Thomas Paine, 1776. Pamphlet. Philadelphia: R. Bell, January 10, 1776. Library of Congress, Prints and Photographs Division.

Fifteen. Common Sense Revisited

tection, Matlack said it had "constantly tended to expose us to the Tyranny of the Mistress of the Seas." When Paine contradicted himself later in the text Matlack underlined the passage in triumph: "*Commerce diminishes the spirit both of Patriotism and military defence.*" Matlack approved of Paine's assertion, "'*Tis not in the power of England or of Europe* to conquer America." This he underlined and pointed at with a little hand. Matlack wrote in the margin that it had been "A bold sentiment for its day."

Timothy agreed that "there is something very absurd, in supposing a *Continent to be perpetually governed by an island.*" He also concurred that the two lands "*belong to different systems, England to Europe; America to itself.*"

Paine had suggested Congress frame a "CONTINENTAL CHARTER." Reading this, a cranky Matlack scrawled a grandiose objection to the second word: "I hate the word *Charter*. It has always conveyed the idea of a Grant from a Superior. This is the trembling quick sand on which the liberty of Europe was quaking — until the idea of Grants is totally obliterated Europe never can be free." Paine's proposed system for rotating the office of president, to give each colony a turn, now horrified the writer's friend as a source of corruption: "For the smaller the majority the more readily our foreign enemy could purchase that number at a less price!!!!"

Matlack must have enjoyed Paine's jab at John Dickinson and his 1775 instructions to Pennsylvania's delegates in Congress: "A Set of instructions for the Delegates was put together, which in point of sense and business would have dishonoured a school-boy."[17]

But, perhaps above all, holding that copy of *Common Sense* in his hands, Timothy remembered how he had felt when he first read Paine's inspiring words: "We have it in our power to begin the world over again." When the pamphlet was published in January 1776 the former cockfighter and debtor was working for Congress as assistant secretary; commissary and clerk-in-chief of the Committee of Claims; and secretary of the Marine Committee. He had been elected colonel of Philadelphia's Fifth Battalion and was about to be made an officer of the Committee of Inspection. Two months after the publication of *Common Sense,* Matlack's committee would challenge the authority of the Pennsylvania Assembly. Thirty-nine at the time, Timothy *had* started his life over again: he had become a revolutionary.

Now it was time for others to remember as well. In 1821, on the forty-fifth anniversary of independence, America took special care to honor its aging revolutionary generation: no one knew how many of the old heroes would be alive for the semicentennial five years later. Newspapers around the country picked up the story of Philadelphia's Fourth of July celebration. The eighty-five-year-old patriot was honored as "the man, who, by order of the Old Congress, wrote the first commission for General Washington — who fought in defense of the same principles, and through life has maintained them — Our Venerable Chairman, TIMOTHY MATLACK — who, on the verge of *ninety* years of age, distinctly read the Declaration, to the adoption and establishment of which he had not inconsiderably contributed."[18] Another account called him "an early and persevering asserter of the principles of liberty, both in the cabinet and in the field.[19]

> At the Republican celebration of Independence in Philadelphia, the Declaration was read by TIMOTHY MATLACK : the subjoined toast, given at the dinner, is descriptive of this veteran.
>
> The man, who, by order of the Old Congress, wrote the first commission for General Washington—who fought in defence of the same principles, and through life has maintained them—Our Venerable Chairman, TIMOTHY MATLACK—who, on the verge of *ninety* years of age, distinctly read the Declaration, to the adoption and establishment of which he had not inconsiderably contributed.

News item printed in the *Providence Patriot* and other newspapers heralding Timothy Matlack reading of the Declaration of Independence on its 45th anniversary. Newspaper. *Providence Patriot*, July 14, 1781, v. 3 n. 56. Free Library of Philadelphia, infoweb.newsbank.com.

On September 27, 1824, a giant procession welcomed a universally known hero of the Revolution to Philadelphia. At the invitation of President Monroe, the Marquis de Lafayette had recently begun a triumphant year-long tour of the United States. In cities and towns and along country roads Lafayette, a man Washington loved like a son, was welcomed by Americans with an outpouring of love and respect. In 1781, as a secretary of the American Philosophical Society, Matlack sent a letter to Lafayette which anticipated this moment: "The breast of every virtuous American pants for an opportunity of expressing their gratitude and affection of the Marquis LaFayette from whom we have received so many important benefits and love of liberty." Lafayette answered that America

> Had formed itself upon a more liberal bazis, and here only the rights of mankind have been fully respected in a popular constitution — every American soldier must than cherish a society which, in keeping alive the sacred flame of liberty, shall answer the great purpose for which he fought and bled.[20]

Matlack's nephew, William Allinson, wrote that Lafayette visited his uncle Timothy in Holmesburg, Pennsylvania, "on his way from Bristol [back] to Philadelphia." This visit probably took place in July 1825, near the end of Lafayette's grand tour.[21]

* * *

Fifteen. Common Sense Revisited

In 1825 Timothy Matlack and his wife Elizabeth were living in a house owned by Timothy's daughter Martha and her husband Guy Bryan. The Matlacks employed a cook, Sarah M. Snyder, who had started working for them in April 1823, a few months after Timothy's retirement. Sarah's salary was $8.50 a week but now, two years later, she complained that she not been paid during her entire tenure in the Matlack kitchen. Martha paid her for her service, and Timothy signed a statement stating, "my wife and myself have been entirely dependent upon Mrs. Martha Bryan for support and the said Martha Bryan has paid for our maintenance from the above mentioned period to the present time." Timothy transferred to his daughter "all my household furniture of every description including the plate and plate ware of which I am possessed." As Timothy was almost ninety years old, he and Elizabeth were likely moved into the main Bryan house, where they could be better cared for. Their furniture was arranged in their rooms, to make them comfortable.

Early in that same year, 1825, Timothy was visited by a cousin named Asa Matlack. Asa described his arrival:

> Journeying along the Turnpike Road towards Holmesburgh or Goose Town.... I came to the Road leading from the Turnpike ... to Bustletown (to the west). A dwelling house belonging to Guy Bryan situate on the SW corner of these Roads, wherein I understood Timothy Matlack now lived, and calling in, was invited to sit down: in a short time came in Timothy; leaning on two large canes, holding one in each of his hands, by which he was enabled to walk about; now in his (89th year) he asked about Haddonfield the place where he was born in N.J.

Timothy sat down and got to talking about his childhood and his family. He could picture the Haddonfield of his youth, a colonial village with a meeting house and scattered shops surrounded by fields, woods, and a creek the boys followed down to the Delaware River. He told his cousin he remembered his three half-sisters, Priscilla, Letitia and Achsah, but that he had no memory of Abi (who died years before his birth). Timothy and Asa talked through the morning. At the end of his visit Asa wrote that "having been agreeably entertained at the house where I am from 9 till 12 Oclock; I took my farewell of Timothy Matlack and proceeded on the road towards Bustletown, passing the academy on my left."

But all was not well at the Bryan residence. Asa Matlack had wanted to talk to Timothy's son-in-law, Guy Bryan, but decided against it, "from the appearance of the house wherein they live & some account given me by J Enochs being unfavorable to my calling at this time."[22] Timothy's daughter, Martha Bryan, a woman who gave birth to fourteen children, was apparently sick. She died the following year at the age of fifty-five. Timothy's last living daughter was Catherine Murray.

Timothy Matlack in 1826. Print. Philadelphia: Samuel Sartain, 1895, after a painting by Charles Wilson Peale, Holmesburg, PA, 1826. Library of Congress, Prints and Photographs Division. (The painting is owned by Independence National Historic Park and is on display at the Portrait Gallery in the Second Bank.)

In June 1826, Charles Willson Peale came to paint Timothy Matlack's portrait for a second time.[23] Matlack had also sat for his son, Rembrandt Peale. Peale was impressed by the Bryan home, called Spring Hill, where he enjoyed "garden walks, distant views of the river, and the sumptuous table within—we feasted on raspberries and cream morning, noon and night."[24] Matlack and Peale had been friends and associates from the days when Timothy's brother Titus served as a lieutenant in Peale's company. Charles had "sat long and often across the table from Timothy, discussing the ins and outs of politics, the perpetual state of crisis in which they worked, seeing the man firm and blunt and belligerent."[25] Peale's earlier portrait of Matlack, "painted during those stormy years when they were so closely allied, is a strong and clear conception unsurpassed anywhere in his work."[26] Talk in town of the "patriarchal and venerable appearance of this solitary relic of a former century" had convinced Peale to paint a last portrait for his museum. He was also inspired by America's semicentennial. Of the painting he now made—which captured Timothy's long white beard and his red cap of liberty—Peale said only, "It is a good picture."

The following month Timothy Matlack quietly celebrated the fiftieth anniversary of American independence. Timothy was told of the passing of both Thomas Jefferson and John Adams on that day of national festivities. Charles Carroll of Carrollton, Maryland, was left as the last living signatory of the Declaration of Independence. Matlack and Carroll lived on.

Two years later William Allinson visited Timothy Matlack, now ninety-two years old. Allinson wrote, "He was clad in a loose morning gown, and a white cap somewhat resembling a turban, and his highly interesting countenance, his sightless, but expressive eyes and long white beard, indicated an age not normally allotted to mortals." Allinson inquired after his health, and Timothy replied, "I scarcely know how I am, or who I am, — where I am or what I am — I only know that I am alive and that's all."[27]

Perhaps Timothy wondered why. Why had he lived so long when so many in his family had died long ago? But another Matlack who lived a long life was Timothy's grandfather William. William Matlack lived to be ninety or ninety-one years of age and "would have lived longer (it was believed) if his tools had not been hid from him — for he took delight or pleasure in having his accustomed tools to work with — which when he could not have, it was remarkable he went away like the snuff of a candle — i.e. deceased."[28] Like his grandfather, Timothy's passion for life kept him alive. Timothy's delight was in discovering the world. Whether riding on Fitch's steamboat, proposing changes to Rittenhouse's open stove, writing about a remarkable thunderstorm, dissecting rattlesnakes, or examining a dinosaur bone, Matlack immersed himself in the world around him. In 1787 Timothy Matlack and Dr. Caspar Wistar read a paper before the American Philosophical Society, which was probably the first written report of the discovery of a dinosaur bone in America. Their paper described "a large thigh bone found in Upper Cretaceous deposits near Woodbury Creek, Gloucester County, N.J." Timothy also submitted a paper titled: "A large tusk found in the back country."[29]

The Revolution and the War of Independence took place during Philadelphia's Enlightenment: a period of rapidly expanding knowledge through scientific study. A product of his time, Timothy Matlack was fully absorbed in his city's intellectual environment. What Timothy loved most was to reason: to think and understand, to solve problems, and to persuade others by rational argument. But now Timothy's time had come to an end. Finally, when there was nothing left of him physically; when he could no longer think or see; when he could no longer discover; he let himself go. Timothy Matlack died on April 14, 1829. Two days later a procession carried his body from Holmesburg to the Free Quaker Burial Ground, on the west side of Fifth Street below Locust, where he was buried. A man named William Cannon was paid for the use of a hearse and two carriages. Peter Lesley provided a coffin with a red-cedar top, and Robert Dunn was the gravedigger.[30] Elizabeth moved in with her son, and the couple's furniture, which belonged to Martha's estate, was sold off in June.

In the Revolution, Timothy Matlack saw that the pursuit of liberty and democracy was the only reasonable course of action. If his main object was reason, not riches, he died contented. Knowing all he had lived, all he had done, and all that he left behind, he died in peace.

Epilogue

Charles Thomson was secretary of the Continental Congress throughout its fifteen years of existence: September 5, 1774, to March 2, 1789. Thomson kept a record of the proceedings in the Journal of the Congress. The Journal was published contemporaneously in thirteen volumes (the secret journal was published in 1821). Gaillard Hunt, chief of the Division of Manuscripts of the Library of Congress from 1909 to 1917, wrote of the original journal: "I have said that sometimes an entry was made in the journal of the Congress by another hand than Thomson's." The first such entry was made by Timothy Matlack on June 12, 1775. On that day he recorded a resolution for a day of fasting and prayer.

Hunt was introducing the subject of the identity of the Declaration scribe. In an effort to determine who he was, in 1916 Hunt compared the Declaration of Independence to Washington's commission, a document known to have been penned by Matlack:

> The first peculiar letter in the commission is the capital "N" in New Hampshire, and we find its counterpart in "Nature's" in the second line of the body of the Declaration. The graceful flourish at the top of "T" in the word "To" in the commission is repeated in the second of the sentences beginning "That" in the Declaration. In the word "offer" in the commission there is a marked peculiarity in the double "f"; the first "f" is made like the old fashioned long "s." It appears in the word "effect" in the Declaration, then in "suffer" and "sufferable." That is the most noteworthy peculiarity in Matlack's writing. The capital "D" in the commission and in the last line of the Declaration; the whole word "Congress" in both documents.[1]

Hunt concluded that these and other details "establish beyond a doubt that the writer of the great Declaration was Timothy Matlack."

For this author, who has seen numerous documents and letters signed by Matlack, the engrossed Declaration is his work. Hunt refers to Timothy's graceful capital "T." "T" is not only the most frequent first letter in the English language, is the first letter in the name Timothy. Capital "T" is Matlack's signature character. Timothy had the opportunity to wield his distinctive *T* repeatedly in the Declaration. Examples include the words *That*, *The*, *To*, and *Tyrant*. Timothy's *T* is his signature on the Declaration of Independence.

We know Matlack was in Philadelphia in the period between Congress's engrossment order and August 8, the day delegates began to sign. He had established himself as the delegates' preferred scribe for important documents. Timothy was not the only man who could produce a fine English round hand, but his calligraphy was especially graceful. Returning to handwriting analysis, Hunt, the Library of Congress official, did not mention the letter *M*, as in Matlack. Matlack's distinctive capital *M* can be found near the middle of the Declaration, in the word *Murders*.

* * *

In May 1779, Benedict Arnold contacted Sir Henry Clinton to offer his paid services to the British commander. His secret messengers were Joseph Stansbury and Dr. Jonathan Odell. In the months that followed both Stansbury and Odell published political satire in New York's *Royal Gazette*. Stansbury's "The Town Meeting" appeared in June and Odell's "The Word of Congress" in September.[2] One individual who figured in both of these works was Timothy Matlack. It was Stansbury's "sagacious Matlack" who harangued the town meeting that wanted to fix prices. His "artful Gaff" could not sway the "Rabble Rout" and the meeting chose a Committee. Jonathan Odell's verse offered the version of Timothy Matlack's life story most loved by his foes:

> Tim Matlack once had credit and esteem —
> His follies made them vanish as a dream —
> By his sober friends abandon't quite
> Game-cocks and negroes were his whole delight.
> Vagrant, and poor, his reputation slurr'd,
> He hasten'd to obey the factious word:
> Who now so active in the cause as Tim —
> Tho' death to honour, it was life to him —
> Restor'd to consequence tho' not to grace
> Behold him fill the secretary's place —
> His pen can write you paragraphs by scores
> His valor kick two Quakers out of doors
> Tim for their champion let the People dub
> Yet virtue still must hold him for a scrub.

We can thank Odell for reminding us that nobody was more active in the cause, the fight for American independence, than Timothy Matlack. Matlack was the people's champion. Bishop William White, who once declined Colonel Matlack's invitation to preach to his battalion, called him "one of the warmest spirits of the day."[3] During the War of Independence, few men in Pennsylvania were as visibly, or passionately, committed to the fight for liberty.[4]

Timothy Matlack has suffered historically for lack of a definitive identity. Even in his own time he was a political enigma. Matlack's fellow congressman, Ezekiel Cornell, wrote: "Mr. Matlack is a strange mortal for a man of sense. I never know one day were to find him the next." Matlack stuck to what he thought was the best course for Pennsylvania and America. It was his independent streak which got him in trouble with Constitutionalists. As we have seen, this was especially true in his opposition to price fixing and his support of the bank. His acceptance of a bank directorship, on the other hand, was opportunistic, as was his Federalist-supported candidacy for clerk of the Senate.

In the Revolution the people adopted Timothy Matlack as their tribune, and this status earned him powerful enemies. A prominent radical in 1776, he was a lightning rod for his party throughout the war. In the mid–nineteenth century, Timothy Matlack's detractors carried forward the negative persona constructed by his contemporary enemies. His problematic public image drew a shade on the private life of a loving father and compassionate friend. Timothy's friends always recognized his "gentleness of spirit." Jacob Hiltzheimer wrote that after the death of his wife, in March 1790, "several of my friends came to see me. Mr. Timothy Matlack stayed with me yesterday from 8 in the morning till 8 in the evening whose conversation was a great support to me."

The story of Timothy Matlack's religious life is one of a complicated relationship. In 1862, William Allinson wrote, "He was in his youth a serious friend and seemed likely to become a minister of the gospel of the Prince of Peace, but imbibing the war spirit, he wandered for many years in devious ways." In the nineteenth century Quakers remembered Timothy Matlack as an adversary. Matlack did in fact jail Samuel Fisher and beat two emissaries with his walking stick. He also led the Free Quakers' campaign for property rights. For these sins Timothy's coreligionists carried a lingering hostility, as the following anecdote confirms.

In the early twentieth century a Matlack family was still living on the original New Jersey homestead. One of these people, distant relatives of the patriot, recalled the discovery of a badly damaged picture during the reconstruction of a cider-mill. In the year 1899,

> when the building was torn down the portrait of Timothy Matlack was found. It had slipped from its original position and was so covered with dust and dirt as to scarcely show that it had ever been a painting, and, being too soiled to deserve preservation, it was consigned to the fire.

When they incinerated Timothy, these Quakers were unaware of his efforts to help their ancestors, in the time of persecution. During the War of Independence, although in direct conflict with Quaker Tories, "he sometimes secretly used his power as an American officer, to favor his former religious associates." They also did not know the disowned Quaker returned to the fold. They were unaware "that during the long evening of his life, he evinced steadfast love for friends, and great diligence in attending their meetings for worship." Later in life Timothy went back to what he had been before: a devout member of the Society of Friends.

* * *

Pennsylvania's 1776 Constitution inspired Benjamin Rush to lament, "All our laws breathe the spirit of town meetings and portershops." But the authors of this frame wanted to create a world in which people with less property did not have to live their lives under prejudicial dominance. The radical Constitution of 1776, which Matlack had helped write, "brought into power a class of people hitherto denied political privileges." It was the most democratic of all revolutionary constitutions and the first step in the long struggle for equality in America.[5] Matlack and his fellow radicals "deserve praise for defying the traditional theories of government and for framing a constitution which breathed the spirit of Eighteenth Century Enlightenment and of the principles of the Declaration of Independence."[6]

The Pennsylvania Constitution's failure to address slavery was rectified by 1780s Act of Gradual Abolition. While this compromise measure did not emancipate Pennsylvania's existing slaves, it established that their grandchildren would be born free.

The radical constitution written by Pennsylvania radicals in 1776 laid the groundwork for the triumph of Jeffersonian democracy in the early nineteenth century.

* * *

Timothy Matlack is making another comeback. He was mentioned in the movie *National Treasure*, and his handwriting was the inspiration for a handful of fonts, including American Scribe. His Charles Willson Peale portrait hangs prominently in the Museum of Fine Arts in Boston, and in Philadelphia his Free Quaker Meeting House is open to the public. And now he has a biography.

Timothy Matlack pushed the people to act for themselves and led them in a revolution. For these achievements he paid a heavy price. In 1783, after his removal from office, Timothy's friends rallied to his support by presenting him with a silver urn. This they engraved with words of appreciation for his "patriotic devotion to the cause of the Colonies in their struggle for Freedom and the many valuable services rendered by him during the entire period until the acknowledgment of their Independence by Great Britain in the Treaty of Peace."

Timothy Matlack believed in himself and his ability to reason; he believed in the people and their ability to govern; he believed in the thirteen colonies and their right to freedom; and he believed in the United States of America and its destiny for greatness.

Chapter Notes

Preface

1. Gary B. Nash, *First City: Philadelphia and the Forging of Historical Memory* (Philadelphia: University of Pennsylvania Press, 2006), 102.

Chapter One

1. Peter Force, ed., *American Archives*, ser. 4, vol. 6 (Washington, 1837–53), 965.
2. William S. Stryker, *The Battles of Trenton and Princeton* (Boston, 1898), 36.
3. "Selections from the Military Papers of General John Cadwalader," *Pennsylvania Magazine of History and Biography* 32, no. 2 (1908): 151.
4. Force, ser. 5, vol. 1, 557, 1,289.
5. Ibid., ser. 4, vol. 3, 860.
6. Richard M. Ketchum, *The Winter Soldiers* (New York: Holt and Co., 1973), 121.
7. Stryker, 232.
8. Joseph Reed, "General Joseph Reed's Narrative of the Movements of the American Army in the Neighborhood of Trenton in the Winter of 1776–77," *Pennsylvania Magazine of History and Biography* 8, no. 4 (December 1884): 391–402.
9. Thomas Rodney, *Diary of Captain Thomas Rodney, 1776–1777* (Wilmington: The Historical Society of Delaware, 1888), 22–3.
10. Stryker, 233.
11. Rodney, 22–3.
12. David Hackett Fischer, *Washington's Crossing* (New York: Oxford University Press, 2004), 254–55.

Chapter Two

1. Matlack Family Papers, Quaker Collection, 1120, Haverford College Library, Haverford, PA.
2. Matlack, Haverford College.
3. Wyck Association Collection, American Philosophical Society, Philadelphia.
4. George Powell, *The History of Camden County New Jersey* (Philadelphia: L. J. Richards & Co., 1886), 609.
5. Matlack, Haverford College.
6. Frank H. Stewart, ed., "Notes on Old Gloucester County, New Jersey," New Jersey Society of Pennsylvania, Gloucester County Historical Society, vol. 1 (1917).
7. Samuel Mickle, *The Diaries of Samuel Mickle: Woodbury, Gloucester County, New Jersey, 1792–1829, Volume 1* (Woodbury, NJ: Gloucester County Historical Society, 1991).
8. Matlack, Haverford College.
9. Julia Bedford Gill, *The Story of a Short Life, Letitia Matlack 1724–1752*, unpublished paper read at a meeting of the Historical Society of Pennsylvania, June 12, 1926, 5.
10. Julia Bedford Gill, 4–5; Matlack Family Papers *(*Asa Matlack's notebooks), Haverford College, 1120.
11. Misc. Benjamin Franklin Collections 1710–1822, American Philosophical Society, Philadelphia, PA, Shop book B F85f6.15.
12. Wyck Coll., b. 227, n. 280, APS.
13. Steven Rosswurm, *Arms, Country and Class* (New Brunswick: Rutgers University Press, 1987), 35.
14. John Fanning Watson, *Annals of Philadelphia* (Philadelphia: E. L. Carey & A. Hart, 1830), 405, 435.
15. John W. Jordan, "The Fellowship Fire Company of Philadelphia, Organized 1738," *Pennsylvania Magazine of History and Biography* 27 no. 4 (1903): 476.
16. Hannah B. Roach, "Benjamin Franklin Slept Here," *Pennsylvania Magazine of History and Biography* 84, no. 2 (April 1960):127–174; Wyck Collection, APS; William Penn Charter School Archives, Deed Book of the Overseers

of the Quaker School, Quaker Collection, 1115, Haverford College Library, Haverford, PA.

17. Harrold E. Gillingham, Elias Bland, and Edward Wilsonn, "Some Colonial Ships Built in Philadelphia," *Pennsylvania Magazine of History and Biography* 56, no.2 (1932): 156–186.

18. Wyck, APS.

19. Jeffery M. Dorwart, *Camden County, New Jersey* (New Brunswick: Rutgers University Press, 2001), 29–31.

20. The Book of Discipline of the Society of Friends in Pennsylvania and New Jersey, 1719, "From an (antient) Copy in the possession of Timothy Matlack Esq.," 289.6 S01, American Philosophical Society, Philadelphia.

21. Timothy Matlack Sr., advertisement, *The Pennsylvania Gazette*, June 27, 1751. Free Library of Philadelphia.

22. Timothy Matlack Sr., advertisement, *The Pennsylvania Gazette*, July 5, 1750. Free Library of Philadelphia.

23. Roach, 127–174.

24. Timothy Matlack Sr., advertisement, *The Pennsylvania Gazette*, August 22, 1751, Free Library of Philadelphia.

25. Wyck, ASP.

26. Wills, Philadelphia, PA, book K, n. 14 (1752), Historical Society of Pennsylvania, Philadelphia.

27. William Penn Charter School Archives, Coll. 1115, Deed Book of the Overseers of the Quaker School, Quaker Collection, Haverford College Library.

28. Timothy Matlack to William Findley, 11 January 1817, *Collections of the Massachusetts Historical Society* 2d ser., vol. 8 (1819), 184–192.

29. Timothy Matlack Jr. Indenture Contract, Historical Society of Pennsylvania, Philadelphia, PA.

30. Catherine LaCourreye Blecki and Karin A. Wulf, *Milcah Martha Moore's Book: A Commonplace Book from Revolutionary America* (College Park, PA: Penn State University Press, 1997), 107.

31. Catherine Phillips, *Memoirs of the Life of Catherine Phillips* (London: James Phillips and Sons, 1797), 109–110.

32. Timothy Matlack to John Peters, June 17, 1756, Peale-Sellers Family Collection, American Philosophical Society, Philadelphia, PA.

33. *New Jersey Archives: Documents Relating to the Revolutionary History of the State of New Jersey*, 2d ser., vol. 1 (Newark: New Jersey Historical Society, 1917), 63.

34. Samuel Rhoads and Enoch Lewis, eds., *Friends' Review*, vol.15 (Philadelphia: Merbiew & Thompson, 1862): 564.

35. Roach, 158.

36. Indian 1683–1794 Collection, (Phi), 1,297, Historical Society of Pennsylvania, Philadelphia.

37. *Pennsylvania Gazette*, October 9, 1760, Free Library of Philadelphia.

38. Timothy Matlack, "*An Oration Delivered March 16, 1780 Before the Patron, Vice President and Members of the American Philosophical Society*" (Philadelphia: Styner and Cist, 1780).

39. W. Nelson, "Beginnings of the Iron Industry in Trenton New Jersey," *Pennyslvania Magazine of History and Biography* 35, no. 2 (1911): 241.

Chapter Three

1. *Provincial Delegates*, vol. V, Historical Society of Pennsylvania, Philadelphia, 77.

2. Brooke Hindle, "The March of the Paxton Boys," *William and Mary Quarterly*, 3d ser., vol. 3 (October 1946), 474; Lorett Treese, *The Storm Gathering: The Penn Family and the American Revolution* (Mechanicsburg, PA: Stackpole Books, 2002), 38.

3. Kevin Kenny, *Peaceable Kingdom Lost: The Paxton Boys and the Destruction of William Penn's Holy Experiment* (New York: Oxford University Press, 2009), 11.

4. Treese, 36.

5. Hindle, 464.

6. Ibid., 466.

7. "Early Quaker Monthly Meeting Minutes," *Pennsylvania Genealogical Magazine*, Genealogical Society of Pennsylvania Historical Society of Pennsylvania, UPA F 146.G32, v. 13, 29, 30, 32, 211, 215.

8. Bertha Cochran Landis, "Col Timothy Matlack A Revolutionary Patriot in Lancaster" Papers of the Lancaster Historical Society, v. XLII n. 6 (1938): 150.

9. Hindle, 478.

10. Hindle, 476; Pemberton Papers Coll. 34, 128, Historical Society of Pennsylvania, Philadelphia.

11. "A Testimony given forth from our Yearly-Meeting at Philadelphia" (Oct. 4, 1777), Library of Congress.

12. A. M. Stackhouse, "*Col. Timothy Matlack Patriot and Soldier: A Paper Read Before the Gloucester County Historical Society at the Old Tavern House, Haddonfield, NJ April 14, 1908*" (Higginson Book Company, 1994), 67.

13. Moore, 107.

14. Peter Thompson, *Rum Punch & Revolution* (Philadelphia: University of Pennsylvania Press, 1999), 8.

15. Arthur J. Mekeel, *The Quakers and the American Revolution* (York: Sessions Book Trust, 1996), 22.

16. Edmund S. Morgan, *Benjamin Franklin* (New Haven: Yale University Press, 2002), 153–54.
17. Mekeel, 24.
18. Jacob Hiltzheimer Diaries, April 14, 1766, American Philosophical Society, Philadelphia.
19. Hiltzheimer, June 4, 1766.
20. Carl Bridenbaugh, *Cities in Revolt* (New York: Alfred A. Knopf, 1955), 363.
21. Lynn M. Brooks, "Against Vain Sports and Pastime: The Theater Dance in Philadelphia, 1724–90," *Dance Chronicle* 12, no. 2 (1989):172.
22. Hiltzheimer, APS February, 1767.
23. Wyck, APS.
24. Timothy Matlack to Abiel Holmes, October 12, 1819, Documents, 1726–1816, 974.8. D65, American Philosophical Society, Philadelphia.
25. Haines & Twells, account book, 1767–1770, 657-H11 American Philosophical Society, Philadelphia; Tobias Lear, "Washington's Household Account Book, 1793–1797," *Pennsylvania Magazine of History and Biography* 29, no. 4 (1905): 385.
26. Rosemary Troy Kill, *Early American Decorative Arts 1620–1860* (Lanham, MD: Altamira Press, 2010), 151.
27. *Pennsylvania Gazette*, May 8, 1766, Free Library of Philadelphia.
28. "NEXT MORNING (After a Debauch)," *Pennsylvania Packet*, February 13, 1775, Historical Society of Pennsylvania.
29. Peter Thompson, 48.
30. The Book of Discipline, APS.
31. Hiltzheimer, September 4, 1767, APS.
32. Court of Common Pleas Execution Docket, March, 1768. Philadelphia City Archives.
33. Hiltzheimer, March 18, 1768, APS.
34. Timothy Matlack, advertisement, *Pennsylvania Chronicle* 3, no. 36, October 2, 1769.
35. Timothy Matlack, "Observations on making and fining Cyder, and on Peach Trees," *Memoirs of the Philadelphia Society for Promoting Agriculture* v. 1 (1808): 112.
36. Wyck, APS; Peter Thompson, 1.
37. Hiltzheimer, APS, September 30, 1769.
38. Miscellaneous Coll., 1676–1937, n. 425, box 7B, HSP.
39. J. W. Cooper, *A Treatise on Cocking* (Media, PA: Cooper & Vernon, 1859), 9. Vk. 37., HSP, Philadelphia.
40. Sharon Salinger, *Taverns and Drinking in Early America* (Baltimore: Johns Hopkins University Press, 2002), 73.
41. Robert Aitken, "Cruelty to Animals Exposed" *Pennsylvania Magazine* (1775); Peter Thompson, 102.
42. Carl Bridenbaugh and Jessica Bridenbaugh, *Rebels and Gentlemen: Philadelphia in the Age of Franklin* (New York: Reynal & Hitchcock, 1942), 182.
43. Hiltzheimer, March 6, 1770, APS.
44. Francis Hopkinson, "The Cockfight," Commonplace Book, 1778. AM .005, Historical Society of Pennsylvania, Philadelphia.
45. John W. Cooper, *A Treatise on Cocking* (Media, PA 1859).
46. Steven Rosswurm and Stephanie Wolf, "Leisure Time in Colonial Philadelphia," June, 1776 (Unpublished paper).
47. Hopkinson, HSP.
48. Jonathan Odell, ed., *The Loyal Verses of Joseph Stansbury and Doctor Jonathan Odell* (Philadelphia, 1857), The World of Congress.

Chapter Four

1. Theodore Thayer, *Pennsylvania Politics and the Growth of Democracy, 1740–1776* (Harrisburg: Pennsylvania Historical and Museum Commission, 1953), 7.
2. Mekeel, 36.
3. Robert F. Oaks, *Philadelphia Merchants and the American Revolution,1765–1776* (Los Angeles: University of Southern California, 1970).
4. Mekeel, 45.
5. Charles H. Lincoln, *The Revolutionary Movement in Philadelphia, 1760–1776* (Cambridge, MA: Harvard University, 1901), 151.
6. Thayer, 150.
7. Rosswurm, 42.
8. Rosswurm, 32.
9. Matlack to Holmes, APS.
10. Hiltzheimer, December 25, 1773.
11. Ryerson, 266, quoted from Lyman H. Butterfield, ed., *Diary and Biography of John Adams: Vol. 3, Diary, 1782–1804* (Boston: Massachusetts Historical Society, 1961), 316.
12. Ryerson, 266, quoted from *Collections of the New York Historical Society*, F116.N5. vol. 13, p. 271.
13. Alexander Graydon, *Memoirs of his Own Time With Reminiscences of the Men and Events of the Revolution* (Philadelphia: Lindsay and Blakiston, 1846), 131.
14. Thayer, 160.
15. Edwin Wolf II, "The Authorship of the 1774 Address to the King Restudied," *William and Mary Quarterly* ser. 3, v. 22, n. 2 (April 1965): 190–224.
16. "Catalog of Franklin Exhibition in the Library of Congress," *Proceedings of the Amer-*

ican Philosophical Society v. 100, n. 4 (August 31, 1956): 385–416.

17. Richard Ryerson, *The Revolution Is Now Begun: The Radical Committees of Philadelphia, 1765–1776* (Philadelphia: University of Pennsylvania Press, 1978), 249.

18. An Epistle from the Meetings for Sufferings: held in Philadelphia for Pennsylvania and New-Jersey, the 5th Day of the First Month, 1775, LCP Ar.75 F91, Historical Society of Pennsylvania.

19. John Thomas Scharf and Thompson Westcott, *History of Philadelphia, 1609–1884*, vol. 2 (Philadelphia,1884), 295.

20. Force, ser. 3, vol. 4, 436.

21. Charles Biddle, *Autobiography of Charles Biddle* (Philadelphia, 1883), 82–83.

22. Minutes of the Philadelphia Monthly Meeting, 1771–1777, The Friends Historical Library, Swarthmore College, Swarthmore, Pennsylvania.

23. Continental Congress, *Journal of the Proceedings of Congress, Held at Philadelphia, from September 5, 1775 to April 30, 1776*. Philadelphia.

24. Peter Thompson, 167.

25. Rosswurm, 58.

26. Force, ser. 3, vol. 4., 1778.

27. Rosswurm, 59.

28. William Duane, ed., *Extracts from the Diary of Christopher Marshall, 1774–1781* (Albany, NY: Joel Munsell, 1877), 50.

29. Scharf and Westcott, vol. 1, 302.

30. Rosswurm, 60.

31. John Coleman, *Thomas McKean, Forgotten Leader of the Revolution* (Rockaway, NJ: American Faculty Press, 1975).

32. *Pennsylvania Packet*, May 27, 1776, Historical Society of Pennsylvania.

33. Massachusetts Historical Society. Misc. Bound Manuscripts. Dec. 16, 1775 United States Continental Congress Marine Committee Minutes about Dimensions of New Gunboats p. 4.

34. Collections, Manuscript Division, n. 397, Library of Congress, Washington, DC.

35. Richard Henry Lee to Arthur Lee, July 6, 1783, James Curtis Ballagh, ed., *The Letters of Richard Henry Lee,1762–1794, vol. 2* (New York: McMillan, 1914).

36. "Diary of Richard Smith in the Continental Congress, 1775–1776," *American Historical Review* 1, no. 3 (April 1896): 494–495.

37. *Pennsylvania Packet*, January 15, 1776, HSP.

38. *Pennsylvania Journal*, Februaty 7, 1776; Samuel Hazard, ed., *Colonial Records of Pennsylvania* vol. 10 (Harrisburg, PA: T. Fenn & Company, 1852): 486–487.

39. Thomas Paine, *Common Sense*, 2nd ed. (Philadelphia: William and Thomas Bradford, February 14, 1776), "*To the Representatives of the Religious Society of the People called Quakers.*"

40. Duane, *Marshall*, 61.

41. Joseph Shippen to Edward Shippen, February 19, 1776, Shippen Papers, 12, Historical Society of Pennsylvania.

42. John Adams to James Warren, March 21, 1776, Warren-Adams Letters Massachusetts Historical Society Collection 62 (1917), 213–14.

43. Richard Ketchum, *The Winter Soldiers* (New York: Doubleday, 1973), 71.

44. David Hawke, *In the Midst of a Revolution* (Philadelphia: University of Pennsylvania Press, 1961), 116–17.

45. Hawke, 118.

46. *Pennsylvania Gazette*, May 15, 1776, Free Library of Philadelphia.

47. *Pennsylvania Gazette*, May 15, 1776, Free Library of Philadelphia.

48. Hawke, 121.

Chapter Five

1. John Adams to James Warren, 20 May, 1776. Robert J. Taylor, ed., *Papers of John Adams*, vol. 4 (Cambridge, MA: The Belknap Press of Harvard University Press, 1979).

2. Ryerson, 24.

3. Duane, *Marshall*, 73.

4. Hawke, 141.

5. Ibid., 147.

6. Ibid., 157.

7. Ibid., 171.

8. Ibid., 160.

9. Ibid., 161.

10. *Pennsylvania Packet*, June 17, 1776, Historical Society of Pennsylvania.

11. Ryerson, 225–26.

12. Proceedings of the Conference of Committees of the Province of Pennsylvania Carpenter's Hall June 18 to June 25, 1776, Pennsylvania Archives, ser. 2, v. 3, 633; Thayer, 184.

13. Ryerson, 234.

14. Force, ser. 4, vol. 6, 965.

15. Ibid.

16. Duane, *Marshall*, 80.

17. Gary B. Nash, *First City Philadelphia and the Forging of Historical Memory* (Philadelphia: University of Pennsylvania Press, 2006), 85.

18. Stackhouse, *Matlack*, 25. Anthony Morris said specifically that he witnessed Matlack's reading on July 4, 1776. He was ten years old at the time. Morris told this story to Benjamin Franklin's great granddaughter Henrietta Constantia Bache. She was married to Charles Abert, Timothy Matlack's great grandson.

19. Charles Biddle, *Autobiography*, 86. Biddle's comment that "There were very few re-

spectable people present" makes it clear that he did not confuse this reading for the event on July 8. For further evidence that the Declaration was read on July 4, see Wilfred J. Ritz, "From the 'Here' of Jefferson's Handwritten Rough Draft of the Declaration of Independence to the 'There' of the Printed Dunlap Broadside," *Pennsylvania Magazine of History and Biography* 116, no. 4 (1992): 507.
20. Julian P. Boyd, "The Declaration of Independence: The Mystery of the Lost Original," *Pennsylvania Magazine of History and Biography* 100, no. 4 (October 1976): 451–2.
21. Force, ser. 5, vol. 1, 1289.
22. John Adams to Samuel Chase, Philadelphia, July 9, 1776, in *Papers of John Adams*, vol. 4, ed. Robert J. Taylor (Cambridge: The Belknap Press of Harvard University Press, 1979), 195.
23. Adams to Chase, July 9, 1776.
24. Duane, *Marshall*, 83.
25. Adams to Chase, July 9, 1776.
26. Adams to Chase, July 9, 1776.

CHAPTER SIX

1. Elisha P. Douglass, *Rebels and Democrats* (Chapel Hill: University of North Carolina Press, 1955), 8.
2. Douglass, 272–73; Ryerson, 245.
3. *Pennsylvania Evening Post*, July 9, 1776, v. II, Free Library of Philadelphia, iw.newsbank.com.
4. Samuel Hazard, ed., *Colonial Records of Pennsylvania*, vol. 10 (Philadelphia: T. Fenn & Co., 1851), 634.
5. Force, ser. 5, vol. 1, 1,287–1,330.
6. Ibid.
7. David McCullough, *John Adams* (New York: Simon & Schuster, 2001), 220.
8. Page Smith, *The Constitution, a Documentary and Narrative History* (New York: Morrow, 1978), 69.
9. Thayer, 186.
10. Hawke, 182.
11. Ryerson, 239 (footnote).
12. Duane, *Marshall*, 81.
13. Thayer, 188.
14. Timothy Matlack Book of Hours, American Philosophical Society. Matlack donated his copy of James Thompson's *The Seasons* (London, 1733) to the Library Company of Philadelphia.
15. American Philosophical Society Archives, 1743–1984, box 4, Timothy Matlack, Concerning the growth of plants, Concerning fireplaces.
16. Thomas Smith to Arthur St. Clair, August 22, 1776, in *The St. Clair Papers*, vol. 1, ed. William Henry Smith (R. Clarke & Co., 1882), 373.
17. Douglass, 15.
18. For evidence that Matlack engrossed the Declaration, see Epilogue.
19. Force, ser. 5, vol. 1, 895.
20. Force, ser. 5, vol. 1, 761.
21. Scharf & Westcott, vol. 1, 331.
22. Hawke, 190.
23. Thayer, 189.
24. "Minutes of the Proceedings of the Convention of the State of Pennsylvania, Held at Philadelphia, July 15, 1776 to September 28," Force, ser. 5, vol. 2, 1–50.
25. Elisha Douglass, *Rebels and Democrats* (Chapel Hill: University of North Carolina, 1955), 271.
26. "The Constitution of Pennsylvania," Force, ser. 5, vol. 2, 51.
27. Douglass, 14.
28. Isaac Kramnick, ed. Introduction to Thomas Paine, *Common Sense* (New York: Penguin Books, 1986), 30.
29. Hawke, 112.
30. "Minutes of the Pennsylvania Convention," Force, ser. 5, vol. 2, 60.
31. Nash, *First City*, 101.
32. John Keane, *Tom Paine* (London: Bloomsbury Publishing, 1995), 126–7.
33. Ibid.
34. Scharf and Westcott, vol. 1, 332.
35. Duane, *Marshall*, 97.
36. Robert L. Brunhouse, *The Counter-Revolution in Pennsylvania 1776–1790* (Harrisburg: Pennsylvania Historical and Museum Commission, 1971), 21.
37. Rosswurm, 125.
38. Rosswurm, 126.
39. Duane, *Marshall*, 105.
40. Ibid., 121.
41. Nicholas B. Wainwright and Sarah Logan Fisher, "A Diary of Trifling Occurrences," *Pennsylvania Magazine of History and Biography* 82, no. 4 (October 1958): 415.
42. Thomas Rodney, *Diary of Captain Thomas Rodney, 1776–1777* (Wilmington: Historical Society of Delaware), 13.
43. Charles R. Smith, *Marines in the Revolution* (History and Museum Division, U.S. Marine Corp, 1975), 96.
44. Parke Godwin, *Cyclopedia of Universal Biography* (New York: A. S. Barnes, 1854), 155.
45. Graydon, 123.
46. Force, ser. 4, vol. 5, 698.

CHAPTER SEVEN

1. Rodney, 24.
2. Joseph Reed, 397.
3. William Young, "Journal of Sergeant William Young," *Pennsylvania Magazine of*

History and Biography 8, no. 3 (October, 1884): 261.
4. David Hackett Fischer, *Washington's Crossing* (New York: Oxford University Press, 2004), 279.
5. Dreer Autograph Collection, 48:1, Generals of the Revolution II, 49–52, Historical Society of Pennsylvania.
6. Joseph Reed, 398.
7. Ibid.; Rodney, 27. The Pearson shooting was also reported by Charles Willson Peale and Sergeant Young.
8. Young, 261.
9. Fischer, 284.
10. Ibid., 307.
11. Ibid., 317.
12. Rodney, 33; Robert A. Selig, Battle of Princeton Mapping Project: Report of Military Terrain Analysis and Battle Narrative, Princeton Battlefield Society, Princeton, NJ, September, 2010.
13. Fischer, 329.
14. Rodney, 33.
15. Sergeant R., "The Battle of Princeton," *Pennsylvania Magazine of History and Biography* 20, no. 4 (1896): 516.
16. Selig, Mapping Project, 66.
17. Rodney, 34.
18. Rodney, 34.
19. Fischer, 336.
20. Rodney, 36.
21. Selig, Mapping Project, 75.
22. Young, note, 264.
23. Cadwalader Coll., ser. 2, b. 21, f. 21, Historical Society of Pennsylvania, Philadelphia.
24. Young, 267.
25. Hazard, ed. Pennsylvania Archives, ser. 1, vol. 6 (1853), 186.
26. John C. Fitzpatrick, ed., *The Writings of George Washington*, vol. 7 (Washington: Government Printing Office, 1931–1944), 79.
27. Fischer, 355.
28. Ibid.
29. "Selections from the Military Papers of General John Cadwalader," *Pennsylvania Magazine of History and Biography* 32, no. 2 (1908): 162–3.
30. Hazard, ed., Pennsylvania Archives, ser. 1, vol. 6 (1853), 186–87; Cadwalader Collection, ser., 2, b. 21, f. 19 Historical Society of Pennsylvania.
31. Young, note, 256.
32. Rosswurm, 131.
33. Young, 266.
34. Fischer, 335.

Chapter Eight

1. Wainwright and Fisher, Diary, 425.
2. Rosswurm, 138.
3. Elaine Forman Crane, *The Diary of Elizabeth Drinker*, vol. 1 (Boston: Northeastern University Press, 1991), 224.
4. Wainwright and Fisher, Diary, 431.
5. Wainwright and Fisher, Diary, 419.
6. Samuel Hazard, *Colonial Records of Pennsylvania*, vol. 11 (T. Fenn, 1852), 173.
7. Ibid., 140.
8. Ibid.
9. Benson Bobrick, *Angel in the Whirlwind* (New York: Simon & Schuster, 1997), 262–3.
10. Hawke, 195.
11. Wainwright and Fisher, 437.
12. Ibid.
13. *Pennsylvania Evening Post*, v. 3, n. 392, August 16, 1777, Free Library of Philadelphia, iw.newsbank.com.
14. James Donald Anderson, "Thomas Wharton, Virginia Exile, 1777–1778," *Virginia Magazine of History and Biography* 89, no. 4 (October 1981): 425–447.
15. Wainwright and Fisher, 447.
16. Anderson, 425–47.
17. Wainwright and Fisher, 448.
18. John W. Jackson, *With the British Army in Philadelphia, 1777–1778* (San Rafael, CA: Presidio Press, 1979), 17
19. Wainwright and Fisher, 450.
20. Wainwright and Fisher, 458.
21. Duane, *Marshall*, 149.
22. Wainwright and Fisher, 461–2.
23. Wainwright and Fisher, 458; Rosswurm, 150.
24. Matlack to Unknown, April 18, 1778, Gratz Collection, case 1, box 8, Historical Society of Pennsylvania.
25. Duane, *Marshall*, 170.
26. Rosswurm, 158.
27. William Bell Clark, "Letters of Captain Nicholas Biddle," *Pennsylvania Magazine of History and Biography* 74, no. 3 (1931): 393–4.
28. Clark, 396–97.
29. Stackhouse, 19.
30. Clark, notes, 399.
31. Daniel J. Crooks, *Charleston is Burning. Two Centuries of Fire and Flames* (Charleston, SC: The History Press, 2009); *South-Carolina and American General Gazette*, January 29, 1778.
32. Charles Biddle, *Autobiography of Charles Biddle, Vice President of the Supreme Executive Council of Pennsylvania* (Philadelphia: E. Claxton, 1883), 394.
33. Scharf and Westcott, vol. 1, 302.
34. Clark, 402.

35. Duane, *Marshall*, 157–8.
36. Hazard, Pennsylvania Archives, ser. 2, vol. 3, 160.
37. Samuel Rhoads, ed., *Friends' Review* vol. 15 (Philadelphia, 1862): 614.
38. Matlack to Samuel Allinson, Lancaster, April 1, 1778, Historical Society of Pennsylvania.
39. Crane, vol. 1 (1991), 302; "Extracts from the Journal of Mrs. Henry Drinker," *Pennsylvania Magazine of History and Biography* 13, no. 3(October, 1889): 305.
40. Crane, *Drinker* (1991), 306.
41. Rosswurm, 159.
42. Elizabeth Forman Crane, *The Diary of Elizabeth Drinker, Abridged Edition* (Philadelphia: University of Pennsylvania Press, 2010), 79.
43. Wainwright and Fisher, 462.
44. Wainwright and Fisher, 465: Crane, *Drinker* (2010), 77.
45. *Pennsylvania Packet*, July 4, 1778, Historical Society of Pennsylvania.
46. Crane, *Drinker* (2010), 78.
47. John Franklin Reigart, *The Life of Robert Fulton* (Philadelphia, 1856), 33.
48. Crane, *Drinker* (2010), 78.
49. Charles Biddle, 162.
50. Rosswurm, 154–5.
51. *Pennsylvania Packet*, August 4, 1778, Historical Society of Pennsylvania.
52. Raymond C. Werner, "Diary of Grace Growden Galloway," *Pennsylvania Magazine of History and Biography* 55, no. 1 (1931): 37.
53. Werner, "Galloway," 48.
54. Peter C. Messer, "'A Species of Treason & Not the Least Dangerous Kind:' The Treason Trails of Abraham Carlisle and John Roberts," *Pennsylvania Magazine of History and Biography* 123, no.4 (October 1999): 303.

Chapter Nine

1. Howard Peckham,"Dr. Berkenhout's Journal, 1778," *Pennsylvania Magazine of History and Biography* 65, no. 1 (January 1941): 79–92.
2. Ray Thompson, *Benedict Arnold in Philadelphia* (Ft. Washington, PA: Bicentennial Press, 1975), 41.
3. William Reed, *Life and Correspondence of Joseph Reed*, vol. 2, (Philadelphia: 1847), 39.
4. Rosswurm, 55, 62.
5. *Pennsylvania Packet*, November 14, 1778, Historical Society of Pennsylvania.
6. *Pennsylvania Packet*, April 22, 1779, Historical Society of Pennsylvania.
7. *Pennsylvania Packet*, November 19, 1778, Historical Society of Pennsylvania.

8. *Pennsylvania Packet*, April 22, 1779, Historical Society of Pennsylvania.
9. "To the Quakers, Bethlemites, Moderate Men, Refugees and other the Tories whatsoever, and wheresoever, dispersed," *Pennsylvania Packet*, February 27, 1779, Historical Society of Pennsylvania.
10. Clare Brandt, *The Man in the Mirror* (New York: Random House, 1994), 166–7; Duane, *Marshall*, 211.
11. Messer, 321.
12. William Reed, (notes), 36.
13. Rosswurm 157; "The Second Troop Philadelphia City Cavalry," *Pennsylvania Magazine of History and Biography* 45 (1921): 283.
14. Rosswurm, 161.
15. William Reed, 38.
16. William Reed, note, 37.
17. Messer, 321.
18. Ray Thompson, 88.
19. Rosswurm 161; *Pennsylvania Packet*, March 2, 1779, Historical Society of Pennsylvania.
20. *Pennsylvania Packet*, March 25, 1779, Historical Society of Pennsylvania.
21. *Pennsylvania Packet*, March 30, 1779, Historical Society of Pennsylvania.
22. William Reed, 388.
23. *Pennsylvania Packet*, February 27, 1779, Historical Society of Pennsylvania.
24. *Pennsylvania Packet*, March 2, 1779, Historical Society of Pennsylvania.
25. *Pennsylvania Packet*, March 6, 1779, Historical Society of Pennsylvania.
26. Anna Wharton Morris, "Journal of Samuel Rowland Fisher, of Philadelphia. 1779–1781," *Pennsylvania Magazine of History and Biography* 41, no. 2 (1917): 145.

Chapter Ten

1. Rosswurm, 170.
2. Winthrop Sargent, ed., *The Loyal Verses of Joseph Stansbury and Doctor Jonathan Odell* (Albany, NY: J. Munsell, 1860).
3. *Pennsylvania Packet,* May 24, 1787, Historical Society of Pennsylvania.
4. "Robert Morris and the Episode of the Polacre 'Victorious,'" *Pennsylvania Magazine of History and Biography* 70, no. 3 (July 1946): 248–52.
5. James Curtis Ballagh, ed., *The Letters of Richard Henry Lee*, vol. II (New York: Macmillan Company, 1914), 92–93.
6. Ibid.
7. Keane, 178–9.
8. Rosswurm, 210.
9. *Pennsylvania Packet*, July 24, 1779, Historical Society of Pennsylvania.

10. *Pennsylvania Packet*, July 1, 1779, Historical Society of Pennsylvania.
11. John K. Alexander, "The Fort Wilson Incident of 1779: A Case Study of the Revolutionary Crowd," *William and Mary Quarterly* 31 (October, 1974), 600.
12. Alexander, 596; Frederick D. Stone, "Philadelphia Society One Hundred Years Ago, or the Reign of Continental Money," *Pennsylvania Magazine of History and Biography* 3, no. 4 (1879): 384.
13. Rosswurm, 211.
14. Alexander, 598.
15. William Reed, vol. 2, 423.
16. Ana Wharton Morris, "Fisher," 169.
17. William Reed, vol. 2, 426.
18. Hiltzheimer, October 5, 1779, American Philosophical Society.
19. William Reed, vol. 2, 425–6.
20. C. Page Smith, "The Attack on Fort Wilson," *Pennsylvania Magazine of History and Biography* 78, no. 2 (April, 1954): 187.
21. C. Page Smith, 188.
22. Ibid.
23. William Reed, 427.
24. William Reed, 153.
25. Morris, "Fisher," 172.

Chapter Eleven

1. Nathanael Greene to Joseph Reed, June 2, 1779, Library of Congress.
2. Washington to Matlack, June 2, 1779, Dreer Coll., v. 178, 31–2, Historical Society of Pennsylvania.
3. *Proceedings of a General Court Martial.... For the trial of Major General Benedict Arnold June 1, 1779* (Philadelphia: Francis Bailey, 1780), 8.
4. Brandt, 149.
5. *Proceedings of a General Court Martial*, 51.
6. George Nelson Diary, 1780–92, Am. 107, Historical Society of Pennsylvania.
7. Brunhouse, 77.
8. Ibid., 78.
9. Philip Sheldon Foner, *The Complete Writings of Thomas Paine* (New York: Citadel Press, 1969), 22.
10. Benezet taught at the Friend's School in Philadelphia from 1742 to 1754, during Timothy's tenure as a student.
11. William Henry Smith, *A Political History of Slavery* (New York: G. P. Putnam's Sons, 1903), 9.
12. *The Independent Gazetteer*, September 4, 1784, Free Library of Philadelphia, iw.newsbank.com.
13. Philip Foner, 15, 18.
14. Force, ser. 4, vol. 5, 715.
15. *Freeman's Journal*, September 26, 1781, Revolution Newspaper Series, microfilm XN 10:3, Historical Society of Pennsylvania.
16. Brunhouse, note, 254.
17. George Nelson Diary, HSP.
18. Allinson Family Papers, Coll. 968, b. 9, f. 108, Quaker Collection, Haverford College Library.

Chapter Twelve

1. Quillsylvania, "An Epistle From Titus to Timothy," 1781, Am 1781, Epi 962, F. 155, Library Company of Philadelphia.
2. Ibid.
3. Ezequiel Cornell to Nathaniel Greene, July 21, 1780, *Letters of Members of the Continental Congress*, n. 299, v. 5, Edmund C. Burnett, ed., (Washington: Carnegie Institute of Washington Publication, 1931).
4. *Pennsylvania Packet*, October 10, 1780, Historical Society of Pennsylvania.
5. *Pennsylvania Packet*, October 3, 1780, Historical Society of Pennsylvania.
6. Crane, *Drinker* (2010), 88.
7. *Pennsylvania Packet*, October 3, 1780, Historical Society of Pennsylvania.
8. *Pennsylvania Packet*, November 18, 1780, Historical Society of Pennsylvania.
9. Ibid.
10. Brunhouse, 90.
11. Ibid, 103.
12. William Barton, *Memoirs of the Life of David Rittenhouse* (Philadelphia, 1813), 397.
13. Brunhouse, 111–112.
14. *Pennsylvania Packet*, March 1781, Historical Society of Pennsylvania.
15. Mekeel, 331; Free Quaker book, b. 1, Free Quaker Archive, American Philosophical Society.
16. Samuel Rhoads, ed., *Friend's Review*, vol. 15 (Philadelphia, 1862), 706.
17. Morris, "Fisher," 145.
18. Free Quaker Documents, Collections of the Manuscript Division, Library of Congress.
19. Pemberton Papers, v. 37, f. 14, 135–137, Historical Society of Pennsylvania.
20. "To the General Assembly of Pennsylvania An Address and Memorial on behalf of the People called Quakers, Philadelphia, Nine Month 7th, 1782," Collections of the Manuscript Division, Library of Congress.
21. Hazard, ed. Pennsylvania Archives, ser. 1, vol. 9, 762; ibid., ser., 1, vol. 10, 9.
22. Pemberton Papers, v. 37, f. 12, 120.
23. Hazard, ed., Pennsylvania Archives, ser., 1, vol. 9, 762.

24. John Cantazariti, ed., *The Papers of Robert Morris, 1781–1784,* vol. 7, (Pittsburgh: University of Pittsburgh Press, 1988), note, 7.
25. "Timothy Matlack, Late Secretary of Pennsylvania to Jacob Rush Esq. Late Member of the General Assembly," *Freeman's Journal,* Philadelphia, January 21, 1784, Historical Society of Pennsylvania; Hazard, ed. Pennsylvania Archives, ser. 1, vol. 10, 227.
26. Hazard, ed., Pennsylvania Archives, ser. 1, vol. 10, 9, 201.
27. Ibid., 227; Timothy Matlack Account Book, American Philosophical Society; Society Coll., Flying Camp of the Revolution, Historical Society of Pennsylvania (Location of the 13 pages missing from the account book).
28. Etting Collection, Members of Congress, v. 2, 90, Historical Society of Pennsylvania.
29. Robert Smith, ed., *The Friend. A Religious and Literary Journal,* vol. 23 (Philadelphia, 1850), 196.
30. Free Quaker Documents, Collections of the Manuscript Division, Library of Congress.
31. Rhoads, Samuel, ed., *Friends' Review: A Religious, Literary, and Miscellaneous Journal,* vol. 15 (Philadelphia, 1862), 705.
32. Hazard, Pennsylvania Archives, ser. 1, vol. 10, 199.
33. Free Quaker Documents, Collections of the Manuscripts Division, Library of Congress.
34. Hazard, ed., Pennsylvania Archives, ser. 1, vol. 10, 229.
35. *Freeman's Journal,* January 21, 1784, Historical Society of Pennsylvania.
36. "An Address to the Freemen of the State of Pennsylvania," Journal of the Council of Censors, 1783–1784, 235, Historical Society of Pennsylvania.
37. Brunhouse, 158–9.
38. *Pennsylvania Packet,* May 7, 1785, Historical Society of Pennsylvania.

Chapter Thirteen

1. Matlack to Guy Bryan, Savannah, February 12, 1786, courtesy of Malcolm Bryan.
2. *Pennsylvania Herald,* May 26, 1787, Free Library of Philadelphia, iw.newsbank.com.
3. See image of the invitation held by the Rosenbach Library Collection; *New-Hampshire Gazette,* August 25, 1787, Free Library of Philadelphia, iw.newsbank.com. For White Matlack see also *History Detectives,* Season 7, Episode 9, George Washington Miniature.
4. John Meginness, ed., *Journal of Samuel Maclay* (Williamsport, 1887).
5. American State Papers, v. 1, 1789–1814, 140–1.
6. Ibid., 142.
7. Marcus Gould, ed., *The Friend; or Advocate of Truth,* vol. 3 (Philadelphia, 1830): 75–6.

Chapter Fourteen

1. Rhoads, ed., *Friends' Review,* vol. 16, no. 14 (1862), 209.
2. Graydon, 154–5; Stackhouse, 103–5.
3. J. Worth Estes and Billy G. Smith, *A Melancholy Scene of Devastation: The Public Response to the 1793 Philadelphia Yellow Fever Epidemic* (Canton, MA: Science History Publications, 1997), 4.
4. Ibid., 2, 5.
5. Tamar Roberts' Book, July 29, 1796, Private Collection.
6. The Highlands Mansion and Gardens, Fort Washington, PA, highlandshistorical.org.
7. Hiltzheimer, American Philosophical Society.
8. Charles Biddle, 275–8.
9. Sanford W. Higginbotham, *The Keystone in the Democratic Arch: Pennsylvania Politics 1800–1816* (Harrisburg: Pennsylvania Historical and Museum Commission, 1952), 5.
10. A. Kirsten Foster, *Moral Visions and Material Ambitions,* (Lanham, MD: Lexington Books, 2004), 39.
11. Ibid., 14.
12. Ibid.,13, 22, 23.
13. *Gazette of the United States* 18, no. 2494, September 24, 1800, Free Library of Philadelphia, iw.newsbank.com.
14. *Aurora General Advertiser,* n. 4567, August 21, 1805, Free Library of Philadelphia, iw.newsbank.com.
15. Higginbotham, 27.
16. *Washington Federalist,* October 14, 1800, Free Library of Philadelphia, iw.newsbank.com; Higginbotham, 69.
17. Higginbotham, 10–11.
18. *Gazette of the United States* 18, no. 2500, October 1, 1800, Free Library of Philadelphia, iw.newsbank.com.
19. *Aurora General Advertiser,* August 21, 1805, Free Library of Philadelphia, iw.newsbank.com.
20. *Aurora General Advertiser,* September 28, 1805, Free Library of Philadelphia, iw.newsbank.com.
21. Simon Gratz Coll., c. 14, b. 31, Historical Society of Pennsylvania.
22. *Aurora General Advertiser,* August 21, 1805, Free Library of Philadelphia, iw.newsbank.com.
23. Ibid.

Chapter Fifteen

1. Harry M. Tinkcom, ed., "Sir Augustus in Pennsylvania: The Travels and Observations of Sir Augustus J Foster in Early Nineteenth Century Pennsylvania," *Pennsylvania Magazine of History and Biography* 75 (1951): 381.
2. Edwin Morris Betts, ed., *Thomas Jefferson's Garden Book* (Chapel Hill: University of North Carolina Press, 2001), 343.
3. Ibid., 352.
4. "A Series of Essays on Manufactures," *Grotjan's Philadelphia Public Sale Record* 3, no. 7 (June 20, 1814), Free Library of Philadelphia, iw.newsbank.com.
5. *Memoirs of the Philadelphia Society for Promoting Agriculture*, vol. 1 (1808), 113, 270.
6. "On the cultivation of the Vine, in a letter to the President of the Society, by Timothy Matlack, Esq.," *The American Farmer* 6, no. 42 (Baltimore, January 7, 1825): 329.
7. John Hill Martin, *Martin's Bench and Bar of Philadelphia* (1883), 169.
8. *Poulson's American Daily Advertiser*, June 13, 1810, Free Library of Philadelphia, iw.newsbank.com.
9. Roberts Vaux, *Memoirs of the Lives of Benjamin Lay and Ralph Sandiford*, annotated by Timothy Matlack, Massachusetts Historical Society.
10. "An Epistle from Titus to Timothy," Library Company of Philadelphia.
11. "Letters on the Origin and Progress of Attempts for the Abolition of Slavery in Pennsylvania," Collections of the Massachusetts Historical Society, ser., 2, v. 8 (Boston, 1819), 191.
12. *Pennsylvania Packet*, February 1, 1783, Historical Society of Pennsylvania.
13. Letters on Slavery, 191.
14. Peter A. Browne, Reports of Cases Adjudged in the Court of Common Pleas (Philadelphia, 1811), 369–74.
15. Jefferson to James Madison, May 25, 1812, *The Works of Thomas Jefferson*, vol. 11, Paul L. Ford, ed. (New York: G. P. Putnam's Sons, 1905), 246.
16. Charles Biddle, 337–8.
17. Thomas Paine, *Common Sense*, a copy annotated by Timothy Matlack, Am. 1776, Pai., Ar76, 149, HSP Collection held by the Library Company of Philadelphia.
18. *Providence Patriot*, July 14, 1821, v.3, n. 56, Free Library of Philadelphia, iw.newsbank.com.
19. *Haverhill Gazette*, July 20, 1821, v. 35, n. 58, Free Library of Philadelphia, iw.newsbank.com.
20. Lafayette to Matlack, Secretary of the American Philosophical Society, February 15, 1781, Collections of the Manuscript Division, Library of Congress.
21. Stackhouse, 61. (Lafayette's visit may have occurred in July, 1825.)
22. Matlack Family Collection, Asa Matlack notebooks, 975A, Quaker Collections, Haverford College Library.
23. Nash, 95.
24. Charles Coleman Sellers, "Portraits and Miniatures by Charles Willson Peale," *Transactions of the American Philosophical Society* 42, no. 1 (1952), 140; Irma B. Jaffe, *The Italian Presence in American Art 1760–1860* (New York: Fordham University Press, 1989), 31.
25. Charles Coleman Sellers, "Portraits and Miniatures by Charles Willson Peale," *Transactions of the American Philosophical Society* 42, no. 1 (1952).
26. Sellers, 141.
27. Rhoads, ed., *Friend's Review*, vol. 15, no. 45 (Philadelphia, July 12, 1862), 706; *The Casket*, v. 5, n. 2 (1831), 63.
28. Asa Matlack Notebooks, Quaker Coll., Haverford College Library.
29. Justin B. Delair and William Sarjeant, "The Earliest Discoveries of Dinosaurs,"*Isis*, The University of Chicago Press, v. 66, n. 1 (March 1975), 10; Timothy Matlack and Caspar Wistar, "A Large Thigh bone found near Woodbury Creek in Gloucester County, N.J.," *Proceedings of the American Philosophical Society*, n. 22 (1791), 154; Timothy Matlack, "A large tusk found in the back country," *Proceedings of the American Philosophical Society* 22 (1791), 193.
30. On November 20, 1905, Timothy Matlack's remains were removed from the Free Quaker Graveyard to Wetherills' Cemetery in Audubon, Pennsylvania.

Epilogue

1. Gaillard Hunt, "The Penmanship of the Declaration of Independence," *The Youth's Companion* (June 29, 1916). This article was picked up by various newspapers including the *New York Sun*.
2. Cynthia D. Edelberg, *Jonathan Odell, Loyalist Poet of the American Revolution* (Durham: Duke University Press, 1987), 98; Sargent, 39.
3. Bird Wilson, *Memoir of the Life of the Right Reverend William White* (Philadelphia, 1839), 50–1.
4. Thayer, 189.
5. John Paul Selsam, *The Pennsylvania Constitution of 1776: A Study in Revolutionary Democracy* (Philadelphia: University of Pennsylvania Press, 1936), 70.
6. Thayer, 197.

Bibliography

Aiken, Robert. "Cruelty to Animals Exposed." *Pennsylvania Magazine*, 1775.

Alexander, John K. "The Fort Wilson Incident of 1779: A Case Study of the Revolutionary Crowd." *William and Mary Quarterly* 31 (October 1974): 600.

"Allinson Family Papers." Quaker Collection. Haverford College Library, n.d.

Anderson, James Donald. "Thomas Wharton, Virginia Exile, 1777-1778." *Virginia Magazine of History and Biography* 89, no. 4 (October 1981): 425-447.

Bailyn, Bernard. *The Ideological Origins of the American Revolution*. Cambridge, Massachusetts: The Belknap Press of Harvard University Press, 1967.

Ballagh, James Curtis, ed. *The Letters of Richard Henry Lee, 1762-1794*, vol. 2. New York: McMillan, 1914.

Barton, William. *Memoirs of the Life of David Rittenhouse*. Philadelphia, 1813.

Betts, Edwin Morris, ed. *Thomas Jefferson's Garden Book*. Chapel Hill: University of North Carolina Press, 2001.

Biddle, Charles. *Autobiography of Charles Biddle, Vice President of the Supreme Executive Council of Pennsylvania*. Philadelphia: E. Claxton, 1883.

Biddle, Henry, ed. *Extracts from the Journal of Elizabeth Drinker*. Philadelphia: J. B. Lippincott, 1889.

Blecki, Catherine LaCourreye and Karin A. Wulf. *Milcah Martha Moore's Book: A Commonplace Book from Revolutionary America*. College Park: Pennsylvania State University Press, 1997.

Bobrick, Benson. *Angel in the Whirlwind*. New York: Simon & Schuster, 1997.

Boyd, Julian P. "The Declaration of Independence: The Mystery of the Lost Original." *Pennsylvania Magazine of History and Biography* 100, no. 4 (October 1976): 451-452.

Brandt, Clare. *The Man in the Mirror*. New York: Random House, 1994.

Bridenbaugh, Carl. *Cities in Revolt*. New York: Alfred A. Knopf, 1955.

Bridenbaugh, Carl, and Jessica Bridenbaugh. *Rebels and Gentlemen: Philadelphia in the Age of Franklin*. New York: Reynal & Hitchcock, 1942.

Brooks, Lynn M. "Against Vain Sports and Pastime: The Theater Dance in Philadelphia, 1724-90." *Dance Chronicle* 12, no. 2 (1989): 172.

Browne, Peter A. *Reports of Cases Adjudged in the Court of Common Pleas*. Philadelphia, 1811.

Brunhouse, Robert L. *The Counter-Revolution in Pennsylvania 1776-1790*. Harrisburg: Pennsylvania Historical and Museum Commission, 1971.

Burnett, Edmund C., ed. *Letters of Members of the Continental Congress*, vol 5. Washington: Carnegie Institute of Washington Publication, 1931.

Butterfield, Lyman H., ed. *Diary and Biography of John Adams: Vol. 3, Diary, 1782-1804*. Boston: Massachusetts Historical Society, 1961.

"Catalog of Franklin Exhibition in the Library of Congress." *Proceedings of the American Philosophical Society* 100, no. 4 (August 1956): 385-416.

Clark, William Bell. "Letters of Captain Nicholas Biddle." *Pennsylvania Magazine of History and Biography* 74, no. 3 (1931): 393-394.

Coleman, John. *Thomas McKean, Forgotten Leader of the Revolution*. Rockaway, NJ: American Faculty Press, 1975.

Cooper, J. W. *A Treatise on Cocking*. Media, PA: Cooper & Vernon, 1859.

Crane, Elaine Forman. *The Diary of Elizabeth Drinker*, vol. 1. Boston: Northeastern University Press, 1991.

Crane, Elaine Forman. *The Diary of Elizabeth Drinker, Abridged Edition*. Philadelphia: University of Pennsylvania Press, 2010.

Crooks, Daniel J. *Charleston is Burning. Two Centuries of Fire and Flames*. Charleston, SC: The History Press, 2009.

Delair, Justin B, and William Sarjeant. "The Earliest Discoveries of Dinosaurs." *Isis* (The University of Chicago Press) 66, no. 1 (March 1975).

"Diary of Richard Smith in the Continental Congress, 1775–1776." *American Historical Review* 1, no. 3 (April 1896): 494–495.

Doren, Carl Van. *Secret History of the American Revolution*. New York: Viking Press, Inc., 1941.

Dorwart, Jeffery M. *Camden County, New Jersey*. New Brunswick, NJ: Rutgers University Press, 2001.

Douglass, Elisha P. *Rebels and Democrats*. Chapel Hill: University of North Carolina Press, 1955.

Duane, William, ed. *Extracts from the Diary of Christopher Marshall, 1774–1781*. Albany, NY: Joel Munsell, 1877.

"Early Quaker Monthly Meeting Minutes." *Pennsylvania Genealogical Magazine* (n.d.): 29, 30, 32, 211, 215.

Edelberg, Cynthia D. *Jonathan Odell, Loyalist Poet of the American Revolution*. Durham, NC: Duke University Press, 1987.

Ellis, Joseph J. *His Excellency George Washington*. New York: Alfred A. Knopf, 2004.

"An Epistle from the Meetings for Sufferings: held in Philadelphia for Pennsylvania and New-Jersey, the 5th Day of the First Month, 1775." Vol. LCP Ar.75 F91. Historical Society of Pennsylvania, 1775.

Estes, J. Worth, and Billy G. Smith. *A Melancholy Scene of Devastation: The Public Response to the 1793 Philadelphia Yellow Fever Epidemic*. Canton, Massachusetts: Science History Publications, 1997.

"Extracts from the Journal of Mrs. Henry Drinker." *Pennsylvania Magazine of History and Biography* 13, no. 3 (October 1889).

Fischer, David Hackett. *Washington's Crossing*. New York: Oxford University Press, 2004.

Fitzpatrick, John C., ed. *The Writings of George Washington*, vol. 7:79. Washington: Government Printing Office, 1931–1944.

Foner, Eric. *Tom Paine and Revolutionary America*. New York: Oxford University Press, 2005.

Foner, Philip Sheldon. *The Complete Writings of Thomas Paine*. New York: Citadel Press, 1969.

Force, Peter, ed. *American Archives*. Washington, 1837–1853.

Ford, Paul L., ed. *The Works of Thomas Jefferson*, vol. 11. New York: G. P. Putnam's Sons, 1905.

Foster, A. Kirsten. *Moral Visions and Material Ambitions*. Lanham, Maryland: Lexington Books, 2004.

Foster, Joseph S. *In Pursuit of Equal Liberty: George Bryan and the Revolution in Pennsylvania*. University Park: The Pennsylvania State University Press, 1994.

"Free Quaker Documents." Manuscripts. Library of Congress, n.d.

"George Nelson Diary, 1780–1792." Historical Society of Pennsylvania, n.d.

Gill, Julia Bedford. "The Story of a Short Life, Letitia Matlack 1724–1752." June 12, 1926.

Gillingham, Harrold E., Elias Bland, and Edward Wilsonn. "Some Colonial Ships Built in Philadelphia." *Pennsylvania Magazine of History and Biography* (1932): 156–186.

Godwin, Parke. *Cyclopedia of Universal Biography*. New York: A. S. Barnes, 1854.

Graydon, Alexander. *Memoirs of his Own Time with Reminiscences of the Men and Events of the Revolution*. Philadelpia: Lindsay and Blakiston, 1846.

"Haines & Twells Account Book, 1767–1770." Philadelphia: American Philosophical Society, n.d.

Hawke, David. *In the Midst of a Revolution*. Philadelphia: University of Pennsylvania Press, 1961.

Hazard, Samuel, ed. *Colonial Records of Pennsylvania*, vol. 10. Harrisburg, PA: T. Fenn & Co., 1852.

Higginbotham, Sanford W. *The Keystone in the Democratic Arch: Pennsylvania Politics 1800–1816*. Harrisburg: Pennsylvania Historical and Museum Commission, 1952.

Hindle, Brooke. "The March of the Paxton Boys." *William and Mary Quarterly* 3rd Series, no. 3 (October 1946): 474.

Hopkinson, Francis. "The Cockfight, Common Place Book." Historical Society of Pennsylvania, 1778.

Hunt, Gaillard. "The Penmanship of the Declaration of Independence." *The Youth's Companion*, June 1916.

"Indian 1683–1794 Collection (Phi) 1297 ." Philadelphia: Historical Society of Pennsylvania, n.d.

Jackson, John W. *With the British Army in Philadelphia, 1777–1778*. San Rafael, CA: Presidio Press, 1979.

Jaffe, Irma B. *The Italian Presence in American Art 1760–1860*. New York: Fordham University Press, 1989.

Jordan, John W. "The Fellowship Fire Company of Philadelphia, Organized 1738." *Pennsylvania Magazine of History and Biography*, 1903: 476.

Keane, John. *Tom Paine: A Political Life*. London: Bloomsbury Publishing, 1995.

Kenny, Kevin. *Peaceable Kingdom Lost: The Paxton Boys and the Destruction of William Penn's Holy Experiment*. New York: Oxford University Press, 2009.

Ketchum, Richard M. *The Winter Soldiers*. New York: Holt and Co., 1973.

Kill, Rosemary Troy. *Early American Decorative Arts 1620–1860*. Lanham: Altamira Press, 2010.

Kramnick, Isaac. "Introduction to Thomas Paine." In *Common Sense*, by Thomas Paine. New York: Penguin Books, 1986.

Landis, Bertha Cochran. "Col. Timothy Matlack: A Revolutionary Patriot in Lancaster." *Papers of the Lancaster Historical Society* XLII, no. 6 (1938): 150.

"Letters on the Origin and Progress of Attempts for the Abolition of Slavery in Pennsylvania." *Collections of the Massachusetts Historical Society* 8 (1819).

Levy, Barry. *Quakers and the American Family British Settlement in the Delaware Valley*. New York: Oxford University Press, 1988.

Lincoln, Charles H. *The Revolutionary Movement in Philadelphia, 1760–1776*. Cambridge, MA: Harvard University, 1901.

Maier, Pauline. *American Scripture: Making the Declaration of Independence*. New York: Alfred A. Knopf , 1997.

Martin, John Hill. *Martin's Bench and Bar of Philadelphia*. 1883.

"Matlack Family Papers." Quaker Collection. Haverford, Pennsylvania: Haverford College Library, n.d.

Matlack, Timothy. "A large tusk found in the back country." *Proceedings of the American Philosophical Society*, no. 22 (1791).

——. "An Oration Delivered March 16, 1780 Before the Patron, Vice President and Members of the American Philosophical Society." Philadelphia: Styner and Cist, 1780.

——. "Observations on making and fining Cyder, and on Peach Trees." *Memoirs of the Philadelphia Society for Promoting Agriculture* 1 (1808): 112.

——. "On the cultivation of the Vine, in a letter to the President of the Society." *American Farmer* 6, no. 42 (January 1825): 329.

Matlack, Timothy, and Caspar Wistar. "A Large Thigh bone found near Woodbury Creek in Gloucester County, N.J." *Proceedings of the American Philosophical Society*, no. 22 (1791).

McCullough, David. *John Adams*. New York: Simon & Schuster, 2001.

Meginness, John, ed. *Journal of Samuel Maclay*. Williamsport, 1887.

Mekeel, Arthur J. *The Quakers and the American Revolution*. York: Sessions Book Trust, 1996.

Messer, Peter C. "A Species of Treason & Not the Least Dangerous Kind: The Treason Trials of Abraham Carlisle and John Roberts." *Pennsylvania Magazine of History and Biography* 123, no. 4 (1999): 303.

Mickle, Samuel. *The Diaries of Samuel Mickle: Woodbury, Gloucester County, New Jersey, 1792–1829*, vol. 1. Woodbury, NJ: Gloucester County Historical Society, 1991.

"Misc. Benjamin Franklin Collections 1710–1822." Philadelphia: American Philosophical Society, n.d.

Morgan, Edmund S. *Benjamin Franklin* . New Haven: Yale University Press, 2002.

Morris, Anna Wharton. "Journal of Samuel Rowland Fisher, of Philadelphia. 1779–1781." *Pennsylvania Magazine of History and Biography* 41, no. 2 (1917).

Nash, Gary B. *First City: Philadelphia and the Forging of Historical Memory*. Philadelphia: University of Pennsylvania Press, 2006.

——. *The Unknown American Revolution:*

The Unruly Birth of Democracy and the Struggle to Create America. New York: Viking Penguin, 2005.
Nelson, W. "Beginnings of the Iron Industry in Trenton New Jersey." *Pennsylvania Magazine of History and Biography* (Historical Society of Pennsylvania) 35, no. 2 (1911): 241.
New Jersey Archives: Documents Relating to the Revolutionary History of the State of New Jersey.1917, 2nd Series ed.: 63.
Oaks, Robert F. *Philadelphia Merchants and the American Revolution, 1765–1776*. Los Angeles: University of Southern California, 1970.
Odell, Jonathan, ed. *The Loyal Verses of Joseph Stansbury and Doctor Jonathan Odell*. Philadelphia, 1857.
Paine, Thomas. "Common Sense, 2nd Edition." Philadelphia: William and Thomas Bradford, February 14, 1776.
Peckham, Howard. "Dr. Berkenhout's Journal, 1778." *Pennsylvania Magazine of History and Biography* 65, no. 1 (January 1941): 79–92.
Phillips, Catherine. *Memoirs of the Life of Catherine Phillips* . London: James Phillips and Sons, 1797.
Pierce, Arthur D. *Smugglers' Woods Jaunts and Journeys in Colonial and Revolutionary New Jersey*. New Brunswick, NJ: Rutgers, The State University, 1960.
Powell, George. *The History of Camden County New Jersey*. Philadelphia: L. J. Richards & Co., 1886.
Proceedings of a General Court Martial ... For the trial of Major General Benedict Arnold June 1, 1779. Philadelphia: Francis Bailey, 1780.
R., Sergeant. "The Battle of Princeton." *Pennsylvania Magazine of History and Biography* 20, no. 4 (1896): 516.
Reed, Joseph. "General Joseph Reed's Narrative of the Movements of the American Army in the Neighborhood of Trenton in the Winter of 1776–1777." *Pennsylvania Magazine of History and Biography* (December 1884): 391–402.
Reed, William. *Life and Correspondence of Joseph Reed*, vol. 2. Philadelphia, 1847.
Reigart, John Franklin. *The Life of Robert Fulton*. Philadelphia, 1856.
Rhoads, Samuel, and Enoch Lewis, eds. *Friends Review*, 1862: 564, 614.
Rigal, Laura. *The American Manufactory: Art, Labor, and the World of Things in the Early Republic*. Princeton, NJ: Princeton University Press, 1998.
Roach, Hannah B. "Benjamin Franklin Slept Here." *Pennsylvania Magazine of History and Biography* (April 1960): 127–174.
"Robert Morris and the Episode of the Polacre 'Victorious.'" *Pennsylvania Magazine of History and Biography* 70, no. 3 (July 1946): 248–252.
Rodney, Thomas. *Diary of Captain Thomas Rodney, 1776–1777*. Wilmington: Historical Society of Delaware, 1888.
Rosswurm, Steven. *Armys, Country and Class*. New Brunswick, NJ: Rutgers University Press, 1987.
Rosswurm, Steven, and Stephanie Wolf. "Leisure Time in Colonial Philadelphia." June 1976.
Ryerson, Richard. *The Revolution is Now Begun: The Radical Committees of Philadelphia,1765–1776*. Philadelphia: University of Pennsylvania Press, 1978.
Salinger, Sharon. *Taverns and Drinking in Early America*. Baltimore: Johns Hopkins University Press, 2002.
Sargent, Winthrop, ed. *The Loyal Verses of Joseph Stansbury and Doctor Jonathan Odell*. Albany, NY: J. Munsell, 1860.
Scharf, J. Thomas, and Thompson Westcott. *History of Philadelphia 1609–1884*. Philadelphia: L. H. Everts & Co., 1884.
"Second Troop Philadelphia City Cavalry, The." *Pennsylvania Magazine of History and Biography* 45 (1921): 283.
"Selections from the Military Papers of General John Cadwalader." *Pennsylvania Magazine of History and Biography* 32, no. 2 (1908): 151.
Selig, Robert A. *Battle of Princeton Mapping Project: Report of Military Terrain Analysis and Battle Narrative*. Princeton, NJ: Princeton Battlefield Society, 2010.
Sellers, Charles Coleman. "Portraits and Miniatures by Charles Willson Peale." *Transactions of the American Philosophical Society* 42, no. 1 (1952).
Selsam, John Paul. *The Pennsylvania Constitution of 1776: A Study in Revolutionary Democracy*. Philadelphia: University of Pennsylvania Press, 1936.
"Shippen Papers." Historical Society of Pennsylvania, n.d.
Smith, C. Page. "The Attack on Fort Wilson." *Pennsylvania Magazine of History and Biography* 78, no. 2 (April 1954): 187.
Smith, Charles R. *Marines in the Revolution*.

History and Museum Division, U.S. Marine Corp, 1975.
Smith, Page. *The Constitution, a Documentary and Narrative History.* New York: Morrow, 1978.
Smith, William Henry. *A Political History of Slavery.* New York: G. P. Putnam's Sons, 1903.
Smith, William Henry, ed. *The St. Clair Papers,* vol. 1. R. Clarke & Co., 1882.
Soderlund, Jean R. *Quakers & Slavery: A Divided Spirit.* Princeton, NJ: Princeton University Press, 1985.
Stackhouse, A. M. "Col. Timothy Matlack Patriot and Soldier: A Paper Read Before the Gloucester County Historical Society at the Old Tavern House, Haddonfield, NJ April 14, 1908." Privately printed, 1910.
Stewart, Frank H., ed. "Notes on Old Gloucester County, New Jersey." New Jersey Society of Pennsylvania, Gloucester Country Historical Society, 1917.
Stone, Frederick D. "Philadelphia Society One Hundred Years Ago, or the Reign of Continental Money." *Pennsylvania Magazine of History and Biography* 3, no. 4 (1879): 384.
Stryker, William S. *The Battles of Trenton and Princeton.* Boston, 1898.
Taylor, Robert J., ed. *Papers of John Adams,* vol. 4. Cambridge, MA: The Belknap Press of Harvard University Press, 1979.
Thayer, Theodore. *Pennsylvania Politics and the Growth of Democracy, 1740–1776.* Harrisburg: Pennsylvania Historical and Museum Commission, 1953.
Thompson, Peter. *Rum Punch & Revolution.* Philadelphia: University of Pennsylvania Press, 1999.
Thompson, Ray. *Benedict Arnold in Philadelphia.* Ft. Washington, PA: Bicentennial Press, 1975.
"Timothy Matlack to Abiel Holmes, 12 October 1819." Documents, 1726–1816. Philadelphia, Pennsylvania: American Philosophical Society, n.d.
"Timothy Matlack to John Peters, 17 June 1756." Peale-Sellers Family Collection. Philadelphia, Pennsylvania: American Philosophical Society, n.d.
"Timothy Matlack to William Findley, 11 January 1817." Collections of the Massachusetts Historical Society. Vol. 8. 1819.
Tinkcom, Harry M., ed. "Sir Augustus in Pennsylvania: The Travels and Observations of Sir Augustus J. Foster in Early Nineteenth Century Pennsylvania." *Pennsylvania Magazine of History and Biography* 75 (1951).
Treese, Lorett. *The Storm Gathering: The Penn Family and the American Revolution.* Mechanicsburg, PA: Stackpole Books, 2002.
Wainwright, Nicholas B., and Sarah Logan Fisher. "A Diary of Trifling Occurrences." *Pennsylvania Magazine of History and Biography* (October 1958): 415.
"Warren-Adams Letters." Massachusetts Historical Society Collection 62. 1917.
"Washington's Household Account Book, 1793–1797." *Pennsylvania Magazine of History and Biography* 29, no. 4 (1905): 386.
Watson, John Fanning. *Annals of Philadelphia.* Philadelphia: E. L. Carey & A. Hart, 1830.
Werner, Raymond C. "Diary of Grace Growden Galloway." *Pennsylvania Magazine of History and Biography* 55, no. 1 (1931).
Westcott, Thompson. *The Historic Mansions and Buildings of Philadelphia.* Philadelphia: Porter & Coates, 1877.
"William Penn Charter School Archives, Coll. 1115, Deed Book of the Overseers of the Quaker School." Quaker Collection. Haverford, Pennsylvania: Haverford College Library, n.d.
"Wills, Philadelphia PA." no. 14. Philadelphia: Historical Society of Pennsylvania, 1752.
Wilson, Bird. *Memoir of the Life of the Right Reverend William White.* Philadelphia, 1839.
Wood, Gordon S. *The Radicalism of the American Revolution.* New York: Alfred A. Knopf, 1992.
Wolf, Edwin, II. "The Authorship of the 1774 Address to the King Restudied." *William and Mary Quarterly* 22, no. 2 (April 1965): 190–224.
"Wyck Association Collection." Philadelphia: American Philosophical Society, n.d.
Young, William. "Journal of Sergeant William Young." *Pennsylvania Magazine of History and Biography* 8, no. 3 (October 1884).

Index

Abeel, Johannes, Jr. 168
Abolition Society (Philadelphia) 183
Act for the Gradual Abolition of Slavery (Pennsylvania) 135–36, 137, 181, 183, 195
Act of Attainder (Pennsylvania) 95
Active (sloop) 104, 105, 106
Adams, John 38, 49, 53, 55–56, 84, 100, 131, 191; opposition to unicameralism 64, 65; president 174, 177; resolution in Congress 47–48, 50
Adams, Samuel 47, 48, 51
Adlum, John 165
agriculture, farming 12–13, 40, 132–34, 173–74, 185
The Alarm (broadside) 49
Albany, N.Y. 88
Aliquipiso 168
Alison, Frances 59
Allegheny River, Pennsylvania 97, 167, 170
Allen, Andrew 58
Allen, James 88
Allen, John (sheriff of Hunterdon County) 22
Allen, John 70
Allen, Richard 172
Allen, William 70
Allentown, N.J. 70
Allinson, Martha Cooper (TM's niece) 21, 171
Allinson, Samuel 21, 93, 147
Allinson, William 188, 191, 195
American Company (theater) 28
The American Crisis (Paine) 9
American Philosophical Society 131, 148, 188, 191
American Scribe (font) 196
Andre, John 88, 95, 126, 141, 142
Anticonstitutionalists (Pennsylvania) 66, 81, 82, 107, 108, 124
apprenticeship 19, 20
Army, British 25, 83, 85–86, 88, 95–96, 194; in

New England 41–42; in New Jersey 8, 70–76, 78, 80; in New York 63; stationed in the colonies 23–24, 27; threatens Philadelphia 7; in Virginia 148
Arnold, Benedict 194; commandant of Philadelphia 98–99, 102–7, 123; court-martial 111–12, n125–31; West Point, plot discovered 141–42,
Articles of Confederation, U.S. 58, 145
artillery 10, 41, 52, 69, 71–74, 80, 122
artisans 30, 34, 38, 42, 49; *see also* Philadelphia: artisans
Assembly, Pennsylvania (After July 4, 1776) 81, 131, 135, 144, 149; abolition law 136–37; convention calls 109; militia laws 67, 78, 121
Assembly, Pennsylvania (Before July 4, 1776) 43; elite control of 34; refusal to support independence 38–39, 46–47, 50–53
Associators (Philadelphia militia) 61, 47, 75–76, 80, 116; formation after Lexington and Concord 41; ideology 7; threat of the Paxton Boys 24–25; winter campaign (1776–77) 8, 10–11, 69, 71–73, 75–76; *see also* militia
Assumpink Creek, battle of 71–72
Atlee, S.J. 143
auction, vendue 17, 18
Aurora (newspaper) 174, 177–78

Bache, Richard 109–11
Bache, Sarah 120
Baltimore, Md. 7
Bank of North America 144–45
Barnes, William 90
Barton, William 175–77
Bartram, Moses 153
Bayard, John 58, 78
beer 29–30, 134, 181;
Bell, William 159

216   Index

Benezet, Anthony 136
Berkenhout, Dr. John 100-2, 111
Biddle, Charles 41, 54, 91, 97, 162, 173
Biddle, Clement 24
Biddle, John 22
Biddle, Nicholas 68, 81, 89-91, 132
Biddle, Owen 22, 47, 56, 59, 94, 146, 152, 171
Biddle, Sarah 22
Billingsport, Pa. 61
Bordentown, Pa. 8, 9, 69, 70-71
Boston 7, 41, 47; Tea Party 37
Bound Brook, N.J. 78
Boyd, John 120
Bradford, William, Jr. 154, 156
Brandywine Creek, battle of 85-86
brewers, breweries 13, 16, 18, 28-29; resistance measures 35-37; *see also* beer
Bristol, Pa. 8, 11, 69, 188
Britannia (racehorse) 31
Britannia (ship) 39
Brown, John 112, 131
Brunswick, N.J. 67, 70-72, 75
Bryan, George 94, 108, 117, 163; sponsors abolition bill 136; supports constitution 59
Bryan, Guy (TM's son-in-law) 158, 189
Bryan, Martha Matlack (TM's daughter) 92, 158, 189
Bryan, Samuel 174
Bull, John 59, 120
Bunker Hill, battle of (1775) 42
Burgoyne, John 88
Burlington, N.J. 8-10, 12, 69, 73, 76
Burlington Island (Chygoes) 8
Burr, Aaron 176-77
Burr, Elizabeth (TM's aunt) 136
Burr, Henry (TM's grandfather) 182

Cadwalader, John 50, 78, 110; as militia commander 8, 9, 68-70, 72, 74-76
Cambridge, Mass. 41
Cannon, James 49; committee leader 46, 50, 64-66; convention leader 56, 58-60
Cannon, William 191
Carlisle, Abraham 99, 107, 108, 149
Carlisle Peace Commission 100-11
Carmalt, Hannah (TM's daughter-in-law) 159, 171
Carpenter's Hall, Philadelphia 52, 53, 84
Carroll, Charles 112, 191
Carson, Joseph 159
Carter, William 24
The Case Knife (mercantile) 22
Cato (play) 28
Chalkley, Thomas 13
Charlestown, Mass. 41
Charlestown, S.C. 89-90, 158

Charming Nancy 127-28, 130
Charming Polly (malt ship) 35
Charter of Privileges, Pennsylvania 58
Chautauqua Lake, N.Y. 169-70
Chesapeake Bay 44, 84
Christ Church (Philadelphia) 165, 172
cider, apple 31, 92, 181
City Tavern, Philadelphia 34, 97, 109, 122, 143-44, 170
Clarion River, Pa. 170
Claypoole, David 172
Claypoole, James 115, 172
Clinton, George 178
Clinton, Sir Henry 96, 126, 194
clothing, attire, fashions 16, 22, 35, 95, 97, 133
Clymer, George 58
Coates, Mary 17, 22
cockfighting, cockmain 31-33, 40
College of Philadelphia 32, 134
committees: claims 44; correspondence 39; inspection 39, 41, 43, 45-47, 55; Marine 44; officers 42; price fixing 117, 120; safety 52-53, 55, 58; secrecy 53
Common Sense (Paine) 2, 44-45, 64, 135, 185-87
Concord, battle of (1775) 41, 51
Conemaugh River, Pa. 170
Conewango Creek, Pa. 169
Conference of Committees, Pennsylvania (1776) 50, 52, 53
Congress, U.S. 38, 41, 119, 144, 193; actions against Tories 84; conflict with Pennsylvania 106
Connecticut 105
Constitution, Pennsylvania (1776) 64-65, 68; Declaration of Rights 62-63, 96, 162; opposition to 66, 109-10, 156; *see also* Convention, Pennsylvania
Constitution, Pennsylvania (1790) 174
Constitutional Convention (1787) 161
Constitutionalists, Radicals (Pennsylvania) 66, 124; conflict with Tories 108-9; control of government 82, 107, 156; political setbacks 143
Continental Army 10, 83; in New England 41, 47; in New Jersey 11, 71-75; in New York 7, 63, 88; in Pennsylvania 68, 69, 86; in Virginia 148
Continental Association 39-40; debates independence 5, 43, 46; evacuations 7, 86; war management 44
Convention (brigantine) 105
Convention, Pennsylvania (1776) 57-60, 62, 67, 110; unicameralism debated 60, 64
Conway, Cabal 68, 101
Conway, Thomas 68
Cooper, Daniel 17

Cooper, David 21, 171
Cooper, J.W. 32, 33
Cooper, Marmaduke 159
Cooper, Norris 172
Cornell, Ezekiel 141, 195
Cornplanter 168, 169
Cornwallis, Charles, Lord 71–73, 75, 86, 102, 138, 147
Council of Censors (Pennsylvania) 156
Council of Safety, Pennsylvania 58, 76, 78, 81; war management 61–63, 65–68
Cowperthwaite, Joseph 10, 24, 41, 69, 78
Coxe, Tench 175, 176
Cranbury, N.J. 70
Craysford (ship) 90
Cromwell, Oliver 146
Crooked Billet (tavern) 69
Crosswicks, N.J. 96

Dartmouth, Lord 39
Davis, Timothy 152
Deane, Silas 119, 120, 143
Dearborn, Henry 177
death, dying 13, 19, 21, 26, 93, 171
debt, debtors, debtor's prison 18, 26, 30, 64, 160–61
Declaration of Independence, U.S. 51–55, 60–63, 188, 190, 193; Dunlap broadside 55, 60
Delancey, James 30, 31, 33
Delaney, Sharp 122
Delaware 41, 52
Delaware River 8, 9–10, 47, 61, 69, 82
democracy, democratic government 7, 49, 53, 57, 59, 64, 110, 195; and military service 103; *see also* Constitution, Pennsylvania (1776)
Democratic-Republican (Democratic) Party 174, 176–78
Dickinson, Cadwalader 149
Dickinson, John 53–54, 57–58; opposition to independence 43, 46–47; opposition to the Pennsylvania Constitution (1776) 66; resistance leadership 34, 37–39; Supreme Executive Council presidency 150, 156; treasonous letter written by 81–82; *see also Letters from a Farmer in Pennsylvania*
Dickinson, Philemon 78, 79
Drinker, Elizabeth 92–97, 107, 109, 112, 116, 142, 148–49, 153
Drinker, Henry 94, 122
Drinker, John 45, 122
drinking 15, 27, 29; *see also* beer; cider, apple; Philadelphia: taverns; rum; wine
Duane, William 174
Duarte, Juan Garcia 118
Duer, William 84

Dunk's ferry, Pa. 10
Dunlap, John 54, 55, 60, 105, 138; *see also* Declaration of Independence: Dunlap broadside
Dunmore, Lord 44
Dunn, Robert 192
Duponceau, Peter S. 162

Earl of Carlisle (Frederick Howard) 96, 100
East India Tea Company 37
Easton, James 58
economy 34–35, 40, 87, 116, 120, 143, 173
education, schools 15, 19, 60, 135
Egg Harbor, N.J. 128–29
Elizabethtown, N.J. 61
Ellicott, Andrew 177
Elmslie, John 25
Emlen, George 17
Emlen, Samuel 153
England, English 7, 8, 12, 95, 185, 187; colonial policies 22, 27, 34–35; Indian policy 24; Navy of 57, 63, 67, 90–91, 96
entertainment, leisure 13, 15, 19, 28–29, 31, 34, 40, 88, 138, 173; *see also* cockfighting; horseracing
Estaugh, John 13, 15
Ewing, James 9
Ewing, John 131, 135

Fair American (brig) 89
Federalist Party 174–76
Fellowship Fire Company 16
5th Battalion of Rifle Rangers 8, 44, 51–52, 57, 69, 72, 74, 76, 79
fire 16, 90; *see also* Fellowship Fire Company
First Troop of Light Horse, Philadelphia 70–71, 122, 161, 173
Fisher, Esther 147
Fisher, Lydia 147
Fisher, Samuel 113–14, 122, 137, 143, 147
Fisher, Sarah Logan 67, 81–83, 85–88, 94, 96
Fisher, Thomas 112–14
Fitzgerald, John 127–28
Fleeson, Plunket 127
food, diet 12, 18, 87, 92, 116, 120–21, 133, 158, 167
Force, Peter 2
Forrest, Thomas 75
Fort Wilson Riot 122–23
Foster, Augustus 180
France, French 8, 94–95, 118–19, 133, 148, 173, 181; Navy of 116, 118
Franklin, Benjamin 52, 54, 56–57, 131, 135, 164–65; and Constitution, Pennsylvania (1776) 110; and drinking 30–31; President Supreme Executive Council 162; resi-

dences in Philadelphia 15, 18, 21; see also *Poor Richard's Almanack*
Franklin, William 31
Franklin, Pa. 170
Franks, David 103, 126, 128–29
Frankstown, Pa. 170
Free Quaker Meeting House 153, 165
Free Quakers see Religious Society of Free Quakers
Freeman's Journal 137, 178
French and Indian War 23–24
French Creek, Pa. 170
Friendly Association for Regaining and Preserving Peace with the Indians by Pacific Measures 25
fruit, fruit trees 13, 133, 180–81, 190
Fulton, Robert 97

Galloway, Grace 98–99
Galloway, Joseph 39, 46, 49
gamecocks see cockfighting, cockmain
Gates, Horatio 68, 88
George III, King of England 9, 28, 50, 52, 54, 103; Proclamation for Suppressing Rebellion and Sedition 43
Georgia 41, 65, 158, 181
Germantown, Pa. 8, 25, 86
Geyer, Andrew 76, 171
Gilpin, Thomas 93
Gloucester (Gloucester City) N.J. 13
Goodson, Andrew (servant) 15
Gray, George 154
Graydon, Alexander 171
Greene, Nathanael 103, 125, 141
Griffin, Samuel 9
Griffiths, Isaac 18

Haddon, Elizabeth 13, 15
Haddonfield, N.J. 13, 17, 189
Haines, Josiah 13
Haines, Mary 12
Haines, Rueben 16, 18–19, 26, 28–30
Haines and Twells (brewery) 28, 36
Hale, William 74, 75
Hall, Lyman 41, 158
Hamilton, Alexander 176
Hancock, John 42, 44, 46
Hancock, Mary 12
Hand, Edward 71, 74
Harmar, Josiah 168
Hausegger, Nicholas 73
Heister, Joseph 185
Henry, George 10
Henry, Patrick 85
Henry, William 59
Herbert, Lawrence 76
Hessians 9, 10, 43, 47, 52, 66, 71–72, 80, 88, 96; Regimental band 83

Hiltzheimer, Jacob 28, 30–31, 37–39, 49, 86, 109, 122–23, 138, 148, 154, 159, 163, 165, 170–73, 195
Hinchenbrook (ship) 90
Hitchcock, Daniel 10, 74–75
Hoge, Jonathan 59
holidays, celebrations 18, 28, 49, 148; see also Independence Day
Holker, John 118, 119
Holmesburg, Pa. 188–89
Hopkins, James 177
Hopkinson, Francis 33, 109–10
horseracing 29–32, 40
House of Commons, British 27, 39
House of Lords, British 39
Howe, Sir William 7–8, 57, 66, 82–87, 95, 100, 138;
Howell, Isaac 148, 153
Hubley, John 59
Hudson River 83, 88, 125, 126, 141
Humphreys, Whitehead 109, 120, 140–41, 144
Humphries, Charles 53, 58
Hunt, Gaillard 193–94
Hunt, John 93
Hunt, Wilson 138

indentured servants 12, 15–16, 183; see also Act for Gradual Abolition
Independence Day (annual celebration) 1, 83, 97, 118, 173, 187
Indian King (tavern) 18, 22, 185
Indian Queen (tavern) 29, 53
Ingersoll, Jared 140

Jacobs, John 59, 66
James, John 112–14
Jameson, John 141
Jay, John 131
Jefferson, Thomas 131, 141, 184, 191; in Congress 43, 54–55; presidential elections 176–77
Jockey Club, Philadelphia 31
Johns, Matthew 122
Jones, Absalom 172
Jones, John Paul 146
Jones, Owen 84, 85
Jones, Owen, Jr. 84, 93–94
Jones, Susanna 92, 94
Jones, William 138
Jordan, Jesse 129
Juniata River, Pa. 170

Kiskiminetas River, Pa. 170
Kuhl, Frederick 56, 59

Lafayette, Marquis de 188
Lake Erie 165, 169, 170

Index

Lancaster, Pa. 9, 23, 50, 55, 86–87, 92, 95, 118, 173, 175, 180
Lancaster Intelligencer 177
Laurens, Henry 118–19, 131
Lay, Benjamin 182
Lebanon, Pa. 165–66, 170
Lee, Charles 66
Lee, Richard Henry 51, 84–85, 100, 118–19, 141
Lesley, Peter 192
Letters from a Farmer in Pennsylvania (Dickinson) 34, 53
Lewis, William 174
Lewisburg, Pa. 165
Lexington, battle of (1775) 41, 51
Liberty Fishing Company 28
Library of Congress 193–94
Light, John 176
Liverpool (ship) 44, 47
livestock, cattle, beef, slaughterhouses 26, 37, 133, 138, 159, 164, 173
Livingston, John R. 142
Locke, John 60
Loller, Robert 59
London Coffee Shop, Philadelphia 34, 66, 120
Long, Island, battle of (1776) 63

Maclay, Samuel 165–66
Madison, James 182, 185
Maine 181
Marshall, Christopher 47, 52–53, 55, 59, 66, 87–88, 92, 94, 96, 107, 118, 152, 153
Marshall, Christopher, Jr. 86
Maryland 41, 48
Massachusetts 38, 41, 65
Matlack, Abi (TM's half-sister) 13, 189
Matlack, Achsah (TM's half-sister) 13, 189
Matlack, Asa (TM's cousin) 189
Matlack, Elizabeth (TM's niece) 138
Matlack, Elizabeth (TM's sister) 13, 18
Matlack, Elizabeth Claypoole Cooper (TM's second wife) 172, 181, 185, 189, 191
Matlack, Ellen Yarnall (Timothy's first wife) 20, 22, 26, 28, 37, 81, 92, 94, 146, 171
Matlack, James (TM's grandson) 171, 184
Matlack, Josiah (TM's brother) 18, 107
Matlack, Letitia (TM's half-sister) 12, 15, 189
Matlack, Martha Burr Haines (TM's mother) 13, 21, 26, 29
Matlack, Mordecai (TM's son) 21, 81, 89–90, 92, 132
Matlack, Priscilla (TM's half-sister) 12, 189
Matlack, Seth (TM's brother) 18–19
Matlack, Sybil (TM's daughter) 28, 92, 158
Matlack, Sybil (TM's sister) 13, 18, 21, 171
Matlack, Timothy (TM's grandson) 181

Matlack, Timothy C. (TM's great grandson) 184
Matlack, Timothy, Sr. (TM's father) 12, 16, 18, 19
Matlack, Titus (TM's brother) 18, 190
Matlack, White (TM's brother) 18, 35, 138–39, 146, 148, 153, 163
Matlack, William (TM's grandfather) 12, 83, 84, 191
Matlack, William (TM's son) 21, 92, 104, 113, 126, 130, 158, 171–72
Mawhood, Charles 73, 74
McDougall, John 90
McKean, Thomas: chief justice, Supreme Court, Pennsylvania 107, 114; governor, Pennsylvania 174–77, 179, 181; opposition to the Constitution, Pennsylvania (1776) 65–66; resistance leadership 47, 50, 52–53
Mears, John 24
Mease, James 128, 142
medicine, medical practice, illness 13, 18, 21, 93, 138–39; *see also* yellow fever
Meng, Ullrich 76
Mercer, Hugh 61, 73–74
merchants 17, 28, 34, 38, 118; *see also* Philadelphia: merchants; *and individual names*
Meschianza 95, 176
Middlebrook, N.J. 82
Mifflin, Benjamin 24
Mifflin, Thomas 37, 46, 73, 75, 109
militia (Pennsylvania) 9, 55, 57, 62, 66–67, 81, 103–4, 120–23; Assumpink Creek, Princeton, effectiveness at 79–80; Flying Camp 61; winter campaign (1776–1777) 73; *see also* Associators
Miller, George 76
Millstone River, N.J. 78
Mirailles, Juan, Don 98
Mitchell, John 128–30
money, finance 17, 18, 28, 45, 71, 82, 87, 116, 120, 143–45, 155; *see also* economy
Monmouth, N.J. 96
Monroe, James 185
Morgan, Charles 90
Morgan, Jacob 74, 78
Morris, Anthony 54, 172
Morris, Cadwalader 145
Morris, Governeur 106
Morris, Isaac 185
Morris, Joseph 88
Morris, Robert 58, 68, 109, 111, 123; abstention from independence vote 53; committee investigation of 118–20; superintendent of finance 144
Morris, Samuel 78
Morristown, N.J. 72, 76, 82, 126

220 Index

Morrisville, Pa. 8
Morton, John 58
Moulder, Joseph 74
Muhlenberg, Fredrick 155, 175
Murray, Catherine Matlack (TM's daughter) 28, 92, 158
Murray, William, Jr. 162
Museum of Fine Arts (Boston) 196
musket 8

Nancarrow, John 163
Nash, Gary 2
National Treasure (movie) 196
Native American peoples 8, 22; Conestoga (Susquehannock) 23–24; Delaware 24; Huron 24; Lenape 12; Miami 168; Mingo 24; "Moravian" 23–24; Ottawa 24; Seneca 24, 97, 168; Shawnee 24, 168
Navigation Acts, British 27
Navy, British *see* England, English, navy of
Navy, Continental 44, 58, 68, 89–90
Neate, William 30
Nelson, George 138
Neshaminy ferry 9–10
New England 20, 27
New Hampshire 41
New Jersey 8, 10, 55, 69
New York City 7, 8, 23
New York State 35, 53, 60, 95
Nicholson, John 150–51, 163
Nixon, John 55, 76, 78
nonimportation 28, 35–36; *see also under* Congress: Continental Association
Norfolk, Va. 44
Norris, Sarah 13
North Carolina 41
Northumberland, Pa. 165–66
Nova Scotia 95

Odell, Jonathan 33, 194
O'Kelly, John 115
Olmstead, Gideon 105, 106

Paine, Thomas 140, 185–87; Act for Gradual Abolition 135–36, 181–82; influence on Convention, Pennsylvania (1776) 49, 53, 64–65; Morris committee and Silas Deane Affair 119–20; price fixing committee 117–18; *see also American Crisis; Common Sense*
Paisley, Mary 19
Palmer, Terrance 138
Paoli, battle of 86
Parker, John 25
Parliament, British 34–35, 39
Patriotic Association, Philadelphia 107
Patriotic Society, Philadelphia 98, 107
Paxton Boys 23, 25

Payton, Catherine 19–20, 26
Peale, Charles Willson 76, 140, 142, 190, 196; Act for Gradual Abolition 136; Fort Wilson Riot 121–24; government, committee service 98, 110, 118
Peale, James 172
Peale, Rembrandt 175, 190
Pearson, Isaac 70
Peggy (schooner) 23
Pemberton, Israel 20, 25, 35, 98
Pemberton, James 25, 63, 149, 150, 152
Pemberton, Phoebe 92, 94
Penn, John (delegate from North Carolina) 38
Penn, John (governor) 23–24, 28
Penn, William 24, 30, 42, 49
Penn Creek, Pa. 28
Pennsauken Creek 12
Pennsylvania 7, 35, 38, 41, 48, 57; democracy 1, 177; population diversity 45
Pennsylvania Gazette 22
Pennsylvania Journal 148
Pennsylvania Packet 100, 105, 113, 142, 144–45, 156
Percy, Hugh 41
Perseus (ship) 90
Perth Amboy, N.J. 23, 57, 60
Peters, John 20
Petty's Run (steel mill) 22
Philadelphia, Pa. 7–8, 15–16, 81–82, 95–96, 174; artisans, craftsmen, mechanics, tradesmen 15, 34–36; British occupation of 87–88; Enlightenment 191; horseracing 31; merchants 28, 34–36, 116; Municipal Corporation 36; taverns, dram shops 15, 27, 68; town meetings 38, 41, 50
Pickney, Charles Cotesworth 177
Pittsburgh, Pa. 165
Plain Truth (pamphlet) 64
Polly (tea ship)
Pontiac's War 24, 50
Poor Richard's Almanack (Franklin) 15
Porter, Thomas 59
Portugal, Portuguese 118
Presbyterians 24, 45; *see also* Scots-Irish
prices, price fixing 116–18, 120; *see also* economy; money
Primus (slave belonging to Elizabeth Haddon) 17, 28
Princeton, N.J. 71–72; Battle of 73–75, 80; College at 75
Province Island, Pa. 24
Pumpkin Fields, battle of 168
Putnam, Israel 8–9, 68
Puzzletown, Pa. 170

Quaco (slave) 17
Quakers 13, 50, 52, 58, 67, 81, 96, 108, 135,

146–47, 149; alcohol, taverns, drinking 29, 31; and American Indians 24; American Revolution 44–45; committee activity 35, 40; disowned members 32, 41, 113; exiles 85, 92; members who joined militia 24–26; ministry 19–20; opposition to horseracing, gambling, frivolous leisure 13–14, 31; opposition to pacifism 25, 41–43, 97; pro-independence faction 84, 121–22; relationship with TM 8; and slavery 17, 137; trade boycott 28; violence against 83–84, 148; Yearly Meeting 25, 121, 182

Rall, Johann 102
Randolph (frigate) 43, 68, 81, 89–91, 132
Randolph, Peyton 39
Raritan River, N.J. 82
Read, James 157
Reading, Pa. 173
Reed, Joseph 10, 103, 130, 135; congressman 111; military leadership 69–71; president of the Supreme Executive Council 109, 121–24, 143–44; prosecutor 106–9; resistance leadership 37–38, 46
religion 45, 135, 146, 172
Religious Society of Free Quakers 138, 146–53, 164, 171, 191
Republican Party 185
Republican Society, Pennsylvania 82, 109, 111
Revere, Paul 37
Reynell, John 17, 19, 20, 34–35
Rhode Island 41, 152
Richeson, Joseph 32–33
rifle, riflemen (Pennsylvania and Kentucky) 8, 57
Ristine, Elizabeth 184
Rittenhouse, David 132, 135, 153; committee activity 47, 49, 118; convention leadership 58–60, 64–65
Roberdeau, Daniel 62, 93, 121
Roberts, John 99, 107–8, 149
Roberts, Tamar 172
Rodney, Thomas 9–10, 67–68, 74
Roebuck (ship) 44, 47
Romeo & Juliet 28
Ross, George 58
Ross, James 175
rum, sugar, molasses 12, 17, 18–19, 27, 35
Rush, Dr. Benjamin 58, 89, 101, 117, 123–24, 132; committee activity 47, 52, 109; opposition to Constitution, Pennsylvania 1776 65, 196
Rush, Jacob 155–56

St. Clair, Arthur 124
Sandtown, N.J. 73
Sandy Hook, N.J. 82
Saratoga, battle of 88
Savannah, Ga. 158, 163
Schlosser, George 56, 59
Schuylkill River 24
Scots-Irish 23–24, 45, 58–59
Seaton, Alexander 19
Selim (racehorse) 30
servants, indentured 12, 15–16
Shewell, Robert 127
Shippen, Edward 162–63
Shippen, Edward, Jr. 70
Shippen, Joseph 46
Shippen, Peggy 88, 95, 103, 141
Shoemaker, Rebecca 99
shops, mercantile 13, 16, 22, 88, 127–28
Shute, Henry 24
silver urn 196–97
Simms, Buckridge 122
Sinnemahoning Creek, Pa. 167
slavery, slaves 17, 44, 54, 95, 135–37, 182–83; *see also* Quakers: slavery
Smith, Adam 60
Smith, Charles 177
Smith, Francis 41
Smith, James 58, 66
Smith, J.B. 93, 118, 160
Smith, Richard 44
Smith, Thomas 60
Smith, William 135
Snyder, Samuel 178
Snyder, Sarah M. 189
Society for the Relief of Free Negroes unlawfully Held in Bondage 137
Society of Friends *see* Quakers
Somerset, N.J. 75
South Carolina 41
Southwark Theater, Philadelphia 28
Spain 98, 148
Stackhouse, A.M. 1
Stackhouse, Kemble 183
Stamp Act 27–28
Stamp Act Congress 27
Stansbury, Joseph 117, 126, 144, 194
Stanton, Daniel 20
State House (Independence Hall) Philadelphia 1, 15, 38, 47, 54–55, 66
Staten Island, N.Y. 23, 57, 82, 84
steel, steel furnace 22, 33, 60, 71, 163; *see also* Petty's Run
Stephens, Adam 66
Stiegel, Henry William 29
Story, Thomas 122
Strickland, Miles 18
Stroud, Jacob 59
Sullivan, John 73, 75
Sunbury, Ga. 158
Sunbury, Pa. 167
Supreme Court (Pennsylvania) 144, 155
Supreme Executive Council, Pennsylvania

Index

78, 82, 100–1, 109, 150, 156, 162, 166; conflict with Congress 106–7; conflict with Tories 95–97; economic crisis 116, 121; Quaker exiles 84–85, 93
Susquehanna River, Pennsylvania 24, 97, 166–67
Swede's Ford (Schuylkill River) 25, 86

Taggert, Robert 87
Tallaca (Lenape chief) 12
Tarrytown, N.Y. 141
taxation without representation 27, 34–35; *see also* Stamp Act; Townshend Acts
Taylor, George 58
Tertian Quids 178
Tetsworth (ship) 17
Thomson, Charles 35–39, 41, 46, 55, 57, 109, 178, 193
Thomson, James 60
To the King's Most Excellent Majesty for Council (petition) 21–22
Tories (Loyalists) 52–53, 81, 99, 108, 121, 135
Towne, Benjamin 120
Townshend Acts 34–35, 37
Trenton, N.J. 7–10, 71; Battle of 9–11, 69
Two Sugar Loaves (shop) 16

University of the State of Pennsylvania (University of Pennsylvania) 134–35

Valley Forge, Pennsylvania 127–28
Van Horn, William 59
Vermont 65
Victorious (ship) 119–20
Virginia 38, 41, 44, 51, 65, 84–85, 93, 97; Declaration of Rights 62
von Steuben, Friedrich Wilhelm 127

War of Independence 52
Washington, George 28, 79, 161, 163–64, 184; and Benedict Arnold 102–3, 125–26, 128, 131, 141–42; commander-in-chief, Continental Army 8, 41, 47, 68, 71–76, 78–79, 85, 87, 96, 148; crossing of the Delaware 9–10; president 165, 168–70

West Point, N.Y. 141
Wetherill, Samuel, Jr. (TM's brother-in-law) 146, 153, 172
Wharton, Thomas, Jr. 23, 65, 82, 88, 93
Whig Society, Pennsylvania 82
Whigs (Supported Independence) 43, 52, 81, 86, 108, 117
White, Joseph 80
White, Peter 182
White, William 194
Whitehall, Robert 59
wildlife 16
Wilkinson, Jemima 153
Williams, Isaac 16
Willing, Charles 18
Willing, Thomas 58, 144–45
Wilson, James 83, 145, 154; congressman 48, 51, 58; defense of Tories 107, 122; Fort Wilson riot 122–23; opposition to Constitution, Pennsylvania (1776) 109
wine 27, 30, 35, 40, 109, 133, 181
Wing, Cornelius 152
Wirt, Joseph 121
Wistar, Caspar 29
Wistar, Dr. Caspar 191
Wister, Dan 31, 32, 49, 139
Wister, John 18
Wister, Sally 139
women, daily life of 15, 20–21, 179, 189
Woodbury Creek, N.J. 191
Woolman, John 136, 182
Wynkoop, Henry 143
Wyoming Valley, Pennsylvania 97

Yard, Benjamin 22
Yarmouth (ship) 91
Yarnall, Mordecai (TM's father-in-law) 171
Yarnall, Peter (TM's brother-in-law) 171
Yarnall, Sarah 146
yellow fever 171–73
York (Yorktown) Pa. 50, 86, 173
Yorktown, battle of 148
Young, Dr. Thomas 47, 59, 65–66
Young, William 69, 76, 80

www.ingramcontent.com/pod-product-compliance
Ingram Content Group UK Ltd.
Pitfield, Milton Keynes, MK11 3LW, UK
UKHW041952140426
5217IPUK00015B/762